Diverse World-Views
in an English Village

Diverse World-Views in an English Village

NIGEL RAPPORT

EDINBURGH UNIVERSITY PRESS

© Nigel Rapport, 1993

Edinburgh University Press Ltd
22 George Square, Edinburgh

Typeset in Linotron Palatino
by Koinonia Ltd, Bury, and
printed and bound in Great Britain by
The Redwood Press, Melksham, Wilts

A CIP record for this book is available from the British Library

ISBN 0 7486 0417 0

To
Anita
Anthony
Ben
Claude
and
Frances

If we do not do descriptive justice to individuals, it is hard to see how we could do it for societies.

Anthony Cohen, *Self-Conscious Anthropology*

Contents

List of Maps, Figures and Tables   viii

Foreword: The Style of the Book   ix

Part I. The Dale of Wanet   1

Chapter 1: The Geographical Landscape   3
Chapter 2: The Historical Landscape   11
Chapter 3: The Landscape as Biography   25
Chapter 4: The Landscape as Idyll   31
Chapter 5: The Landscape as Community   43

Part II. Individual Lives in Wanet   53

Chapter 6: Identities and Relations in the Field   55
Chapter 7: The Ethics of the Research   69
Chapter 8: The Habits of Interaction   78
Chapter 9: Doris's Personae and World-Views   83
Chapter 10: Sid's Personae and World-Views   106
Chapter 11: A Routine Conversation   122
Chapter 12: The Conversation Analysed   150

Part III. Meaning versus Form: The Individual and the Community   159

Afterword: Style Reconsidered   193

Bibliography   201
Index of Names   208
Index of Subjects   211

List of Maps, Figures and Tables

Map 1.1: The Dale of Wanet.   4

Figure 2.1: Population curves of Wanet and Leyton between
            1801 and 1971.   16
Table 2.1: A comparison between population distribution in
            Wanet in 1871 and 1981.   17
Table 2.2: A comparison between occupations in Wanet in
            1871 and 1981.   22

Figure 9.1: Doris Harvey's family.   83

Figure 10.1: Sid Askrig's family.   106

Figure III: A. F. C. Wallace's simple equivalence structure.   183

Foreword: The Style of the Book

This is an account of the diversity of perception and the ambiguity of interaction in an English village. It originates from a piece of anthropological research, largely by participant-observation, which I carried out over twelve months in 1980 and 1981 and have been writing about and considering, in one way or another, since. The research was my first piece of sustained fieldwork, undertaken as part of the process of gaining a doctorate, in my early twenties – these facts playing a significant part in my stay in 'Wanet', the small village and dale in rural, rugged Cumbria, in the north-west of England, as will become apparent.

I remember relishing the moment when, on first returning to the university from the field and feeling laden with experiences, I told my doctoral supervisor that I knew what I wanted to write about: the complexity, the inconsistency of things. Social life was not about neat, mechanical models, about overarching systems, whatever may be the conventional wisdom about structure and function, synthesis and consensus. Social life was farcical, chaotic, multiple, contradictory; it was a muddling-through, which turned on the paradoxical distinction between appearance and actuality.

Intervening years have enabled me to reflect upon my early ideas about Wanet. Some have altered, all have hopefully developed but the memory of that momentary outburst in the department at Manchester (and Tony Cohen's complicitous grin) has stayed with me, and I have wanted to remain true to its sentiments and tone in this book. That is, the book attempts to escape from singularity – or at least from dealing with singularity in the absence of its sociological fellow, diversity. So here is one book, written in a number of rhetorical styles, borrowing from a number of paradigms, narrated by a number of voices, and telling of a number of views of life in Wanet. These multiplicities intersect and overlap, collide and diverge, influence and oppose one another, but I do not present them as necessarily adding up to one authoritative, authorial picture, and they do not reflect just one experience. Of course they all emanate from 'me', but my singularity is but a conventional shorthand too, and in these pages I travel between social milieux, between definitions of meaning, between talking-relationships, between prejudices and conceits, between personal identities –

my own (as nervous field-worker, as social theorist, as neophyte Englishman, as apprentice farm-hand, as darts and domino enthusiast) and others' (most notably those of two longtime inhabitants of Wanet, Doris Harvey and Sid Askrig) – without causally interrelating all of these or tying them back to a monolithic book-structure which connects all. Wanet entails a family of experiences for me, if you will, and it is this polythetic category of information that I seek to present here. The book represents juxtaposition without essence, without 'closure' as Simmel put it, except in the subjective sense that it recounts everything that the intellectual needs of the author, at a given time, have caused him to see.

Writing a text is also an experience, and it is an appreciation of Simmel which has matured during the drafting of this book. I have come to feel like symbolic interactionist Hugh Duncan when he observes that on so many excursions into social scientific theory it is Simmel's figure which appears at our journey's end, already returning from a point we have just recognised as there to be reached (1959, p. 108). I wish that I had appreciated him sooner, and, indeed, that social anthropology had taken on board his brand of phenomenology – of an individual construction of social experience which is endlessly creative, manifoldly fragmented and inherently contrastive – in place of the sterile and extraneous Durkheimian emphasis on societal requirements and normative constraints.

Without in any way wishing to implicate them in this opinion, I should like to thank those who, over the years of this drafting, in Manchester, St John's (Newfoundland), Sde Boker (Israel), and again Manchester, have given me direction, counsel and support: Anthony Cohen, Paul Baxter, Richard Werbner, Emrys Peters; Marilyn Strathern, David Turton; Robert Paine, Jean Briggs, Judy Adler, Victor Zaslavsky, George Park, Joanne Prindiville, David Anderson; Emanuel Marx, Gideon Kressel, Frank Stewart, Moshe Schwartz; Alan Macfarlane, Edwin Ardener, Marc Hobart; Paul Stoller, Dan Rose; Patricia Smith, Vivian Bone, Maureen Prior. And while a list of words and names can sometimes convey very little, there is something to be said (as every Englishman gone abroad knows) for volume and repetition: ANTHONY COHEN, MARILYN STRATHERN, RICHARD WERBNER.

This book is in three parts. In the first I introduce the dale of Wanet by approaching it from five different perspectives, five different routes to the place, as it were. In Chapter 1 I explain something of Wanet's geography and economy; in Chapter 2 I give a short history of settlement in the dale; in Chapter 3 I reveal some of the dale's important cognitive landmarks, as seen through the eyes of a number of its inhabitants, both indigenous and more recently arrived; in Chapter 4 I show

how rural communities like Wanet have traditionally been described in the literature, from the travelogue to the social scientific tract: how Wanet would likely be described in the idiom of the rural idyll; and lastly, in Chapter 5 I offer a view of the nature of community in Wanet by showing how two neighbouring families think of one another, and make one another into parts of their respective lives. These five perspectives cannot always be brought together into one focus; the five routes do not necessarily give on to quite the same place. Rather, the view of Wanet from one Chapter, say as rural idyll, provides us with an entire picture of a particular kind, a kind which may be hard to reconcile with the picture of another Chapter, say Wanet as lived in by the Rowlands and the Whitehouses. But this is in the nature of constructions of the social world, and of the information with which it is filled. Different landscapes are perceived in the 'same' social space; and even if the landmarks perceived, such as 'Wanet', overlap, this need not mean they are perceived alike. Rather, different perceptions will connect with, abut, and relate to one another in all manner of tangential, situational and non-prescribable ways. Indeed, these are major themes of the book to which, in one guise or another, I shall repeatedly return. Nor is there a final conciliation or coming together of perspectives and perceptions in conclusion – except inasmuch as it is I who here interpret and voice them all; and that seeming-singularity of construction is questionable too, as we shall see. Hence, the book represents a juxtaposition of routes which lead through Wanet and, with their particular experiences behind them and their own expectations ahead, make of it what they will.

In the second part of the book I introduce its main protagonists on to the Wanet stage: Doris Harvey, Sid Askrig and myself. In Chapter 6 I recount my own route to Wanet, as a student of anthropology hoping to become an ethnographer, and the way I came to share relationships and engage in a number of interactional routines with quite a few local people and in particular with Doris and Sid. In Chapter 7 I look askance and question, in hindsight, the ethics of my behaviour in adopting the persona of observing-participant which I did; I explain why I have felt able to publish my experiences as this account. In Chapter 8 I return to the former narrative and describe the theoretical questions and analytical paths which my regular relations with Doris and Sid began to open up and develop for me – notions of a diversity of world-views and a multitude of personae within both of them. In Chapter 9 I then give a detailed account of the different ways Doris constructs her world, and the positions she grants herself within them; and in Chapter 10 I provide a similar account of Sid. In Chapter 11 I finally bring the speaking voices of Doris, Sid and myself, as field-worker, together in one conversation to show how our personae are regularly brought to life, and world-views routinely used, in everyday interaction. Lastly, in Chapter 12 I spell out what I see as the important analytical points of the above interaction, including (without pre-empting my argument too much at this stage) its ambiguity and miscommunication, its habituality and mutual gratification.

The primary focus of the book, then, is on two individuals (Doris Harvey and Sid Askrig) apart and together, as I construe them (three individuals including me). I feel justified in doing this and still calling the book an 'anthropological' study, firstly, because I believe that the simple dyad contains the germ of the complex, that the macro-social is only to be appreciated via the micro-, and secondly, because I believe that interaction – the regular coming together of individuals in symbolic exchange – is the basis of sociation: it is interaction which precedes and entails social order. The third part of the book is a theoretical essay in which I relate some of the implications of this study and these views to a wider literature. I still keep one foot in Wanet, with Doris and Sid in interaction, but with the other I step on some anthropological toes, go some way in following the lead of a few others, and lastly suggest my own path from Wanet to an anthropological appreciation of sameness and difference, sharing and diversity, sociality and idiosyncrasy. I depict society as emanating from cultural forms and individual intentions, as constituted by public behaviours and personal meanings.

Finally there is an Afterword in which I introduce alternative possible approaches to my data, and explain why I maintain a preference for the one offered here.

Author's Note

The ideas I shall explore in this work do not call for the people, places and relationships which gave rise to them being identifiable. To preserve their anonymity, therefore, I have altered names and other details as necessary.

Nigel Rapport
Manchester 1993

Part I

The Dale Of Wanet

Landscapes can be deceptive.
Sometimes a landscape can seem to be less a setting
for the life of its inhabitants than a curtain behind which
their struggles, achievements and accidents take place.

For those who, with the inhabitants, are behind
the curtain, landmarks are no longer only geographic
but also biographical and personal.

John Berger, *A Fortunate Man*

1

The Geographical Landscape

Wanet. Nearly 650 people live here, between the skylines of Tarn Fell and Wanet Wold, Robb Coum and Riggdale Reth. These hills, rising up 1,600 feet from the dale bottom to heights of 2,000 feet or more, stride north-eastward for about ten miles, not two miles apart, enclosing the valley. On the steep slopes people have built stone cottages, farmhouses and barns. With meadows and pastures and allotments, with dry-stone walls, once-used water mills and lime kilns, they have tried to domesticate the fells. But here is still Wanet, from Wanet Foot to Wanet Head, 18,500 acres of limestone, gritstone and slate, of gills and beck, of clayey bottom-land, thistled slopes and high, peaty tops.

And here is Wanet Town, snug in its meadow bed: grey-stone cottages, dressed and whitewashed, dour churches and draughty graveyards, and the narrow, windy streets looking in at misted windows. Wanet is a small valley in rural, eastern Cumbria, locked in a mountainous fastness. Within motorway contact of Preston and Carlisle, Wanet is well buffered from their noise for first there are the intervening dales, villages and small towns such as Leyton and Hogart, Willen and Prongten, Gapton and Bedgedale. And the narrow wall- and hedge-lined roads protect Wanet further, by their meanderings and their wild ordeals over fell-tops.

Wanet's first inhabitants are said to have been the Norsemen. They gave it topography in the names 'dale' (valley), 'beck' (river), 'gill' (stream), 'fell' (hill) 'garth' (yard), 'laith' (barn), and 'tarn' (moorland water). The Norsemen settled in dispersed farmsteads on the fell sides in order to rear their stock, and their isolated farms are still here but now, thick stone buildings from the eighteenth and nineteenth centuries replace the Norse peat sod-roofed and cruck-constructed huts. Only after the Norsemen did the Angles fight their way into the dale, and it was they who first settled in strings of cottages, gathered together into hamlets and villages on the flatter bottom-land.

The tension between Norseman and Angle still finds an expression in Wanet. Today it is that between the pastoral farmsteads of the fell slopes and the cottages of the artisans and shopkeepers, the tradesmen and the retired, which line the now-metalled roads through the dale to its neighbours.

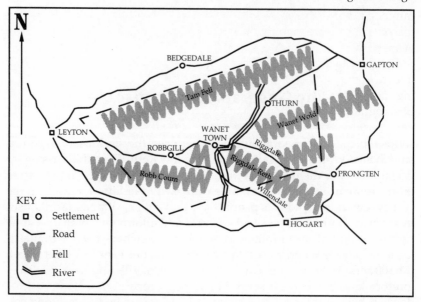

Map 1.1: The Dale of Wanet.

There are four main gatherings of cottages in Wanet, the largest of these is Wanet Town, with over two hundred of the dale's inhabitants living there. Their painted cottages huddle around a primary school, a garage, a village green, an Anglican church and Victorian vicarage, a Congregationalist chapel, a Methodist chapel, a grocery-shop-cum-post-office, a tea-house, an antique shop, a sweet shop, a number of bric-a-brac and craft shops and two residential pubs: the Eagle and the Mitre.

Next in size, with half the number of cottages, is Thurn. Thurn lies to the north-east of Wanet Town and near the head of the dale. It boasts a small grocery shop, a guest-house-cum-restaurant, the Hilltop pub, and another Methodist chapel.

To the south-west of Wanet Town, and about a quarter of its size, nearer the foot of the dale, is Robbgill. Its cottages assemble around a grocery shop, another Anglican church and a small tea-house.

And fourthly, Riggdale, which is about the same size as Robbgill but lying to the east of Wanet Town, and already starting to climb over Riggdale Reth alongside the road to Prongten. Its cottages boast a nearby Methodist chapel too.

Wanet receives less sunshine and more rain than many parts of England: 58 to 70 inches per year so there may be flooding in November and December – when the River Tan and the numerous gills and shake-holes burst – and intermittent snow from January to April, and showers or damp drizzle from May to October. Yet the dale is beautiful, panoramic. And after blowing into Wanet from head or foot, a feeling of discovering a secret habitation can draw you winding on to the hearth – Wanet Town.

But people are jostling for space here now. Of the 635 people who live in Wanet, almost 200 were not born here, nor even in the surrounding dales. They have moved in from distant towns and cities such as Birmingham, Manchester, Edinburgh, Leeds, even London. They come here to retire and rest, or they come here to live and find local work as shopkeepers, caterers or builders or teachers, or they 'farm' their own smallholdings. Some come to Wanet to live but still commute to jobs down the motorways. They are doctors and artists, civil servants, bankers, factory supervisors, business executives.

Touring outsiders have also broached Wanet and been shepherded in by its pastoral image. They visit in their hordes, from Whitsuntide right through the summer until the Harvest festivals of early October. On a hot bank-holiday weekend, these visitors can outnumber the local inhabitants. They trek and camp or stay in caravans; use the local pubs, guest-houses or bed-and-breakfasts here; or they come to air out the damp in their own second homes and holiday cottages.

There is a lot of bickering over land and houses. The natives quarrel with the newcomers – whether working or retired or second-homers. And the farmers compete with each other for every spare field. They need more land because the small farmsteads of the nineteenth century (often of less than twenty acres) are no longer viable so small farms in the dale are being bought up by larger eighty-acre ones and outsiders, planning lumber afforestation, or just fancying a few unspoilt rural acres, often bid in the auctions for the land too – as well as for the old farmhouse. And these outsiders can often bid higher for their house or cottage than the existing inhabitants of the dale in need of a new home after they marry or retire.

There is a shortage of jobs here too. In the mid-nineteenth century, Wanetdale found gainful employment for 1,900 folk. Even in the early years of this century, Directories were reporting the existence of Wanet drapers, tailors, butchers, boot- and shoe-makers, carters, gardeners, gamekeepers, jewellers, clock-repairers, cycle manufacturers, carriers, railway platelayers, coal agents, bakers, coachmen, dressmakers and confectioners. Now the farmers scarcely afford paid adult help on their farms – even the residential village 'bobby' has been moved out of the dale to more pressing beats. People shop and drink outside the village too, for with better roads and more cars to use places are closer at hand. Those living in the dale's cottages and even the small farmers must earn their living in building or joinery, renovating buildings or the expanding farms, or renovating houses and shops and pubs and restaurants for their newcomer owners. Or they work on the dale's roads and verges and drains for the County Council, or for the Gas and Electricity Boards. Some find jobs as cleaners and cooks and shop-assistants and odd-job men in the dale, and an increasing number of Wanet natives are driving outside each day to jobs in quarries and garages and on the railways. Some go as far as Hogart and Gapton, Kendal and Kirkby Stephen, to work as company representatives and salesmen, or as factory labourers.

There is also tension nowadays over organising the dale. Some natives feel that the newcomers are robbing them of their Parish Council and Church Committee, of their Holiday Committee and Youth Club Committee, of their Charity Commission and School Governors' Board. And the women feel robbed of their Women's Institute and Mothers' Union, of their Methodist Guild and Barn Evenings, of their Meals-on-Wheels and Playgroup, of their Christian Aid Committee and Polio Research Charity, of their Sunday School and Whist Drives.

It is easy to feel preyed upon in Wanet, and to resent it. One can recall that in the past the dale was private and thriving, with Wanet Town as its social centre. Now local people often cannot find somewhere to live and work. It is easy for locals to perceive this as a conspiracy by the country's economy and politicians, by the immigrants and the laziness and loose morals of the working classes in the cities, and all assisted by the Government, the County Council . . . and especially the National Park Committee.

National Parks were set up in Britain after the Second World War by Acts of Parliament, to ensure that areas of 'outstanding natural beauty' were conserved and their recreational enjoyment by visitors was promoted. Just over a fifth of England and Wales has now been accorded some form of official 'protection' for the beauty of its countryside or the rarity of its wildlife. Local Councils delegate some of their powers and responsibilities to National Parks committees consisting of around eight Secretary of State appointees and sixteen District and County councillors (only a number of whom have to actually reside within the park area). Wanet has been under National Park jurisdiction since their inception in the early 1950s. However, there is a feeling among some of the people born here that they do not need to be shown by outsiders how to enjoy and preserve their dale through footpaths and stiles, car parks and public lavatories. To them the Park committee, the wardens, the Park officers and all the walkie-talkie wielding patrolmen seem to be legalising and even assisting the dale's invasion and demise for while the Park is home to around 40,000 people, they will play host, over the year, to millions. Hence although the land in Wanet is still owned by people who live here, natives can feel that grants offered for refurbishment of stiles, paths and copses are mere kid-glove coverings of compulsory orders for tourist access. And while the Park maintains the 'settled harmony' of the dale, natives perceive that all development is controlled – farm buildings to factory space, reservoirs, quarries and overhead electric cable.

Moreover, when Wanet natives try to make do, and use any available avenue for securing a local income, such as by providing bed-and-breakfast, or a camping field, or a caravan site, or a pub, or a shop, or by selling their labour for building or painting or cleaning, or even converting an old barn into a holiday cottage themselves, their efforts can still be thwarted. Permission is denied, deemed inessential for 'normal life' or not fitting the existing scene while building grants go to newcomer outsiders, and private conifer forests (albeit sanctioned by now-defunct Development boards) eat away hay meadow and rough grazing, and radically alter the traditional skyline. It can become easy to regard National Park regulations on advertising, dumping, littering, caravan and camp site placements as spiteful. And even when the Planning Committee grants permission, and all the duplicate paperwork in distant offices is complete, it can still seem that development may only be carried out in the stipulated and often more costly materials, styles and colours. For the Wanet farmers in particular, the National Park appears to be a deliberate, extra bureaucratic hurdle, separating them from the EEC and government grants and subsidies which many now need to survive on this hard land. The struggle to rear stock in these wet hills is enough.

Hardy breeds of sheep and cattle are the farmers' wealth and pride in Wanet. It is these flocks and herds which tramp and dung the fells (and in the past there were geese and ponies too), bleating and lowing before they are sold off to replenish the breeding stock of farmers further south on dryer, flatter lands. At least, to this end the farmer will sell his gimmer (female) lambs (crosses between Rough Fell, Blue-faced Leicester, Swaledale and Dalesbred breeds) at markets in Kendal, Leyton and Gapton, when about six months old. At the same time, wether (castrated male) lambs are sold for fattening and butchering in England or the EEC. The farmer only keeps a few purebred lambs for himself each season, rearing them on his fells from lambs to (weaned) hoggs, to (clipped) shearlings, to (mothering) sheep so as to replenish his own flock of 30 to maybe a few hundred Roughs or Swaledales.

All farmers in the dale have at least some sheep. Some grow beef too. This may be in the form of 'suckler' herds, where the cows run with the bull and then suckle their calves for six months before the latter are sold for fattening further south. Growing beef may also be in the form of 'store' cattle. Here, the same Hereford, Aberdeen Angus or Welsh Black calves are reared for longer on the Wanetdale farms, before final fattening on the lowlands of the south. Still other farmers in the dale operate with more 'flying' herds, buying and selling adult cattle at rapid rates. And besides the traditional beef breeds, some farmers are experimenting with sperm from the continental Charollais, Semantol and Limousine breeds, and attracting high auction bids for their cross-bred calves.

A more popular option with Wanet farmers, when available, is to grow dairy cattle alongside their sheep for the government's Milk Marketing Board guarantees to buy all the milk produced here at a fixed price. A few farmers are also issued with licences to bottle and sell their own milk to local customers. The popular dairy breeds are Friesian and Holstein which have now superseded the traditional Northern Dairy Shorthorns. By including some Jersey or Guernsey cows in the herd (whose milk has more butterfat), milk quality can be assured as well as gross yield. Again, the dairy farmer rears the best of his herd's progeny himself, from calves, to (weaned) stirks, to (bulled) heifers, to (second-time lactating) cows. Bull-calves, crosses, and poor heifer-calves are auctioned off shortly after birth but all stock in Wanet have to be smallish animals, from hardy breeds, which calve and lamb late in the spring to avoid the frosts. Beasts which are too large eat too much, and sink into the wet soil, pot-holing the fields, and the farmer's success in rearing and selling his stock, and their wool or milk, is very much a matter of making the best use of his land.

Most of the land here is sloping and wet, the soil is thin, and the little flat bottom-land is clayey and periodically flooded by the River Tan. And all the land here has been individually owned by different farmers since the last patches of common grazing land on the peaty fell-tops were stone-drained and enclosed as walled allotments, following the Acts of Enclosure of between 150 and 200 years ago.

Farmers often divide up their land by quality into the different categories of meadow, pasture, and allotment but it is a struggle to maintain quality. Thistles and poorer grasses (moss, heather, bracken, purple moor-grass, matweed and rough cotton grass) are threatening to spread down the fells from the top allotments (at 1,100 to 2,000 feet) to the pastures and even the meadows. And the farmer, although armed with mechanical sprayers, is often unable to maintain the drainage and other improvements to the fell-tops afforded by the labour-intensive farming of the past. The marshes can seem to be reclaiming them. The problem is further exacerbated by the declining system of dry stone walls. Six feet high and, at base, three feet wide, when built by the nineteenth-century gangs of expert wallers at a rate of one rood (seven yards) per day, they used to march in straight lines up and across the fells and over into the next dale. Now it is often hard to keep the widening gaps within them in check.

The meadows (at 400 to about 700 feet, on the dale bottom) are the best land in the dale, and of vital importance for the hay harvest. Hay is the only crop which farmers grow here. The soil, altitudes, mean temperatures, and irregular and heavy rainfall all are said to militate against further arable exploitation (wartime enforcements of barley or potatoes were disastrous). So the meadows are carefully engineered. The farmers 'till' them with chemical fertiliser, spread cow dung or slurry on to them, drain them and destone them, all in an effort to maintain grasses of a higher feeding value (such as perennial rye grass, Bent grass, sheep's fescue, clover and vetches).

Above the meadows (between roughly 700 feet and the start of the allotments at 1,100) lie the pastures. The pastures in Wanetdale do not play as important a role in the hay harvest as the meadows. None the less, farmers will often still muck-spread and till them, spraying against docks and thistles, for they must provide good quality grass for the stock (the cows, especially) throughout the year.

It is on the allotments (and higher pastures) that the farmers can keep their sheep for much of the time, for they are better scavengers of grass than cattle. Sheep are 'put to the tup' in late October and November, and are then brought down to the lower pastures and meadows to lamb in March and April. For most of the year the farmers leave their sheep to fend for themselves, only supplementing their diet in the worst of the winter (from December to February) with hand-fed hay, protein nuts and other nutrient concentrates. The sheep are also helped to fight sheep-scab, maggots, foot-rot, wicks, ticks, the staggers, and so on, by injections, drenchings and dipping, and they are often de-tailed to protect against anal infection and mastitis. Most importantly, the farmers want to 'heath' their flocks, a practice from the days of common grazing land of rearing sheep from one generation to the next on one 'gaited' section of fell. For then the learnt knowledge of the flock – the best areas to feed in different months, the safe tracks, the protective hollows in the wind and walls in the snow, the reliable gills – is also passed on from ewe to lamb. Flocks which are not heathed on a home range will be forever jumping rickety walls and wire fences into the lusher grasses below, or into neighbours' fields (where they can become prey to neighbours' dogs).

In the worst of the winter, the farmers keep their cattle warm in barns all day, but from the last of October right through the 'back-end' until May, cattle will always be housed for at least some hours. Cows being wintered in barns have to be fed, watered and mucked-out by the farmer daily. The lactating cows need the most attention, and are fed carefully measured quantities of hay, straw, dairy nuts, protein nuts, minerals, and carbo-hydrates (in the form of a treacle-like liquid or as brewers' left-over grains). The farmer will reserve his barn space near the central milking shippon for his lactating cows, while his dry or resting cows, calves and stirks can be housed on any of the barns dispersed around his land. There is a string of barns in Wanetdale built at the base of the allotments (as part of the old small farmsteads of the last century) which can be used in this way, as well as for storing supplies of sheep hay. Then only in May can all the cattle enjoy the luxury of fresh grass again.

There is great skill in juggling the use of the farms' best meadow and pasture for this land is needed by the newly-lambed ewes (especially the mothers of twins and the very occasional triplets), the newly-calved cows, the lactating herd and also by the growing hay. The more land which is reserved from May to August for the hay crop, the less avail-able to the stock. And yet, even after this investment, the hay crop can never be assured in Wanetdale because of the weather. The mowing, 'scaling' (turning and drying), rowing-up, baling and final 'leading' (transporting the collected bales for stacking on barn 'moos') of the hay are anxious operations, in the few dry hours before the next possible shower. Therefore, some farmers are compromising by only haytiming a few of their fields and buying waggonloads of guaranteed, good hay from the lower lands further south, via trusted local dealers. And other farmers are turning to the production of silage, if they can afford to build a silo and buy the necessary 'forage waggons' for when making the highly nutritious silage, grass can be mowed and picked up wetter, and then left to leak and decompose in the sealed sheds. Thus the farmer becomes slightly more independent of the weather.

With their machines, their families and their children, farmers often work more or less independently of each other now. Young farm-hands may be hired for a few months, and odd-job men and small farmers for a few hours or days for some specific digging or walling, but otherwise extra-familial labour, help, or cooperation is not common. Even the gangs of Irish workers who used to be hired in Wanet for the haytiming (before going south for other harvests) are no longer afforded. For any extra services which are needed, the farmers can drive out of the dale, or have the services drive in. For example, easing the work surrounding cow-calvings by spreading these throughout the warmer parts of the year, farmers now telephone the Artificial Insemination Board when-ever they notice a heifer or cow in oestrus, and one of their men in the area simply injects the bull semen of their choice.

With all this driving to and fro, by locals as well as outsiders, what kind of community is left within the fells? That is a further issue, as we shall see.

2

The Historical Landscape

There *has* been a community here, as mentioned, since the Dark Ages. The settlement pattern, indeed, is the same now as it was in the seventh century when, according to one source, Wanet was the capital of its own Brigantes kingdom (Colbeck, 1979). Certainly the odd Celtic place-name survives from the period (as well as Anglo-Saxon), but it was the Vikings coming from the west who really stamped a lasting influence on the dale as they began to clear its heavily wooded fells and moors for their sheep transhumance.

In the twelfth century, monks followed the Norse pastoralists into the area, draining marshes, laying down ways to parent monasteries and setting up lead and charcoal mining (Wright, 1977, p. 55). By the Middle Ages, Wanet had become part of the large manorial estate of the Fitzhugh family, but in 1422 by royal statute of Henry VI a local government of twenty-four 'statesmen' or 'synodsman' (later 'questmen' or 'sidesmen') was instigated. These were yeomen farmers who governed Wanet by council, disbursed certain charities and, together with the Bishop, selected the local Anglican pastor.

The Wars of the Roses brought ravages to dale life, however, and at their end in 1485 Wanet was a royal manor held immediately under the Crown. But the family dynasties of yeomen farmers continued, and although population remained small (still only about 250 families in the sixteenth century) prosperity slowly returned, especially after Henry VIII's dissolution of the monasteries made much land available for purchase. In Elizabethan times, Wanet was home to a flourishing corn industry, with three corn mills. Another economic avenue opened up with the rise of the wool trade, and by the end of the 1500s Wanet had achieved renown for its cottage wool industry. In 1629 Charles I sold Wanet to a Royalist supporter, but the Civil War was to follow and shortly after the Restoration, in 1670, the land returned to a local landowner to be held in trust for the tenants in general, as freehold land.

This return to the conditions of Henry VI's fifteenth-century charter brought great change. The statesmen rebuilt their properties in stone, employing the descendants of the masons who had originally tended the monastic properties. Population increased, family dynasties expanded, occupation of the land grew more intensive, and crafts and trade flourished. As well as cattle and sheep, the statesmen raised herds of dun ponies and geese on the extensive fell-tops, and reached markets as distant as Richmond and Doncaster. Droving, in fact, became big business, along such tracks as Craven Old Way, with trains of pack-horses for the transporting of farm produce as well as livestock to southern markets. Networks of inns and pastures for rent then also developed en route. Along these networks, for example, Wanet exported butter, and specialist trades in coopering and copper sprang up for the making of butter boxes in which the product could be safely transported. Also the wool trade represented an extensive enterprise. In addition to the coarse locally-carded wool, 'bump', which Wanet inhabitants kept for home use, they imported finely combed wool (and later, machine-spun worsted) and knitted these into stockings, mittens and gloves. Indeed, for a number of centuries (until finally superseded by mass-produced, manufactured woollens in the 1890s, in fact) such knit-wear became the area's greatest export. Statesmen would travel to London and act as middlemen between the manufacturers of their dale and the merchants of Cheapside. Later, government agents even re-sided at Kirkby Lonsdale and Kendal to secure the worsted products directly for the army. And with the growth of local markets there was an easy exchange of finished products leaving Wanet, laden on flat-topped carts, with more 'raw' materials returning.

   In the late seventeenth and early eighteenth century, Wanet saw its greatest period of prosperity. Those who were not statesmen on their own land were offered tenancies almost as assured as freehold (Thirsk, 1961, p. 86), or else they prosecuted trades for which there was a large market. Expert hay rakes and scythes, for example, enjoyed a wide wholesale distribution, and there were even reputed to be specialist continental woodcarvers domiciled in Wanet having fled the Plague and Great Fire of London. Circumstances were to keep changing, but the seventeenth century, with its successful intensive production of livestock, its stone farmhouses, stone barns, and first stone walls for the separation of pasture land from wood, vegetable garden and meadow, and the separation of family from family, laid down a pattern of life in the region which was to survive right through the nineteenth century, if not up to the Second World War. It was to give to the dalesfolk what Hartley and Ingilby (loving compilers, from their nearby homes, of compendia of material culture and lore) describe as a certain uniformity and homogeneity, however superficial (1968, p. xiii; also Rollinson, 1974, p. 15). The traditional way of calling for sheep, for example, may have varied from dale to dale (from 'Howe, Howe,' to 'Hoe, Hoe,' to 'Oh, ho, Oh, ho,') as may have the favourite recipe for oatcake and the preferred shape of peat spades, but there was a regional identity none the less, one which twentieth-century institutions – *Cumbria* and *The Dalesman* magazines, the National Parks – then sought to celebrate and preserve, although the latter also presided over a range of new behaviours, as we shall see.

To return to the eighteenth century first, however, we find two happenstances which were to bring particularly significant changes to local life. The population of Britain as a whole in 1700 was five million, and three-quarters of these people lived rurally. Within 100 years population was to more than double, with pressure on the land only slowly being relieved by the Industrial Revolution. In Wanet such increase was exacerbated by gavelkind inheritance in which all progeny had a right to be settled on family land. The outcome was a decrease in the size of farms so as to reach sometimes as low as three to eight acres each. Secondly, in 1750 there began the government Acts of Enclosure, intended to rationalise the sheep-rearing industry and clear and improve the land. Woods had been cleared from the fells since Anglian times and after the Enclosure Acts, this process was speeded up. In particular, the common land on the fell-tops on which, traditionally, grazing sheep, geese and ponies had been able to roam as far north as Scotland, was divided up and allocated to different farming families. Heather was burnt off, stone drains were sunk, and limestone burnt in kilns built nearby in order to sweeten the grass.

The small farms soon proved non-viable and families were forced to modify production. A cotton mill was opened in 1730, but Wanet people seem to have refused to work with the heat and smells, or to have their children do so. Instead they chose to pursue knitting as a cottage industry even more frenetically, and the amount of woollens leaving the dale by tumbrel-cart on the improved roads to weekly markets continued to increase. As the population of the dale topped 2,000, Wanet Town saw artisanal families living in flats in two or three storey houses, and every member engaged in the knitting of jackets, stockings or nightcaps. Farmers also experimented with the growing of oats and potatoes, and around 1750 marble quarrying was successfully begun, and towards 1800, coal mining. Hence, what the later eighteenth century witnessed was the development of occupational bricolage in which the small farmer or artisan combined a number of economic activities, as suited to his particular skills and penchant, and the labour he could muster according to the developmental cycle of his family. Knitting, quarrying, mining, stock-rearing, cheese- and butter-making were all turned to as partial means of securing economic survival. The local social life of 'ganging-a-sitting', cockfighting and gambling, meanwhile, and inter-parish rivalries over wrestling, football, racing and leaping contests, seem to have been maintained with vigour.

In the early nineteenth century, however, population continued to rise. Indeed, the rural population as a whole was greater between 1800 and 1875 than ever before, reaching a peak of 9.1 million. In 1880 there were three times more people in Britain than in 1750, and four times more in 1911 than 1801. The proportion of rural to urban population was of course dropping (from 75 per cent rural in 1700 to 65 per cent in 1801 to 50 per cent in 1851) as labour was soaked up by the development of the manufactory, but the worsening of nineteenth-century rural poverty was still marked. The response (when more fluid occupational strategies, temporary jobs and cottage industry proved impossible) was increasing population movement (Samuel, 1975, pp 10–14). In Wanet, occupational diversity became ever more necessary, and in a small sample of its 1,700-odd inhabitants, besides four gentleman, a solicitor, a headmaster, an independent minister and a perpetual curate, Baines' *Directory* of 1822 records three people practising boot and shoe making, two blacksmiths, one wheelwright, two worsted and stocking yarn manufacturers, one stone-mason, five victuallers (innkeepers), five grocers, one corn miller, one slate dealer, four drapers, three ironmongers, one butcher, one chair maker, one tailor, one hosier, one cooper, two cattle dealers, and three carriers transporting produce out of the dale to Kendal and Lancaster.

The mainstay of Wanet production continued to be knitwear, however, although quarrying also became more of an organised industry. Wanet stone, since it contained no iron pyrites, was found especially suitable for the manufacture of gunpowder, besides its more pedestrian function as millstone. The dark limestone was also polished up into a popular marble which graced fireplaces and chimney-pieces, artists' palettes and mortars, inkstands, and also a number of the portals of those emblems of the rising industrial age: central railway termini. Thus marble joined Wanet's list of pack-horse exports, even reaching destinations as distant as India and Australia before the market collapsed with the arrival of fashionable Belgian and Italian products, deemed superior or at least more classical.

It was also in the nineteenth century that the dale developed as a centre of intensive milk production, an economic avenue that was to challenge the wool business not only for its use of the best meadow land but also for the financial security which was provided. By the end of the eighteenth century Wanet had long had a reputation for the quality of its butter exports, as well as the butter boxes in which factors' open wagons would ferry it to Leyton and Kendal creameries and from the turn of the century, milk was also exported to the rapidly expanding urban markets. The milch cows benefited from the old lime-sweetened soil, and from the army of local and Irish labourers who were available from hiring-fairs for draining marshes, walling-in meadows, haytiming, and keeping the grasses free from docks, ramps (garlic), thistles and moss. Then, as now, the retailing of milk from a patchwork of small farms on high fells depended on getting the most out of locally grown grass without depending too much on the importing of fodder and supplemental feeds, and 1859 in particular saw the start of a number of years of intensive walling work for the procurement of fine hay meadows, or 'holmes'. Even when farmers physically moved their cattle to the new conurbations and set up milk-houses, such as in Liverpool or Manchester, the success of the enterprise depended on the quality of dale grass.

These adaptations notwithstanding, poverty became more widespread in the region as the nineteenth century proceeded. A popular refrain in the western Yorkshire dales advised people to 'do as they do in Dent: got no tobacco, then chew Bent [grass]'. A number of disastrous summers in northern England exacerbated conditions. Finally, unable to procure farm work or else make their remote properties of a few acres support a family, thousands migrated towards the industrial centres of Bradford, Leeds, Halifax, Durham and Keighley. Indeed, between 1871 and 1881, after the British rural population peaked at 9.1 million, 100,000 were to leave the land in search of work and security in cities or overseas, part of that mass movement which, by the century's end, was to make Britain the most urbanised nation in the world.

In Wanet, the rearing of sheep and dairy cattle on fell farms remained the dominant forms of production nevertheless. Indeed, with the departure of many small farmers (the demise, in fact, of many of the original statesmen families) those who were able to remain greatly benefited from the freehold land and barns thus made available. Often land came to be sold to landowners of major estates who lived outside Wanet, but, even so, through the amalgamation of plots within the dale many local enterprises were given a new lease of life. With large mountain pasturages they could become far more economically viable, and their farmer-owners or new tenants or managers more specialised. For traditional hand-knitting was shortly to be overtaken by mass-production, while marble quarrying was ended by the trade in continental products, and the droving of stock to market, like the shallow-mining of coal and lead, was superseded by the arrival of the railway.

The Lancaster–Carlisle railway was begun in 1843 and conveyed its first passengers by 1846. The competing and adjacent Settle–Carlisle route was completed by 1875. Between them, access to the Lake District and Yorkshire Dales in the later years of the century was made easier than ever before. Not only could commodities such as coal now be shipped in with ease (soon causing the local market and pack-horse route to Kendal to collapse), but the weekend tourist, whose horse-

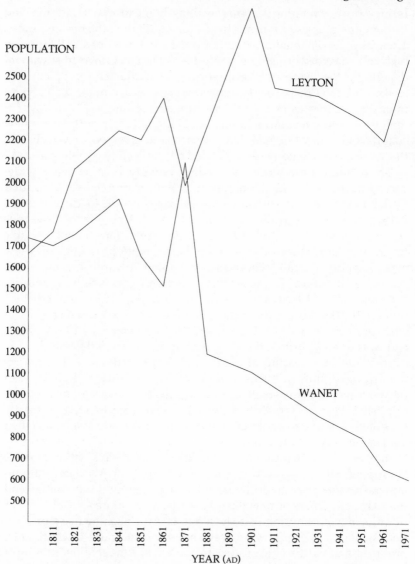

POPULATION

LEYTON

WANET

YEAR (AD)

Figure 2.1: Population curves of Wanet and Leyton between 1801 and 1971.

Table 2.1: A comparison between population distribution in Wanet in 1871 and 1981.

1871	1981
Pop. 2096 (503 surnames =4.16:1)	Pop. 635 (168 surnames =3.78:1) [68 surnames survive from 1871]
0.1 persons per acre	0.03 persons per acre [as against the English average of 1.34]

	1871	1981	
ROBBGILL hamlet and environs	139 persons in 33 houses	73 persons in 25 houses	ROBBGILL hamlet (plus scattered farmhouses)
Houses between WANET FOOT and WANET TOWN	222 persons in 39 houses	138 persons in 53 houses	Farmhouses between WANET FOOT and WANET TOWN
Houses between WANET TOWN and the hamlet of THURN	308 persons in 69 houses	50 persons in 20 houses	Farmhouses between WANET TOWN and the hamlet of THURN
THURN hamlet and east to WANET HEAD	840 persons in 129 houses	114 persons in 46 houses	The hamlet of THURN and farmhouses up to WANET HEAD
Houses from up RIGGDALE to WANET TOWN	231 persons in 46 houses	47 persons in 16 houses	Farmhouses up RIGGDALE
WANET TOWN	348 persons in 91 houses	213 persons in 90 houses	WANET TOWN (including 1 grocery shop, 5 holiday cottages, 1 tea-room, 1 reading-room, 3 barns, 1 restaurant, 3 knick-knack shops, 1 guest-house, 1 drapery shop, 1 post office, 2 art galleries, and 1 smithy; so approximately 75 residences)
	Total: 2096 persons in 407 houses (5.1:1)	Total: 635 persons in 250 houses (2.5:1)	

drawn carriage had formerly foundered along inaccessible fell passes, could now secure a speedy entrance from his new urban home for a walking or cycling tour.

The more-immediate effect of the railway, however, was the arrival in the area of thousands of navvies, on the liberal wage of seven to ten shillings per day. Catering for these caused the erection of steep tramways up the fells, and the dotting of different dales with shanty towns (Jericho, Sebastopol, Belgravia), stores, breweries and workshops; also the extension of local graveyards. Not only was the navvies' work hazardous but their relaxation habits, from the traditional gambling, cock-fighting and drinking to the novel dynamite-throwing and boxing were said to be 'Wild-Western' in their fierceness. For a while, the railway also provided a lifeline to the small farmer. The navvies bought farm produce and knitwear, and many boarded in local homes, and some enterprising farmers sold their labour to the railway companies. When the companies objected to hiring men who were already working, farmers simply signed over their farms to their wives and cared for their stock as and when they could.

The respite was temporary, however. Although the small 'statesman' farmer and rentier may have been able to do without poor relief for a number of years, when railway work petered out and the navvies moved on, many Wanet families moved with them and transfer of land to the more robust or stubborn farming enterprises resumed. The population curves above chart this decline for Wanet while the importance of the nearby market town of Leyton continued to grow (Figure 2.1); here too is a figuring of the changing pattern of residence within Wanetdale (Table 2.1).

Hence, as the nineteenth century came to a close it became clear that the ends of the small fell farm, of the village artisan and of the permanent farm labourer were in sight too. Economic niches that had lasted 300 years were disappearing with the coming to maturity of the Industrial Age. (Not all those left in Wanet became 'large' landowners, needless to say, and still today there are a number of small owner-occupiers and tenant farmers who survive by combining their farming with building or walling or joining, or helping-out as general labourers for a few hours on larger farms. Indeed, even the large farmer has to remain enough of a polymath to turn his hand to the demands of motor mechanics, decorating, building, even veterinary practice, as we shall see.)

If the 1840s and 1850s witnessed the rise of the conurbation – that 'ugly citadel', as Dickens described it in *Hard Times* in 1854, 'where Nature was as strongly bricked out as killing airs and gases were bricked in' – then it was over the next few decades that the effects of this new urban society began making themselves felt in the daily life of the area. People before had been forced to leave to find work, as we have seen (cf. Howitt, 1971, p. 241), but in the latter half of the nineteenth century the generations of those born in the town and city began making their way back out into the country again. There had always been the literary gentleman-traveller in the Lake District and Yorkshire Dales, such as Wordsworth, William Howitt, Coleridge, Southey, and so on, but the influx of railway labourers and those tourists who literally followed in their tracks – riding up from Lancaster, for example, for a day's cycling – heralded the birth of a new social phenomenon, the opening-up of the region to the massed carriers of urban-based cultures.

Perhaps it was this which, at least in part, encouraged the growth and widespread popularity among local dalesmen of independent religious sects such as Wesleyan and Primitive Methodism, and Zion Congregationalism. Quakerism had had a short-lived success in the seventeenth century, and George Fox was said to have preached to a crowd of many hundreds outside the meeting-house at nearby Brigflatts in 1675, but the Quakers were already a diminishing body by the time John Wesley reached Hawes a century later. Even then, according to Cockcroft (1975, pp 11–19), it was not until the mid nineteenth century, with local evangelists such as Richard Atkinson, that Nonconformity really took hold in the area. Before his death at 41 in 1884, Atkinson became something of a spiritual leader, an emblem in fact of local identity. It was claimed that he could predict the future and could cure animals. Striding across the fells in order to save time between gatherings, it was said he always knew where the bogs were and how best to avoid them. Even those who did not choose to follow a Nonconformist sect, and remained with the Anglican church or did without organised religion all together, could see represented in such charismatic figures and the congregations they led symbols of local life which was in stark contrast to that of the conurbation, whose emissaries were becoming increasingly frequent.

The twentieth century has not seen a reversal of this trend (even if the number of practising Methodists in Wanet has now dropped to around seventy, while the number of Congregationalists and Quakers combined is fewer still); yet more 'townies' have rediscovered the Southern Lakes and the Dales. By the 1930s, J. B. Priestley found that the two or three fell-walkers of his childhood, out in the Dales for a week-end stroll, had been overtaken by organised young gangs of twenty or thirty. These were hiking or biking their way into rural territory with such organisation that he was constrained to say that they 'almost looked German' (1934, p. 174). This was shortly to be followed by the age of the private motor car, with the dramatic upsurge in car-borne tourism with which the National Parks were set up to deal, and then, finally, the current process of 'counter-urbanisation' – as some commentators have described the degree of immigration to the region by ex-city-dwellers in search of retirement- or holiday-homes, or the securing of suitable properties for lease. Already in the 1930s, Priestley documented what he saw as the spread of urban habits of relaxation into the countryside. For example, he cited the ways in which new coaching inns were opening, with garage-men and mechanics replacing the traditional ostler and groom (1934, pp 176–7), and by 1979, with 85 per cent of the population living in cities, a 'trip to the country' had become Britain's most popular recreational pursuit (followed by the seaside, the garden and the park), in which 37 million people indulged at least once per year (see Countryside Commission, 1979).

The second half of the twentieth century, then, has seen leisure develop into a growth industry in the region, as the mobility and spending power of city dwellers have increased and their average holidays lengthened. After thirty years of motorway access (even if the provision of local bus and train services has declined) 'offcomers' now seasonally enter Wanet in large numbers, patronising its pubs, souvenir shops and guest-houses, camping- and caravan-sites, youth hostel and outward-bound centre (both buildings converted from old shooting lodges to accommodate visitors' changing predilections).

It is a moot point the extent to which this rise in tourism has led to more jobs for local people as distinct from local jobs. In many cases those catering for the urban tastes are offcomers themselves. Moreover, the urbanite search for rural contrast and the National Park preservation of village harmony have possibly thwarted the 'unsightly' development of noisy, large-scale industries. Certainly the traditional ones have disappeared (Wanet's last marble mills were pulled down in the 1920s), and population figures showing some stability over recent decades (1971: 590; 1981: 635) disguise the fact that young people in search of work are being replaced by the retired or those commuting to jobs elsewhere. Meanwhile, figures showing low unemployment by national standards, and indeed marking a 34 per cent rise in rural self-employment between 1978 and 1985 (*The Economist*, 1985, pp 19–25), in many cases represent the 'enterprise culture' of 'new' dalesmen (the computer-programmer on contract work in Manchester, the water-colourist selling paintings of Lakeland and Dales scenes, the architect mailing planned elevations to Leeds, and the piano teacher tutoring the children of the above), or at least the traditional determination of 'old' dalesmen to get by without losing his independence to the city, its businesses and bureaucracies, and without becoming enmeshed in exhortatory development schemes, benefits and compensations, or other such 'sophistry' (cf. Wright, 1977, p. 174).

Needless to say, with two world wars, the instigation of a welfare state and the emergence of national, then international, economic planning, the traditional agricultural mode of production has not survived the twentieth century unscathed or free from the organising and 'guidance' of the city either. The mass production of the manufactory spelled the end of the dale craftsman as we have seen, and if in the 1920s there were still specialist makers of hay-rakes securing a living from this alone, in general the First World War served to increase the speed with which the artisan was made redundant. In 1933 the Milk Marketing Board was formed, giving stability to the national milk market and fixing an overall price. This also made the procuring of a milk licence of extreme importance to many local farmers, representing the difference between being viable and not. In Wanet, for example, even though sheep outnumber cattle by approximately fifteen to one, dairy production remains the linch pin of many a successful farmer's economic strategy. And yet in order to obtain a licence, the milking process must be modernised and 'rationalised', especially since the introduction of bulk-tanker lorries which will only collect milk from 'accessible' farm tanks. Milking has had to become sanitised and mechanised. Thus, although the last forty years have seen a return to farmer-owners in Wanet, replacing the absentee landlords and managers of the late 1800s, the small or remote farmer has again been squeezed, or at least encouraged by 'golden handshakes' to sell out to his neighbour because the bulk-tanker cannot reach his milking shippon or because his yield is too small, or because a milking licence is in some other way hard to procure.

The Second World War brought the routine possibility of a private car to many a Wanet farmer too, as well as tractors and mechanised tools in place of his horse and what remained of his paid labourers. Since the war, a father and son partnership, or two brothers, has been the largest economic team which most farms have been able to support. Not that productivity has suffered; it could not afford to. The war years were good years in terms of the status granted to farming, of course, and the prices which farm produce could command. Food production was so paramount that agriculture was largely excluded from any of the planning controls established in the 1940s and 1950s, and born of wartime emergency, and nurtured by post-war subsidies, British farming underwent a revolution in method. More specifically, mechanised, capital-intensive farming techniques have enabled the fell farmer to compete with dairy, pig and egg production on lower, more fertile land further south. More recently, grants from the Marginal Production Schemes of London and Brussels governments have also supported the fell farmer in this competition by subsidising his successful rearing and sale of lambs and calves, and financially encouraging him to consoli-

Table 2.2: A Comparison between occupations in Wanet in 1871 and 1981.

1871	1981
Pop. 2096 (1204 males: 892 females)	Pop. 635 (311 males: 324 females)
1280 locals 816 offcomers	450 locals 185 offcomers
average age of death: 26	average age of death: 76
293 scholars	115 children:
	60 primary school: 55 secondary
	159 retired
	[82 locals: 69 offcomers]

1871	1981
169 Farmers	157 Farmers (and spouses)
56 Farm Labourers	[154 locals: 3 offcomers]
26 General Servants	1 Plumber
47 Stone masons	6 Publicans [offcomers]
11 Quarrymen	5 Bar staff
58 Miners	[2 locals: 3 offcomers]
50 Housekeepers	4 Teachers [offcomers]
310 Railway excavators	2 Millworkers [locals]
1 Railway timekeeper	8 Road labourers [locals]
1 Railway inspector	48 Housewives
1 Railway overlooker	[26 locals: 22 offcomers]
6 Engine drivers	6 Joiners [locals]
4 Nippers	4 Cabinet makers [locals]
3 Railway contractors	1 Architect [offcomer]
4 Engineers	2 Carpenters [locals]
782 General Labourers	2 Electricians
12 Knitters	[1 local: 1 offcomer]
1 Auctioneer	2 Artists [offcomers]
12 Dress makers	13 Caterers
2 Marble merchants	[5 locals: 8 offcomers]
10 Innkeepers	3 School staff [locals]
12 Gentlemen	3 Drivers-for-hire [locals]
5 Marble polishers	3 Garage mechanics
4 Lawyers	[2 locals: 1 offcomer]
11 Tailors	7 Shop owners
14 Joiners	[4 locals: 3 offcomers]
6 Shopkeepers	5 Shop assistants [locals]
1 Post messenger	5 Daily maids [locals]
1 Painter	22 Builders
5 Carriers	[20 locals: 2 offcomers]
24 Shoe-makers	3 Quarrymen [locals]
6 Drapers	2 Homesteaders [offcomers]
3 Reverends	2 Textile spinners [offcomers]
1 Lay preacher	2 Waitresses [locals]
1 Curate	12 University students
1 Schoolmistress	[8 locals: 4 offcomers]
6 Commercial clerks	2 Decorators
1 Governess	[1 local: 1 offcomer]
1 Nurse	1 TV Serviceman [offcomer]
2 Police constables	1 Railway signalman [local]
3 Game keepers	2 Railway lengthmen [locals]
1 Turner	4 Lorry drivers [locals]

In the 1871 column the entries from "310 Railway excavators" through "782 General Labourers" are bracketed together with the annotation: 1112 < [296 locals / 816 offcomers]

1 Corn clerk	2 Bank clerks [locals]
1 Surgeon	3 Factory workers [locals]
1 Annuitant	1 Factory foreman [offcomer]
5 Cordwainers	8 Commercial reps. [locals]
1 Butter-dealer	2 Insurance salesmen [locals]
2 Carters	3 Engineers
1 Brass finisher	[2 locals: 1 offcomer]
1 Builder	2 Company directors [offcomers]
1 Traveller	1 National Pk Officer [offcomer]
18 Grocers	2 Lecturers [offcomers]
6 Butchers	2 Computer analysts [offcomers]
20 Carpenters	1 Accountant [offcomer]
1 Brewer	
2 Millers	
1 Shepherd	
1 Cooper	
14 Grooms	
17 Blacksmiths	
2 Gardeners	
3 Sawyers	
1 Flour dealer	
1 Waller	
1 Tea dealer	
3 Hawkers	
3 Bakers	

TOTAL: 1803 Jobs in Wanet

TOTAL: 350 Jobs

293 in Wanet	57 outside
[232 locals:	[46 locals:
61 offcomers]	11 offcomers]

date his assets through improving the land with fertiliser (fertilisers are used eight times more liberally now than before the war), buying tractors, and building pit-silos and, eventually, self-feed cattle parlours (see Patterson, 1959, pp 340–2; also Mercer, 1988). The result has been, for example, a three-fold increase in milk yields from the region since the Second World War.

In sum the last hundred years have seen major changes to a Wanet way of life which might be traced back to the late seventeenth century at least. Of course, more recent changes have a tendency to seem more drastic and revolutionary than earlier ones, with their shock-waves still reverberating, and no doubt the passage of time will provide different perspectives, but the arrival of the railway during the latter half of the last century presaged not only widespread mechanisation but also the rise of tourism, two very major incursions with which twentieth-century Wanet has come to terms. True, pastoral hill-farming has retained its economic prominence as the characteristic mode of production in the dale, but it is farming of a very different kind from a hundred years ago. It now juggles the returns from hay meadows with those from camping fields, and it deals with markets, planners and sponsors whose decisions emanate from more and more distant urban centres and are intended to cover larger and larger hinterlands. A summary of these changes in the character of Wanet's occupational structure since 1870, then, is presented in Table 2.2 above.

Undoubtedly the future holds more challenges again. Upland agriculture may at present be cushioned against falling prices and cuts in production by continuing livestock allowances, even as European governments strive to reduce food surpluses (it is estimated that an area of England at least equivalent to the size of Devon and Derbyshire combined will no longer be needed for farming by the early years of the next century [see Mercer, 1988]) but pressure to consider alternative uses for traditional farm land can still be expected in future. Of course, pundits have been mooting an opening up of more of the region as an explicit tourist playground for decades, if not grouse moors then camping sites, caving centres, spas, whole holiday villages, or at least a move towards wholesale afforestation, as if the hill-farm will always be too vulnerable to cold winters and wet summers to make pastoralism a wholly secure option (cf. Simmonds, 1971, p. 38). But even if agriculture survives, schemes favouring 'set-aside' or 'extensification' (less intensive use of farmland through a curtailment of fertilisers, a reduction in grazing levels, an increase in size of fallow borders near field boundaries and a reintroduction of rotating fallow land), as well as advances in biotechnology (such as embryo transfer, sexual predetermination and cloned offspring) might mean that it comes to involve a very different set of practices.

For the present, however, even as Wanet Town hosts more offcomers than ever before, and traditional whitewashed cottages are transformed into twee weekend retreats, and 'village' threatens wholly to separate from 'valley', it is the family farm which remains the dominant Wanet symbol. That is to say, however much the above figures might speak of native depopulation and suggest a transformation of the dale of Wanet from a place of work to a place of recreation and 'escape', it is farming and the family farm (farm land, farmhouses, farm yards, farm animals and farmers themselves) which nevertheless retain most symbolic significance in connexion with a vibrant Wanet 'way of life'. And this remains true for the offcomer as for the local. There may be intense competition over their definition and ownership, but, as we shall see, they still represent the centre of the dale landscape, around which many other personal landmarks revolve.

3

The Landscape as Biography

Arthur farms up Riggdale and he knows every inch of those hills, he will tell you. Why, if he came back in a hundred years' time he would detect every minor change in Riggdale Reth's height and shape. And he's passed all his knowledge on to his daughter, Rose so that as she's learning to drive her second-hand Morris Minor (so she can get to her new job as barmaid in the Eagle in Wanet Town more easily), she will stick to the hill roads near the farm which she loves, even though they are steep and bendy, and frosty in the early morning. But then there's Kevin, from Wanet Town, who could not agree less with Rose about the wonders of Riggdale. He struggled up the Reth once, on foot, and it took him a month to recover (the one consolation was that it took his mate Alf even longer)! But never again. Even when he's late for his banking job in Kirkby Stephen, Kevin avoids the Riggdale road – those farm gates across it, keeping stock in, are such a headache – and he races his finely tuned Escort over the longer route up Wanet Wold. The only concession he will make to his farming heritage is occasionally to mow his mum's lawn.

Sid also usually avoids the dale's side roads, but for another reason – they get too congested with tourists. The intruders faff about, meandering down the middle of the roads like they own the place and keep real working folk from their jobs. Sid can spot them a mile off, and so steers well clear – unless, of course, he feels like driving an offcomer's car into a hedge. Doris sticks to the main roads, too. It is the only way to keep to her business schedule when she's delivering milk, and the only way to assure her touchy farming neighbours that she's not taking a jaunt past their fields just to be nosy. So Doris saves her investigating for when she's up on her and Fred's allotments. High up there, on her very own land and beholden to no one, she can check up on them all. In fact, that would be a great place to be buried when she dies – still surveying all. Husband Fred feels the same way, when he can finally get away from everyone and be alone with his stock. The exorbitant price this land went for at auction when old Boorwick Farm was parcelled up almost seems worth it. If only old man Rickworth next door would keep his fences in better repair . . . they're more like a clothes-line down the west slope!

On the other side of the mountain, Arthur also checks out his sheep but he wishes there were no fences up at all, like in the olden days when shepherds could map out their favourite routes over miles of common land. At least you still have the old drovers' roads (themselves the old Roman roads) to take you back. They traced the fell tops for hundreds of miles, linking market town and village, and always skirting the peaty bogs and the clayey marshes, as surefooted as the flocks they carried. And they also avoided the belligerent townsfolk in the valleys below. You can see those drovers must have disliked the crowds the way their roads keep walkers up here. They knew what they were doing all right. The Romans and those others on these roads wouldn't have liked the tourists in Wanet Town any more than Arthur does. In fact, it is probably the Vikings that Arthur is descended from. After all, they were self-reliant farmers working quietly and busily alone, on their isolated plots high on the steep fells, and even nowadays, walking the allotments, one can sense that Viking spirit is still present.

Jack agrees. He is a joiner, so he doesn't often get Arthur's opportunities to walk the high fells, but he likes to feel the past all around him too, and he gets a really good feeling from all of Wanet's old stone farmhouses. Take the Blythe family's, for instance. They've been living at Millwood Farm continuously since the 1600s which must be a national record. Inside his own house Jack surrounds himself with the fruits of his historical passion too – antiquarian books. He plans to donate them to the Wanet museum one day, if ever one were opened.

Not too far away from Jack, in Robbgill, live Paul and Anita Smythe. Now that they have finally retired from their civil service jobs in Coventry they enjoy nothing so much as dating and classifying Wanet's topography. They would more or less agree with Jack's claims for the locale, but perhaps elaborate to say that it was in the early fifteenth century that Wanet's farmers stopped being manorial tenants and became independent yeomen, or 'statesmen', with a council of twenty-four owner-farmers who ran local affairs and sat on their own pews in church, with a grammar school granted by James I, and at least since the late seventeenth century with imposing whitewashed farmhouses, with slate roofs, stone mullions and sandstone lintels, to replace the earlier, no doubt draughty, wood and peat constructions. It is this that they tell Mary on a tour of inspection of her fine corbelled chimneys, and how, by rights, her farmhouse should have a porch built on to the front of it too. Mary, indeed, wishes it did, for then it would be a far more presentable sight. As it is, her barn looks more impressive than her house! And just think – with a decent porch Mary wouldn't have to wait for those rare hot days to be out on the terrace on her sun bed. She could sit in the shelter and comfort of the porch even in a breeze or a downpour. Sam, her husband, laughs. When he sees Anita coming he scuttles off in the opposite direction. Let the women go on chittering for the next few hours if they want to, but everyone knows Wanet has nine months of winter and three months of bad weather. You know you are bound to get wet, and that your waterproofs will only turn so much water, so what is there to discuss? And out Sam goes, away from the hen-party huddled round the kitchen fire.

Many tourist travelogues would disagree, however. Wanet's beauty is said to 'sparkle with interesting individuality'. Wanet is somewhere which always 'seems sunny', where you walk in 'still tranquillity', in 'salubrious and peaceful air', and in 'an unbroken desertion'. So the walkers come crowding in – school parties, outward-bound groups, caravanners, campers, cavers and army cadets. It is the cadets that Kevin probably hates most. For at least the fell-walking cronies invariably get themselves lost way out on the high allotments and have to call out the Fell Rescue Team, in their matching knickerbockers and gaiters – and that's a good laugh, and the cavers keep on getting stuck down some shake-hole, because their gear has got wedged in – and that's right funny too. The squaddies, however, out on orientation exercises from their army bases always seem to read their maps aright just when it gets to pub-opening time, so they end up propping up the bar all evening in the Mitre and then wander round the streets all night, making a scrow, and puking in people's gardens. And what do the Wanet girls do but give them the eye! The tarts! So for the cadets Kevin always makes sure he's wearing his Guinness T-shirt which reads 'Genuine Irish'.

But Sid and Arthur don't mind when the army comes. In the Eagle, Sid congratulates the officers for the latest victory against the IRA and gets the low-down on future operations, while Arthur chats about experiences in barracks, like his in East Anglia in the Second War, and gets bought a pint or two. Of course, some Wanet residents are delighted about any visitors the dale can attract, or at least relieved that here is another source of local income. So when the County Council plans some noisy, unsightly and inconvenient roadworks on an August bank holiday, the Wanet Commerce Corporation is up in arms, and a special meeting is called in order to give chairman Hilary Tucker a mandate to use their letterhead and write and complain about such blatant disregard for Wanet business such as the tourist season as well as haytiming. Fred and Doris go along to the meeting, anxious about their custom on the caravan site, and so does Jon, because of his camping ground, and Herbert the garage owner, and Hattie and Barbara the gourmet restaurateurs, and Peter the artist, and Henry, Richard and Charles the Publicans, and Jessica and Rupert from 'By-gones', the home-spun wool and antique furniture and local photography and pottery shop. And they win their case! Well, Hilary is so good with word. It's no wonder she keeps leading the Thurn Thespians to all the finals of the Women's Institute drama competitions.

Cyril, however, could have wished for another result (even if his mini-bus and taxi service would have suffered) if only to take that Hilary Tucker woman with her 'Wanetdale Sweets and Treats Emporium and Tea-House' and her whiskered, surgeon husband, down a peg or two. There she is, claiming her business is of centuries' standing, and using the name of Wanet, and all she provides the place in return is regular evenings of incessant bellowing at the Mitre pub. And who ever heard of 'Wanetdale' anyway? 'Wanetdale' be buggered! The place is called 'Wanet'. And there, Cyril knows, even those jumped-up windbags on the Wanet Parish Council would have to agree with him. For they soon had to complain when the County Council was undergrounding all those overhead electrical wires recently – making the place look more 'untouched' – and suddenly all these signs went up advising motorists of diversions from 'East Wanetdale' to 'West Wanetdale'. People didn't know what the hell was going on! The clerk had to explain right sharp-ish that as far as local people were concerned 'Wanet' was the name of the dale and 'Wanet Town' its centre. Happily, the signs came down.

When faced with such bureaucratic heavyhandedness and hot air, however, Kevin thinks that the only suitable response is immediate action. In a talking-match these offcomers can always come out on top – wordsmithery is the only thing they *are* good at, and look at how they butt their snouts into every stew in the dale. But if there was a Wanet Republican Army and sentries were posted on the approach roads and the railway tracks, then intruders would soon be pushing up daisies. Brian would agree, and considers the National Park wardens dishonest liars. They keep telling the locals that they do appreciate that the visitors are transients and that locals have different interests, and the disruption from tourism would be far worse if it wasn't for the Park's regulations, while without the tourists, local amenities (such as railway service) would be worse again. But Sid knows the Park creates most of the problems it pretends to solve, and he believes its officials are due for a fall. They aren't so high and mighty, and one day soon they might just trip over their wallets and break their necks.

Phil sees it differently, however. He was a railway signalman for nearly fifty years. Retired now, he still keeps in touch and enjoys regaling tourists in the Eagle with railway lore, like how the gradient over some of these fells was so steep (Shap, for instance) that extra steam-engines had to be kept ready just in case carriages started going backwards! He still knows what he's on about, and he can appreciate the Council and Park arguments. He realises, for example, that by the 1970s local railway lines were sometimes operating at an 84 per cent annual loss, and that it is only the Summer Rail Specials – trains for tourists, and for shopping outings to Leeds and Preston – that keep some stations open at all. Closing local lines completely would be a great shame.

Matthew, indeed, would call it a tragedy, because there's so much identity and history caught up in them. He has listened to Phil, enthralled, for so many years that when the visitors come he can answer most of their queries too which makes him really proud. If Phil's son Steve hadn't taken over his dad's job, Matthew reckons he could have left his Leyton bank clerkship and become a right crafty signalman himself. And Hattie is pleased about the railway too, however they manage to keep the lines open. With only one bus per week to Leyton, and then a long wait for the one to Kendal, how are old people meant to get out and about? At least the railway lets them stock up on some cheap supermarket offers.

Fred sees the Inter-City expresses whizzing past on their way to Scotland when he's tending his sheep on the high allotment he's recently rented on Wanet Wold. But when he sits down mid-morning by the barn, with his flask of tea and a biscuit, and looks down into the dale, he doesn't hear the trains at all. For there is the River Tan where he used to fish and swim as a boy. There were forty-pound salmon in the beck in those days – why, you could cross it on their backs and not get your feet wet! And it was only the bridge by Hogart that stopped trawlers sailing up from the sea. Then, in Henry's Paddock (the land he owns below this) there's that hollow of larches. Fred's going to cut down one of them soon for a really smush hardwood gate for the front garden, and there'll still be a lot of cover left for his hoggs to shelter under in next winter's storms. Of course, before all that he'll have to sell this year's lambs and finally decide where to take them. If only their faces weren't quite so white and pasty. Certainly, he'll trim the hair off their faces and necks, and make sure they're all nicely washed and beribboned, but these dealers still seem to look out for that bit of black in the face, and young Timmy, the new ram, didn't quite manage that this year, even if he did a fair job in other respects. It is ludicrous really as the quality of the meat isn't any different but Arthur, Fred's brother, just says to go along with it – dye their faces if necessary – and don't try to reason it out. If that's what it takes to make your lambs a bit more noticeable among the thousands in the Gapton sales, then that's what has to be done – with fickle market prices and tricky auctioneers, you can't risk not giving the dealers the colour they prefer. But maybe Fred will try out a few fat lambs for price at Leyton market this year. It is far smaller than Gapton but it had a good reputation for sheep once, and now it's got a handy new auctioneer – old Cocker's son who learnt his father's craft – maybe things will look up again. And there's always Kendal to consider. Fred usually feels that its cattle market has a habit of attracting such large lowland beasts that they would swamp animals like his, bred for the Wanet fells. But Doris told him that her cousin Michael's father took some lambs there at the back-end of last year's sales and got a fairish price, so that might be worth a try as well. He'll have to wait and see. Anyhow, back to work now, or it'll soon be time for dinner, and his stomach will be touching his backbone with nowt hardly to show for it at all. . .

4

The Landscape as Idyll

I

In 1838, William Howitt, author of *Visits to Remarkable Places* and *A Popular History of the Treatment of Natives by European and Christian Colonisers*, published *The Rural Life of England*, an account of a journey taken by him and his wife Mary around those points of England less well known to polite circles in town. Part of their time was spent in the dale of Dent, in the same upland fell country as Wanet, and one chapter ('Nooks of the World: Life in the dales of Lancashire and Yorkshire') is a description of the region. The chapter is prefaced by a line drawing of strangely garbed natives, in procession through a spreading moon-lit jungle of dense forest depths and forbidding mountain peaks which would not look out of place in New Guinea, and accompanies Howitt's description of a wild, shut-in region of vast and dreary hill and moorland tracts. Here, we are informed, is to be found a 'primitive race' with the most peculiar lingering habits of all England. They exhibit a great simplicity of life and character which goes back even to the days of old English patriarchy and yet, despite their lack of *savoir-faire* and adventure, Howitt sees in them an earnest-hearted people, hospitable, kind, law-abiding and virtuous, with strong social sympathies, an honest sense of property and a moral integrity of mind. Their pre-eminent attachment to their 'back settlements' and 'pleasant hills' is sensible enough, he concludes, for here is perhaps the 'most perfect nook of the world that England holds' (1971, pp 226–47).

Nearly a century later J. B. Priestley wrote his *English Journey*: 'Being a rambling but truthful account of what one man saw and heard and felt and thought during a journey through England during the autumn of the year 1933.' He too travelled through the dale country, finding it 'Tibetan in its height and emptiness' and seeming, in its grey desolation to be 'at the world's end'. Here the stone buildings and walls still seemed less the results of man's labour than natural outcroppings, while the folk, solid and lonely, continued to imagine fairies dancing on the hillsides, as if they had kept hold of originally 'keener senses' which others had lost. In conclusion Priestley concurs that the 'authentic dale country' is the best in England (1934, pp 173–8).

The hundred years between Howitt and Priestley did little to alter the idyllic way in which the visitor from the city depicted the rural, dale landscape, then, despite the historical upheavals of the Industrial Revolution, railway, motorway and tourism which I have described. It was still seen to be populated by natives who were in touch with the earth, with their senses, and time-honoured customs, in ways which urban man had lost. Both Howitt and Priestley find a pastoral simplicity and honesty in the countrymen inexorably tied to that everlasting circle of the fertility cycle (as Blythe has put it [1969, p. 15]), an English version of the noble savage. Nor has this mode of description become less popular to the travel writer in the fifty years since Priestley. Thus we find Scott celebrating the 'unbroken peace' of this inaccessible, remote and 'truly wild, mountain country' where it is possible to die from exposure and also hear larks as in the days of the Norsemen (1965, pp 26–30). While Cockcroft decides that 'the golden thread of continuity' makes dale country an 'inspirational place' (1975, p. 126), and Hartley and Ingilby describe centuries of self-reliant, independent and neighbourly people who have eked out a simple and traditional existence here, in crude houses, on little money and with few resources (1982, pp 11–12). Clearly, for commentators from the 95 per cent of the British workforce which the Industrial Revolution wrenched from their more traditional pursuits of farming, forestry and fishing, village life in a rustic setting like Wanet has retained its charms as the best and 'natural' place to live, and as a home to be one day returned to. Until that time, one creates what rural qualities of life one can in an urban or suburban home and makes frequent trips to the countryside in one's free time. For it is 'a place of sentiment' still and even if only 22 per cent of England represents urban development, the countryside is still there to be preserved (cf. Palmer *et al.*, 1977, p. 739; also Young, 1986, p. 124).

II

The folk concept of the rural idyll has coloured anthropological writing on Britain in a number of ways too, the most striking of these being the notion of the 'traditional rural community'. Here is represented a culture which, as Byron described it for the Shetland isle of Burra, was consensually shared, homogeneous and uniform. The traditional community was close-knit and isolated; it was egalitarian, shunned ostentatious differentiation and esteemed traditional competences (1985, pp 146–9). Community wholeness, moreover, was apparent in all activities as things were 'rarely merely what they appeared to be', as Frankenberg put it; in the village there were more latent functions than in the town (1965, p. 291), as every 'practical' happenstance also had wider social aspects (Rees, 1951, p. 96). In short, in the traditional rural community, all people and events were part of an encompassing social whole. All informed this whole, all added up to this whole, all was granted a place by it. Thus, in the Welsh settlement of Llanfihangel, the community represented itself as a patchwork of connected houses, each of which was granted a special purpose, and each visited according to the nature of the community occasion – theological or poetical or musical or craft (knitting) (Rees, 1951, p. 133). In the English village of Gosforth, the community allocated different emotional and physical attributes to different kinship groupings, tying all surnames together in a picture of a corporeal whole (Williams, 1956, pp 77–8). And in the Scottish hamlet of 'Clachan', the community contrived a system of nicknames which allocated everyone a position in a community-wide jigsaw of collective geographical, genealogical, occupational and historical space, and specified for each individual particular socially identified foibles, virtues and skills (Mewett, 1982, pp 238–41). In sum, in the social anthropological version of the folk concept of a rural idyll, the traditional community came to represent society organised in terms of mechanical solidarity, status relations, multiplex roles, dense interactional networks, equilibrial social structures, and ascription (Frankenberg, 1965, pp 286–92).

As regards the mode of ascription in terms of which membership of the rural community was organised, anthropologists usually seemed to favour one of two kinds: a social system where class was the main load-bearing institution; and one where class considerations (such as differentials of job, house and income) were marks of an outside world only, and locally irrelevant. Williams's study of the Devon village of Ashworthy would represent an account of the latter sort, where villagers lived a total social life of all-pervasive relations, and the social structure was an harmony of cross-cutting kinship – political, neighbourly and religious ties (1963, p. 184). Similarly, for Byron on Burra (1985, p. 155), Mewett in 'Clachan' (1982, pp 102–3), Rees in Llanfihangel (1951, p. 143), and Harris in 'Hennage' (1974, pp 38–9), centuries, perhaps, of accumulated practice had engendered a single moral community with deep-rooted traditions of local behaviour. It was accomplishment in these places which earned local esteem, differentiated members from outsiders and caused the maintenance of a self-sufficient 'social system in miniature'.

In contrast to the above are those social commentators who depicted the rural community as a social structure based on class, even if sometimes under the guise of paternalism. As Newby explained (1975, p. 178), community ought to be seen as a nineteenth-century phenomenon and part of the capitalist ideology of social control. Here was the creation of a little kingdom in which farmers, as rational businessmen, imposed their values and beliefs on their labourers. They, in turn, accepted this 'false consciousness' for want of ideological alternatives, showed deference to what became the 'traditional' system of authority, and partook of a cultural consensus which was in conflict with their underlying class interests (Newby *et al.*, 1978, pp 188–90, 276). Littlejohn's study of a parish in the Cheviot Hills would follow these kinds of lines, for example. Here we find three classes: upper-middle, represented by the vicar and the big farmers; lower-middle, represented by the other farmers, the forestry managers and the teachers; and finally the working class of craftsmen and labourers. The higher an individual's class, Littlejohn explains, the wider and more dispersed his social network, and the more frequent his contacts outside the parish (1963, p. 114). Hence while the community represents an economic platform for the owners of the means of production, with little sentimental significance, for the workers (who outnumber, by five-to-one, the top two classes combined) it forms the bounds of the modal social world and the place where they compete to be part of the best farmers' teams.

For all of these anthropologists of Britain, I suggest one can find the equivalent of the popular rural idyll in the notion of community – something more or less closed, holistic, functionally integrated, and consensual; and something opposed to the associational way of life of the town and city. That is, the anthropologists would follow Tonnies's developmental dichotomy of *Gemeinschaft* to *Gesellschaft* (or else Spencer's, or Durkheim's, or Maine's, or Weber's, or Redfield's, or Becker's) and see in the countryside a way of life diametrically opposed to that of the urban centre. At the least, they would see the rural and the urban as the distant poles of a spectrum of types of social organisation; but more common was the claim, as made by Williams for Gosforth, for example, that Norse and Celtic features differentiated his (Cumbrian) village from the rest of English culture (1956, p. 202). In the community was to be found a traditional order and localness threatened by the homogenising forces of urban change.

III

Indeed, for many commentators community had already been superseded, the idyll overcome. This portrayal is a common one. Two World Wars and the arrival of twentieth-century technology (the first planes seen overhead in 1914 [Cockcroft, 1975, p. 53], the arrival of the private car and telephone after 1945 [Blythe, 1969, p. 15]), were said to have caused extensive links to be forged with the outside world and the introduction of new ways of life. Thus the traditional self-sufficient community had been transformed into a dependent part of a uniform national culture. Communication and travel had become easy, with locality no longer representing the consensual centre of work, recreation, gossip or esteem. For the young especially, urban values had attracted people to new criteria of worth, new sources of status, new notions of monetarised labour and profit, and new social horizons. In short, local community had come to be replaced by a more urban, atomised, individualised type of society. A rural social structure may have survived in stasis for centuries but the arrival of urban institutions, mobile individuals, industrial wage labour and international markets, meant that what community closeness, feeling and cohesion remained would not survive much longer.

Byron's account of Burra is a good example of this rhetoric. An accommodation of local life to the outside, an adjustment of perceptions to international contingencies, had always been part of this busy cultural crossroads, we hear, but the arrival of oil in the 1970s and the technological developments which followed, together with the building of a bridge to the Shetland mainland which was suitable for motors, heralded a change in kind for the traditional local community. Local economic calculi, attitudes to work and preferences for it, were transformed. Self-sufficiency was broken and not only did people start commuting to oil-related jobs, they also drove across the bridge to the mainland in order to work in the fish plants, or attend the courts or hospital or secondary school, or see the doctor or the police, or go to the bank or garage or pub. At the weekend, the island was deserted. Also, the privacy of a post-office off the island meant that dole cheques were easier to receive without incurring neighbours' Calvinistic castigation. In fact not only did oil change old job patterns, material expectations and the evaluation of labour, but state universalism and government welfare programmes abrogated local institutions of self-reliance and care. Local kinship networks fell away as systems of integration and reciprocity, and personal status became less a matter of kinship ascription than individual achievement, measured in terms of cash returns from a national money market. Outside jobs became prized as a source of security and prestige (and education valued as a route to them), while Burra as a local community, to the people who lived there, became equivalent to any other rurality, a place of simplex relations and competition in terms of conspicuous consumption (1985, *passim*). Indeed, on the not-too-distant isle of Lewis, according to Mewett, the cultural artefacts of traditional community life came to be expressly devalued and stigmatised. In the race for more pay, material rewards and mainland recreation, to stay on the island, in Gaelic rusticity, was to be regarded as sentimental and a financial failure (1982, pp 225–33).

As with the folk concept of the rural idyll, then, the anthropological equivalent in the notion of the traditional rural community is seen as becoming an endangered species: a nook increasingly distant and hard to find. Threatened by the introduction of what are claimed to be the universalistic structures of the modern nation-state, the face-to-face, 'total' community splinters. As Rees put it, the spread of urban standards, commercial and business relations, and class solidarities spell the end for traditional 'tribal' reciprocities (1951, pp 166–7); in fifty years, Williams wrote in 1956, community will have completely died (1956, p. 203); for people work outside and relax in private (Newby, 1972: pp 430–1; also cf. Frankenberg, 1957, pp 150–1; Marshall and Walton, 1981, p. 221).

IV

The source of the idyll of rural community is more of a moot point. It has been traced to a Victorian anti-urban bias, as industrialising towns came to be viewed by the middle and upper classes as unhealthy hotbeds of social discontent and political disorder, while the countryside could be seen as remaining the repository of traditional and ideal values and the home of the ultimate status symbol – the country seat (e.g. Phillips and Williams, 1984, pp 2–3). But then Dewhirst cites Fred Morton Eden celebrating as early as 1797 the virtue, intelligence and independence of the healthy peasant of England's north country as compared with those who seek help and charity in the more familiar regions of the populous south (1972, p. 1), while as late as 1890, Gomme can be found describing the village as a primitive element which is of necessity broken under the advance of civilising economic and political conditions (1890, p. 232). Clearly the use of the rhetoric of rural community is a complex issue, and the precise details of English life in town and country referred to, even more so.

For this reason Pahl (1968, *passim*) has argued against the social scientific usefulness of either urban/rural dichotomies or continua for describing English social life, 'urban' and 'rural' being such hackneyed terms that their usage inevitably confuses. Not only does he feel that Britain is now part of one large system of production, communication and information (as we have heard above from others), so that cultural isolation is replaced by one system of transport, one array of consumer goods, one range of media coverage, one set of bourgeois values, but he also opines that urbanised relationships are no less face-to-face, necessarily, than their predecessors, and no more anonymous. In other words, Pahl warns against tying patterns of social relationships to geographical milieux *per se*. Living close together need not entail shared experiences or bounded identities, and living apart need not mean their negation. Lifestyle need not derive from or even relate to locale as externally defined. Of course, according to MacFarlane, rural life as idyllically constituted by peasant sameness and community, holism and social-structural stasis fails to depict accurately how life in England has been lived at least since the thirteenth century. In his thesis (1978, *passim*), there has been an individualism in English social and economic life, of ego-centric kinship, political liberty, rights to property, independence of conscience, market acquisitiveness, geographical mobility, occupational changeability and widely distributed affluence, which pre-dates by some hundreds of years the Protestant Reformation, growth of capitalism and Industrial Revolution said by such classic commentators as Homans (not to mention Marx and Engels) to have given rise to such urbane atomism in the first place.

Indeed, even in the data anthropologists have themselves provided concerning their rural communities, rather different pictures can be seen to emerge if different points in the composition are highlighted. Thus, the image of rural isolation is changed somewhat when we consider the national and international markets of which, as in Wanet, those working on the land seem long to have been aware: exporting wool all over Britain from the Chevïot Hills, and early on taking advantage of opportunities in America and Australia (Littlejohn, 1963, p. 59); buying lamb from New Zealand on Burra, and selling woollen sweaters to Paris and fish to the United States (Byron, 1985, p. 49); making wholesale hosiery deals on the London market from the Craven highlands, and importing the latest tailored styles (Speight, 1892, pp 428–9); feeding silver, illegally clipped from coins in the Yorkshire Dales, into an international black market trade (MacFarlane, 1981, p. 78); and investing wealth in Dentdale which was gleaned from merchandising sugar and slaves in the West Indies (Parker, 1977, p. 90). Moreover, again as in Wanet, many countrymen seem to have been visited by urban tourists *en masse* for centuries, latterly by rail (Wright, 1977, p. 151), previously by road (Howitt, 1971, p. 230). Meanwhile, those who did not leave their localities have long been *au fait* with sending out telephone messages – whether to relatives, vets, or midwives (Mitchell and Joy, 1973, p. 88) – while receiving international news and hearing of the circumstances of their fellow-Calvinists in the Khasi Hills of Assam or their fellow-Independents in the South Seas (Rees, 1951: p. 114).

Similarly, the image of rural continuity and stasis is altered by a highlighting of the details of change. For example, there is the endemic movement between farms in Ashworthy which Williams recounts (far from the peasant's attachment to his land) (1963, p. 57); or Howitt's record in 1838 of artefacts in the western Yorkshire Dales which had even then long fallen into disuse (such as fell tumble-carts and peat sledges), while the scorn of outsiders and the stigma of being seen as old-fashioned had already caused men to be leery of engaging in such traditional local practice as knitting if observed (1971, p. 236); or that native of the Yorkshire Dales, the geologist Adam Sedgewick's tale in 1868 of how the dialect of local children was already different from when he was a boy (1868, p. 80).

Finally, the image of closure in the rural community is ameliorated by an appreciation of demographic movement by various researchers. For example, one part of the village of Elmdon stays on, maintaining a birth-, marriage- and kinship-linked core, while another part is changing all the time – the village as bounded and yet forever seeing people come and go (Robin, 1980, pp 239–41; Richards and Robin, 1975; Strathern, 1982b, pp 273–4). Even those 'exiles' who leave Lewis and work in mainland jobs do not necessarily rescind their relations to the place or lose their membership of the 'Clachan' community (Mewett, 1982, pp 222–3).

In short, in dealing with traditional anthropological descriptions of British rural communities we must be aware of the specifics of the genre in which the data appear, and locate the authors within a particular scriptorial tradition. Like the rural idyll, the notion of village community has a cultural locus and a history, and carries with it certain broad implications of people and life 'in the countryside', as we have seen. In the anthropological as in the lay tradition the village community represents an entity which is prior to the modern conurbation and, as Strathern puts it, something whole and 'natural'; but as she exhorts (1982b, pp 248–9), we must realise that, idiom or no, this is not necessarily so: that, as I began to show above, very different pictures can always be drawn out of the 'same' data and situations. 'The village community' must be seen as an idea, however socially prevalent at a certain time (so that it finds favour among villagers, townies, and their professional social scientific commentators alike). Indeed, it can be seen as a popular idea, a dominant symbol (after Turner), a shorthand in which a multiplicity of cultural themes meet, and a micro-institution which is part of the normative apparatus of a particular modern society (after Zijderveld's account of the authority of the cliche in complex society [1979]).

In other words, the idea is something that we ought to contextualise culturally and not be beholden to adopt uncritically. This is not to say that we need to follow Bell and Newby's course (1975, pp 13ff.) and see the idea of village community as something imposed on society so as to reflect the values and further the control of its ruling echelons, rather that we should not merely accept this idiom of expression at face value. In the ideas of the rural idyll and the rural community we should see part of a society's institutional apparatus, part of the practice of exchanging shared forms of behaviour, which may be instrumental in serving a number of political ends, which may be imparted with a number of possible meanings, which may be personalised in terms of a number of individual lives, whose significance, in short, derives from its particular context of usage and which must be understood as such.

V

In practical terms, this means that we should beware confusing the *form* of a social organisation (such as rural community) or an idiom (such as the natural, enclosed village) or a genre (such as idyllic rusticity) with their content. An idea may be universal but the way it is used is not: the idea of rural community and its supersession by modern urban association, of ascription giving way to contractual achievement, of mechanised means of production ushering in a standard industrial mode of production, and so on, translated into the particularities of different settings and situations become very different creatures. That is, not only should we beware confusing the genre of rural community with the reality of life outside the town, and be aware of the genre as a culturally and historically specific mode of expression, but we should also realise that the seeming sameness of our categories of description – 'rural', 'community', 'kinship-based', 'class solidarity', 'integrated social structure' – disguise a possible diversity of actual social relations. To elucidate and not corrupt these is to step outside the general forms of idiom and genre and accept that we may not be able to generalise social behaviour to Britain as a whole, or to rural Britain, or even to a region of rural England; significant behaviour may belong to particular spans of working social relations, to particular talking-relationships, alone. Thus Cohen has emphasised that merely to see 'North Atlantic fishermen' in Shetland and not 'Whalsay fishermen', to see a 'generalised British family' and not 'Hendry's folk at the Sneugins', to see 'relations between male villagers' and not 'a friendship between Hendry or Charlie and Auld Ertie', is to see the surface and not the substance. For whatever the common public assumption and the implications of its shared idioms, beneath ostensibly similar forms may reside different worlds of meaning in which discrete cultural boundaries continue to be cherished (1982b, pp 13–15). This is not to say that every social network is an isolate, or that every talking-relationship must be treated as unique. Rather it is saying that the particular case is to be greatly respected; that the significance of local social relations need not be seen as determined by outside forces, however powerful and prevalent the latter appear; and that in opposition to a variety of versions of ergodic hypotheses which would see in one case a representative of the many (e.g. Arensberg, 1959, p. 9; or Fox, 1978, pp ix–x), when imbued with local colour and experience, as they invariably are, seemingly 'representative' behaviours may assume meanings of very particular significance.

For example, in his insightful portrayal of the work of a country doctor in a village of foresters, John Berger shows that, far from the seeming surrender to common and universal hazards, the illnesses of Dr Sassall's patients are forms of expression of highly uncommon meanings. Only as a locally ensconced fellow-interactant is the doctor able to diagnose these unique ailments, 'keep them company', and finally return their sufferers to their everyday routines; the paradigm of 'commonsensical' interpretation, meanwhile, is merely 'a temptation to blindness' (1968, p. 62). Similarly, in Strathern's account of the Essex community of Elmdon, we find the universal English idea of the village and the idiom of kinship being used by local people as means of interpreting their own particular class positions, relating the wider world to personal experience and circumstance. Village and kinship become Elmdon symbols which are used to think about and order the world from individuals' local points of view, while national class positions become reference points for their estimations of self (1981, p. 147; 1982a, p. 93). Or again, though we may find on Burra the structural relations of neighbourhood and crew going the same way as the traditions of crofting, and falling into desuetude (Byron, 1985, pp 153–5), Cohen recounts how on nearby Whalsay these structures of behaviour continue to be invested with great symbolic significance. While neighbourhood and crew may no longer be the working frameworks of social organisation, they are vital idioms for the continued legitimation of local association and they create a rhetoric of cultural continuity which overcomes change. While crofting may no longer be economically necessary or even viable, it remains a popular activity and crofts are competed for because as a social structural archetype, crofting maintains local notions of time and distinctive place (1982c, pp 21, 47). Finally when the arrival of Nonconformity (in the shape of Calvinism) polarised the community of 'Clachan' into believers and non-believers, dividing neighbours and kinsmen alike (Mewett, 1982, p. 117), in Williams's Ashworthy (in the shape of Methodism) it cut across prior divisions and was partly responsible for an overcoming of the conflicts of class (1963, pp 195–8).

Of course such examples could be multiplied, and my account of Wanet will bring another case into the lists, but the point is made: the universal structure of behaviour or institution is brought to social life in a diversity of ways, and for a precise appreciation of the behaviour it is to the particular example that one must turn. In a compendium of such cases, moreover, one should not expect a gluey coherence or neat integration (any more than an assemblage of unique isolates). Rather, from case to case there will be an overlapping of behavioural same-nesses and differences, of 'familial resemblances' between features of local social life: from rural emigration in search of salaried employment in one area, for example, to counter-urbanisation in another; from a cutting-back on rural services in one location to a decentralisation of manufacturing in a second; from capitalist secularisation here to Non-conformist revivalism there; from dense kinship networks to individuals being allocated only contextual ties; from stigmatised rusticity to symbolical traditionalism; from inter-farm rivalry to valley-wide co-operative farming work-teams; from membership of a local core of families being measured in terms of competence against a consensual set of norms to competence being evaluated differently per situation and observer. In short, far from simple dichotomies and continua, from generalisable categories of behaviour in village community or town, a compendium of cases of social life in Britain will consist of an aggregation of partially (polythetically) connected behaviours.

In terms of my approach here, which I intend not to be a compendium of British village life so much as the elucidation of one specific case, what this means is that community in Wanet will not be sought as an integrated social structure, a set of certain regular patterns of behaviour (ascribed belonging, dense kinship networks, consensual values, multiplex relationships, and so on) which fit neatly together, like cog-wheels or some such image of a mechanical whole. Wanet will not be approached as an example of a particular type of social grouping at all – anachronistic or otherwise. This is not to say that I shall not have a keen interest in behavioural regularities: I shall. But these regularities will be tied firmly to more micro-social levels of analysis: to individuals and the interactions in which they habitually engage with one another. A precise focus on actual interaction, on features of cultural behaviour in particular use (living with a family, drinking with darts-partners, employing neighbouring farmers), will be the key.

In this way we might find that rather than building blocks which always cause the replication of one kind of collective structure (an overarching, equilibrial community), items of routine behaviour serve as ambiguous and malleable forms which may crop up in very different circumstances, be combined in different ways, and, to their protagonists, mean different things. They are the 'same' behaviours and yet they assume different lineaments in different lives; lives which, therefore, may be said to share certain familial resemblances with one another: the same nose may appear more than once, for example (the same consciousness of Wanet being deluged by newcomers, perhaps), but in combination with different eyes and mouth adding up to very different visages. Hence, far from determinants and exemplars of sameness, behavioural regularities may be the vehicles through which a number of Wanet communities are constructed and lived in at the same time; and, as such, more properly seen as instruments of great diversity.

5

The Landscape as Community

I

As the local proverbial wisdom has it: 'Kick one person from Wanet and next day seven people will be limping'. In this narrow valley, exchange of information, albeit along particular routes, is rapid and regular, and feelings of belonging prevalent. For here is a collection of people linked together closely, possessing many of the same names for pertinent landmarks in their cognitive maps of everyday landscapes. And yet they are not linked by any singular or imperative status. Rather, the dale of Wanet can be seen as an assemblage of individual lives which influence, overlap and abut against one another in a number of ways. The lives exhibit a family of resemblances which mark their owners as Wanet individuals, but with no simple common denomination. To borrow a phrase from one of Rees's Welsh informants (1951, p. 75), they are tied together 'like a pig's entrails'.

II

As an example I shall take the case of the interrelations between two Wanet families, the Rowlands and the Whitehouses. Next-door neighbours in Wanet Town, they see each other, talk about each other and evaluate each other's behaviour a great deal. Each family figures prominently in the local landscape of the other. The Whitehouses – Eric, Eira and grown-up daughter Florence – live at Vaila, a pebble-dash bungalow built near the edge of the village in the 1950s. Eric and Eira Whitehouse are retired now, and elderly, but the family hardware store around the corner near the Eagle Inn is being run by daughter Florence. Eric and Eira still assist with the tidying up, stock-keeping and suchlike, but it is Florence who now leaves the house at half past nine in the morning to open the shop for business. Not that she is busy, necessarily, even when there by herself. Trading has been slow these past few years, with people driving to larger shops and supermarkets in Leyton and Kendal for most of their hardware goods, unless Florence offers a special discount on a run of items like hay-rakes or buckets to bring in the custom for a week or two. Besides the post office and the grocery shop, it seems to Florence that only the shops selling to tourists are potentially viable. Nowadays, most of her energy in 'Whitehouse Hardware' goes on stoking the coal fire, keeping the place warm and the stock from getting damp. But the Whitehouses are not overly worried because Florence is soon to marry and then the store can finally be sold off; and even if the current business is not that attractive a proposition, a premises on the main street of Wanet Town will be much sought after. It could, for example, easily revert to the familial residence it was before – if not to two.

Florence is going to marry Bob Thomas and move on to the Thomases' farm to live. Bob's parents have already moved out of the farmhouse to a bungalow which they had built near by, and the place is waiting for Florence and Bob to move in. What will also be convenient is that the Thomases' farmhouse is less than half a mile from Vaila (albeit uphill) and Florence and her parents will be able to keep in close touch. There is even a footpath across the fells, so in dry weather they will be able to enjoy a walk in the fresh air as well.

The footpath between Vaila and the Thomases' farm crosses Old Gate Farm, home to Rick and Susan Rowland, their teenage daughter Wendy and son Clive. Old Gate does not have the land that the Thomases' farm does, squashed as it is between the Thomases' and many of the outer buildings of Wanet Town, nor is there much room for immediate expansion. But Rick and Susan are in the process of developing their business, buying and renting land around the dale as it becomes available. Looking up the hill at the farm Bob Thomas and his father are running beside them, Rick and Susan always feel that here they have something to aim at.

From the windows of their eighteenth-century farmhouse, nevertheless, it is Vaila that the Rowlands are more likely to be aware of, because the two buildings are immediately adjacent. The five-foot high dry-stone wall of the Rowlands' back garden is that of the Whitehouses' drive as well, linking the bungalow to the road, while over the wall of the Whitehouses' back garden there is a view of the Rowlands' cowsheds and camping fields. Moreover, since Vaila is built on a north-south orientation and Old Gate farmhouse on an east-west, reciprocal vision from inside the two houses is not much obstructed either.

Florence really finds this lack of privacy annoying, and she knows that her parents do too. Indeed it is worse for them because they are not going to move, and yet it is something they can do little to change. Wherever you happen to be in Vaila you can hear the yelping of the Rowlands' farm dogs and the yapping of their pups. The way they are always barking suggests that they are not being properly fed and if it is not the dogs that awake them then it is the banty cock at half past five every morning, standing on the garden wall, making his din. The least the Rowlands could do, according to Florence, would be to lock him in an outhouse or garage. Then there is the smell from the Rowlands' calf hulls. It is hardly pleasant entertaining visitors in the back garden with a stale odour wafting over the wall, but if Florence goes to the front instead she is are accosted by the stares of Rick Rowland and his workmen brushing cow-muck off themselves with some dirty brooms and trough-water before going into the farmhouse, or else Susan has had a family of campers pitch their tents right by the drive wall so that they cannot help but look straight into Vaila dining-room and her parents' bedroom.

The trouble for Florence and her parents is, that unless the Rowlands are either shamed or bullied into doing something they just will not make an effort. When Eric tries to help out and buy a few wheelbarrow loads of manure for the garden from an overspilling midden that Rick has been too inefficient to get out on to the land, Rick rings the bell in what appear to be the filthiest ripped clothes he could find, trailing muck everywhere and still managing to dump the pile in the wrong place (so Eric has to strain himself moving it once more). Or again, when Florence tries to be fair and buy an equal amount of milk for the shop from Doris Harvey *and* Susan Rowland she is forced into having more delivered than she really needs just because Susan (unlike Doris) will not sell half-pints. Even if Susan drops in and buys the occasional little thing from the shop (and is friendly enough, asking about her cousins' health, as Florence shows her old family photos and makes her tea), and however good it was to see Susan's patriotism a while back (going out of her way to sell milk with Royal Wedding souvenir bottletops in silver and black as a celebration of the occasion), it would still be nice if Susan were thoughtful *all* the time and Florence could buy one-and-a-half pints from her and from Doris, not two.

Then there is the question of footpaths on Old Gate Farm land. Far from making it clear where the paths begin, and how exactly they proceed, so that their fellow-villagers can visit one another and tourists enjoy the views from their fells, the Rowlands seem to have gone out of their way to make things confusing. When Eric and Eira tested the footpath route from Vaila to the Thomases' and their daughter's new home, they found traversing Old Gate Farm a bit like negotiating a rabbit warren. But then the Rowlands always have had little concern over getting along with their neighbours. For years there was that rather public and acrimonious dispute over some matter or other between Susan and her brother and sister-in-law, Colin and Irene Blythe, and since then, Rick and Susan seem to have turned their ready ill-temper towards their farming neighbours, the Thomases. When Rick and Susan first married and the farm began to take shape, old David Thomas would offer his help all the time – even during haytime when he had his own place to keep in order. But what did Rick do in return but illegally tip some rubbish into the beck and block up the sewage outlet from Thomas Farm! And when David sent the River Authority officials around to complain, Rick claimed he was only returning the compliment after David had done the same! Of course the River Authority did not listen because David's tipping had merely been soil, done with permission and well out of harm's way but since then, the Rowlands have been as malicious as possible. Susan's latest trick seems to be suddenly to get as friendly as she can with the Thomases' farmhand, Jonty Blythe (her cousin), so as to tease out of him all the gossip from work. Hopefully, after years of kind treatment, Jonty will remain loyal. Meanwhile, when Susan and Rick meet one of the Thomases in the street, or see them across the fields, they ignore them, as if Florence's fiancé and his family simply did not exist.

When Florence becomes a Thomas she realises that she will be step-ping into this feud but just maybe the marriage will occasion a change. After all, she is inviting the Rowlands' daughter Wendy to be a brides-maid at the wedding. Indeed, Florence regards Wendy as something of a protegée. When she began teaching Sunday School, Wendy was one of her first pupils, and ever since she has been a regular caller at the shop or Vaila. Whenever Susan gets fed up with her and throws her out of the house, Wendy pays a visit. They sit and watch telly together ('Dallas' is a favourite), and Florence sympathises as Wendy complains that her parents do not take her seriously and are always criticising her work. Then Wendy helps Florence with the new batches of Sunday School pupils, organising them at parties at the Parish Hall, for exam-ple, and in return, Florence takes Wendy and her girlfriends, like Wendy's cousin Sharon Blythe (Jonty's daughter), out for a drive. They might go to Hogart for an ice cream, or over to Windermere for a paddle. The girls like going anywhere where there are boys, and Florence is keen to show them that being religious and pious does not mean that you cannot also enjoy a bit of fun. Besides being a spiritual and educational occasion, Florence hopes her wedding will be a day Wendy can really relish, a day to show Susan that she is an adult, and could soon be a bride like Florence. Wendy already daydreams about whom she might marry. She even has her eye on Bob Thomas's brother Mike! Then she and Florence would be related, they joke, business-partners too, if Bob and Mike went into the farm together!

But then you never quite know how Susan and Rick will act. Since the Congregationalist Chapel is opposite Old Gate Farm lane, and right beside the Rowlands' camping field, Florence had to ask Susan if she would make sure that there were no tents nearby which could spoil the wedding photographs on the Saturday in question. And Florence thought that as their daughter was being honoured by acting as brides-maid – even though not a relative and after many an acrimonious incident between the Rowlands and the Whitehouses over the years – Rick and Susan would gladly and immediately accede to this request. But obtaining a promise took repeated pestering. As for Wendy's dress-measurements, Florence and her parents have yet to hear. Susan looked put out enough when Florence asked her to make Wendy a simple underskirt from some old nightie. It is as if she does not care about her daughter's spiritual development, or her independence or even her pride in her appearance. All Florence seems to get from Susan are snide remarks about the rigours of being a farm wife and keeping household jobs such as baking, cleaning, washing and ironing, strictly to schedule, and laughter when she has to repeat to Florence some garbled instructions about how to wallpaper her and Bob's new front room, or whatever.

Nevertheless, when she moves into the Thomas farmhouse Florence hopes relations will improve. Looking down from her kitchen window she will be able to see Rick on the land, and compare his schedule and his way of doing things with her Bob's. So even when Bob is up the fell and out of sight, she will have an idea how the land is shaping and when he is likely to be back for his next meal. Susan will be her closest female neighbour and it would be nice to be able to ask her for occa-sional wifely advice, compare notes on lambing successes maybe, and invite her around for a get-together, say over morning coffee or after-noon tea. She must not rush things, of course, or appear nosy or a spy for the Thomases, and with cows of her own, her milk account at the shop will have to stop, but maybe she can keep buying a yoghurt from Susan every now and then. What is more, if Florence maintains the business she recently began in mail-order cosmetics, then she could still deliver to Old Gate Farm and stop for a quick chat. Whatever the history of relations between the Rowlands and Whitehouses, perhaps through her and Bob, and (who knows) young Wendy and Mike too, times might be a-changing. . . .

Rick and Susan Rowland find their neighbours, the Whitehouses, typical of the two-faced sort that Wanet now seems to be home to – all friendly, kind and helpful one minute, and then snobbish and standoff-ish the next. When Rick and Susan were courting, Eric and Eira behaved perfectly, even sending Susan flowers. Then as soon as they married and had kids, secured a milk licence and started making something out of Old Gate Farm, the trouble began. For example, with ducks and calves in the front garden and reams of nappies to dry, Susan had Rick put up a washing line in the back. But the Whitehouses decided they were not having that, so Eric took a photo of the line full of nappies and then Eira asked everyone who came into their shop how they would like to live next door to that sight! They tried to change Susan's household routine, as if it were Vaila and not Old Gate farmhouse which had been there since the 1700s. Sometimes, even lying in bed at night, Susan and Rick have heard Eric and Eira standing in Vaila drive criticising them before guests. The Whitehouses have become like city property tycoons, trying to crowd them out on Old Gate Farm and make life intolerable. Traditionally there was privacy and space in Wanet, and certainly on Old Gate. Then you find the likes of the Whitehouses buying up all the land and suffocating you. Whoever heard of planting a bungalow, with a north-south orientation, a few feet away from a neighbour's farmhouse?

At least Eric and Eira are getting on a bit now. Eric stays at home and Eira goes gallivanting round the world on exotic holidays – and no doubt in search of exotic men, and when Eira *is* home all she seems to do is sip sherry out of teacups and then wave at you tipsily from her bedroom window all hours of the day. But unfortunately their spitefulness seems to have been inherited by their daughter Florence. Now that she is grown up, Susan and Rick try to act neighbourly towards her and give no offence. They might call her barmy once in a while, but surely Florence realises that you don't mean anything unfriendly by that. And how does Florence pay it back but by coming round to complain when Rick's lambs wander up Vaila's drive (through the open gate) and eat some flowers; by reporting the number of campers Susan and Rick site in their fields to the National Park officers (when her shop benefits as much as anything from a village full of tourists); and by sending round threatening letters when Rick's cows accidentally shit-up her shop's front step ('1 bag = 12p, 1 flag = 5p, 1 badge = 15p' – she went on listing damaged items like that and claimed she would get even somehow!).

The trouble is that Florence is still so immature. Eric and Eira never seem to have taught her how a daughter ought to behave. They spoiled her and let her flit about the place in their car all day long instead of having her learn how to cook or clean or otherwise pay her way in the family enterprise and hold up her corner. Nor is Florence's friendship with their Wendy such a good idea either, for here is Wendy, picking up all kinds of wasteful notions, squandering time and money in Florence's company, instead of keeping to her place on the farm doing her chores or schoolwork. And all this wedding and bridesmaid business is just the latest joke in the affair! Firstly, as you might expect with Florence's immaturity, the wedding is going ahead one moment but then is called off the next. On such shaky foundations and doubtful plans, Florence then expects Wendy to spend money on some ridiculous white bridesmaid's shoes which will only be used once, as well as expensive wedding photos afterwards, no doubt, which will be looked at little more. And since Wendy does not yet support herself, this means a drain on the Rowland family resources and for what return? Florence just has no appreciation of familial give-and-take, and here she is encouraging the same in Wendy. In the end, Rick and Susan know, they will pay up, but it would be nice to call Florence's bluff. If Wendy is so eager to waste money on the fripperies of Florence's wedding, but has mismanaged the use of her own pocket-money and savings, then from Florence's purse be it!

It might have been different if Florence had invited Rick and Susan to the wedding as well, but no. Flouting the principles of neighbourliness, the Whitehouses have chosen to add insult to injury and, it seems, invite a host of offcomers to what will no doubt be a flashy, city-like affair. There was even talk of tying a rope across the farm lane in order to direct guests into the Congregationalist Chapel and cut off Old Gate Farm completely! As if the lane did not belong to the Rowlands and they could not prosecute misuse of it if they so chose! Florence asking for a clear view for her wedding photos is one thing but treating the Rowland family as if it were too lowly to be met is quite another. If Florence expects a wedding gift, she is in for a shock.

The irony is that Florence claims to be so religious and charitable and yet that time when a Sunday School party heading for Shap Abbey got stranded in Wanet by snow, Florence would not allow them to spend the night on Chapel premises, or even join in with a local service. It needed Rick and Susan to offer to put them up in a couple of old caravans. Now there is all this meanness over wedding arrangements and invitations. However, the Rowlands will probably end up doing the nice and proper thing, sending her a wedding card and telegram, moving the tents and hoping the weather stays fine.

Of course, no one is all bad and Florence Whitehouse has her good side. She was kind to her cousins at Sandhole Farm when their teenage daughter died tragically, and she has babysat the child which they had to replace her. She has also taken time with Wendy during her pubic (adolescent) years, lending her books and introducing her to some nice people and fancy tastes in clothes and food. It would be nice if her marriage were to herald a change in relations between the Rowlands and the Whitehouses, and there is talk of Rick and Susan visiting her on Thomas Farm, even with the Thomases as well. But when you seriously consider her in the clutches of the Thomases, it hardly seems likely. In fact the whole notion of Rowlands on Thomas land is incredible. For this is the same David Thomas who tried to spoil their hay in the old days, and told them since then that he would prosecute them for trespassing if they ever so much as set foot on his farm, and young Bob

Thomas is still not strong enough to stand up to the old man's cursing and temper. It is far more likely that Florence will soon be part of the Thomas set-up, looking down on them from her farmhouse kitchen, nosing into the secrets of Old Gate Farm, belittling Rowland efforts and wishing them ill. Maybe a new line of conifers to block her view is what is called for; that would cap her efforts! Anyway, a keen eye will have to be kept whenever she creeps out on spying forays down the footpath to the old folk at Vaila.

And what sort of farmer's wife will Florence make? She already heads into the doctor's surgery in the village hall at every little ailment, and then takes to her bed to recuperate. How will she cope when the real work starts and Bob expects her to work through her 'off-days', and gain some respect? How will she take to lambing all night? Won't she find that after her spoilt upbringing and lazy hours in the shop, farming is just too much for her? She will be inviting folks to 'pop up' for coffee, and spending her time baking little pastries, and there will be Bob, wasting away for want of his meat and potatoes! He'll certainly have an awful lot to put up with, and won't the give-and-take of the larger Thomas family also suffer as a result? Bob already looks a bit white and ill, and that is no doubt from him trying to work on what his fiancée is cooking. No doubt he will be acting now as Florence's guinea-pig. In fact their marriage could be a very entertaining affair! You can't really see Bob successfully breaking Florence in because she just won't have the necessary stamina or skills. No, Florence will probably cap all the Thomases' efforts – unless they go mad and drown her in the milk tank first. . .

III

In the affair of Florence's wedding and other day-to-day happenings in Wanet, links between the Rowlands and the Whitehouses can be seen to be informed by considerations of a number of different types: familial, occupational, neighbourly, factional, spatial, bureaucratic, sexual, spiritual, generational, economic, affinal; relations between Rick and Susan and Wendy and Florence and Eric and Eira, as they conceive of them, are coloured by 'events' of all of the above kinds. The outcome is a multitude of significant ties, whereby the Rowlands and the Whitehouses figure prominently in each other's perceptions of life in Wanet.

However, there is no overriding or imperative status which each grants to the other, and which always influences their opinion on each other's behaviour and the way they should interact. It is not as if each sees the other as primarily, as fundamentally English, say, not Welsh, or Protestant not Catholic (*contra* Emmet, 1982, p. 166; Larsen, 1982, p. 135). Nor is it the case that each reduces the other to what Wallman would call 'a total symbolic package', in which an array of varied emotions are condensed and a complex store of diverse meanings knitted together (1977, pp 19–21; also Turner, 1974, pp 55–6). Susan does not always conceive of Florence first and foremost as a local and not an offcomer, for example, nor is the fact that she is interacting with a fellow-villager Susan's initial consideration when they meet. Furthermore, I would not say that as fellow-members of the community of Wanet the Rowlands and the Whitehouses necessarily view each other with more precision and qualifying detail than they would use when dealing with more 'distant' people, for whom inexact stereotypes and shorthands suffice (*contra* Phillips, 1986, p. 144). Florence, for example, does not see the failures in spirituality of Rick and Susan in any less black and white terms than those of others outside her potential flock.

Rather than any common denomination of this sort, the Rowlands' and the Whitehouses' considerations of each other's behaviour – the norms they use for evaluation, the boundaries they construct to mark identity – represent something of a loose aggregation, a pot-pourri. While each depends on the other for much of the social activity in the Wanet landscape upon which they can remark, and while each is helped by the other towards that social security (economic, emotional, and so on) without which these remarks could not be made, there is no constant, or singular or all-encompassing mode of perception which they share as fellow community-members. Perceptions in Wanet, instead, form a family of resemblances, a bundle of partially overlapping cognitive constructions, and, as we shall see, it is individual interpretation of the relations of the moment which determines which consideration is pertinent, and which construction is salient, when.

Part II

Individual Lives in Wanet

As soon as our attention turns from a community as a body of houses and tools and institutions to the states of mind of particular people, we are turning to the exploration of something immensely complex and difficult to know. . . . But it is the thinking that is the real and ultimate raw material; it is there that events really happen.

Robert Redfield, *The Little Community*

6

Identities and Relations in the Field

In the early 1980s I drove down into Wanet on the main road from Leyton for the first time. I was looking for a village in the southern Lake District or the Forest of Bowland in which to undertake anthropological field research, but before reaching Wanet I had had little luck. For accommodation on the basis of a year's or even six months' lease was not easy to procure. It being the summer, rentiers far preferred the chance of the high weekly rate which they could get for a holiday cottage from short-term customers, and what was more, they appeared assured of a regularly returning clientele. The weekly rental rate which I could offer, albeit long-term, paled in comparison. And if there *was* room, it was in villages which seemed dormitory-cum-second-home retreats, emptied of an indigenous population, inhabited by urbanites and deserted in the winter.

However, in Wanet my luck changed. Stopping in the public car park, I walked around the 'Town'. It appeared neither suburban nor in demise. In a small hardware-cum-drapery-cum-souvenir shop (which, I was informed, had originally been purely drapery, in the days when such specialisation in Wanet was called for and viable) I got chatting to Eira. She had recently retired from a shop she owned in Hogart and was looking after the counter for her daughter Florence – today at the doctor's – who had taken over the running of this, her father's shop, at his retirement.

Meanwhile, I explained to Eira that I needed a cottage to rent while I lived for a year in the village to write an anthropology project for college on the recent history and society of a dale which was surviving as a traditional community – like Wanet appeared to be, but unlike, say, Grizedale, empty now but for the ghostly relics of crumbling farm-steads. Short of decent company, Eira invited me to supper in her bungalow, and to meet her husband, Eric, and then to stay the night. They liked a new face, and so in the morning Eira phoned her cousin, Hattie, and then sent me round to meet her because a few years before, Eira had sold Hattie a cottage and it was certain to be vacant over the winter. Eira was sure Hattie would appreciate someone keeping it warm and clean, at least until the Easter tourist season began.

The cottage had once been a Sunday School room tacked on to the back of the Primitive Methodist chapel but when the Primitives amalgamated with the Weslyans round the corner and the buildings fell into disuse, they were bought by Eira's father and refurbished as a garage and badminton hall. Then, when Hattie bought it she converted the chapel into a plush restaurant to attract visitors, and the Sunday School into a lean-to cottage to sleep them. Thanks to Eira's introduction, Hattie agreed to a six months' lease. My search for a suitable fieldwork location could stop.

That autumn I moved in. The first days were mostly spent outside Wanet in the district record office and archives but in the evenings Eira sent me along to the Wanet badminton club, and I found my way to the beer, dartboards and domino tables of the village pubs. Anxious to meet as many people as quickly as possible, I also soon offered my services to Hattie in the restaurant, and began waiting on table and clearing up in return for the excellent left-overs. And it was this local work which really made me begin to feel that I had arrived. I had a local role, a niche, a purpose which other people could recognise and appreciate. Of course, everyone knew of my arrival in the dale long before I knew of them, but at least now I was not just that student friend of Eira Whitehouse's, running round on a year's skive from college on some silly project. Now I was also that lad trying to cook for himself and ending up in a nest of women – Hattie Harris's poncy cafe. I also began to feel I had a few more relevant things to say to people for conversation centred on the dale, and now I could chip in myself with phrases like 'Hattie's business' and 'local rabbit pie' and 'how rude people can be, cancelling without warning: that's the week's profits gone'. I began to have something real, something local to talk about. Hattie's restaurant was a legitimate local issue down the pub, after the opening gambit of the weather, and difficulties driving or walking to work through gale or flood or snow.

Of course, an outsider talking almost exclusively to Wanet locals was an oddity. I was explaining myself as primarily interested in the social history of the dale – how local lives, ordinary not regal lives, had changed since the 1870s – because having used the term 'anthropology' once or twice with Eira and with a new young couple running the youth hostel and being received by a polite but alarmed silence, I realised that history was a far more recognised and potentially appropriate and acceptable subject. For history, Eira knew, would reveal more of the community's glorious past, when, for example, as recently as 1840, people from Leyton had to come to Wanet Town to register their votes; *then* Leyton knew its proper place. And history, Doris knew, was all about rocks and bones,and death. It was beyond her why anyone would want to be so morbid – life and real people were what interested her and what had died was best forgotten – but then these unhealthy, bookish townies were never really understandable anyway. That was just the way they were bred.

However, as I unwittingly barged my way into local social milieux and, in my eagerness to learn of more names and news, exposed my ignorance of the manners of the people, I became more suspect. I was a 'mystery man', I had come from nowhere, without a family or name, and yet I was English, or claimed to be, so why should I be so naive and odd? It was a challenge to *their* Englishness. For being English, we should all know the same things, so why was I asking? *They* were definitely English, so maybe I was not. I must be lying. I was a Baader-Meinhof terrorist – like that Astrid Proll who passed through a few years back. In fact I was probably her boyfriend or I was a spy, for why should some jumped-up city pup presume to come and study them in Wanet? So they called me 'Professor', and 'Joshua', and 'Whiskers'. And didn't I think they were as knowledgeable and modern as anyone else? Doris knew intelligence came in many forms, but folks in Wanet had twice as much common sense as city people, and they worked a lot harder too. And Kevin told me they weren't zoo exhibits or museum relics for people to come and gawp at. He wasn't having me going round telling tales about him and his mates in Wanet for ten more offcomer wankers to laugh at and come and see.

My problem was that I was trying too hard to ingratiate myself and wanting too soon to feel accepted. I knew that the process of getting regarded as 'local' could take years, if not generations. I wanted to procure my data in a far shorter time and however hard I worked, I still depended on the help and friendliness of these strangers. It was a reliance on their giving which I resented, and I found it very frustrating. Here I was with my foot in the door, living, working and relaxing in Wanet, and trying my darndest to show local people how different I was from the rest of the offcomers. All I wanted was for them to show me how to belong.

Belonging! They all seemed to possess it so casually, and assume it so naturally, whereas for me it became the rarest of treasures yet I found the locals unfathomable – if not fickle. There I was, deeply engrossed in conversation with Arthur at the bar one evening, righting everything from the world's rugby teams to its trade unions, only to be ignored by my new-found local patron the very next night! I could not see that what I thought of as a constant testing of progress over the village threshold was to Arthur and others a chance discussion with a visitor on remote topics.

I became slightly neurotic. What more could I do to prove myself and my goodwill? Could they not see how important this was to me? I also felt cheated. Here I was, a native English speaker, yet capable of saying little that my neighbours wanted to hear. After initial welcome, their expressions would become distant, just as I was warming to the opportunity of telling them about the world I had recently come from, its drawbacks when compared to Wanet, and the latest outrages reported by the newspapers or radio. I realised I had little to say that had any local coloration but how *could* I have if they did not tell me anything? I saw that it was only in regular local relationships that I would be able to hold reasonable conversations, but I *had* the linguistic capacity for these and I *was* courting them – all avenues were open, so why did they not respond to my blatant suggestions that we try to become better acquainted?

In my eagerness to belong and my determination to ignore what I regarded as their mistrustfulness, if not coldness, I made some social blunders. For example, of the two pubs in Wanet village I had decided to make the Eagle my nightly watering hole. It presented the more 'olde worlde' image and apart from Friday evenings when everyone met at the Mitre for a darts and domino competition and free supper, the Eagle was the regular haunt of an older clientele. The Mitre, with its brighter decor, jukebox and ex-suburban landlord and lady (employing girls from the cities as barmaids and chambermaids), attracted a younger and rowdier set. By contrast, the Eagle offered piped music and a landlord who, although a relative newcomer, was at least a Yorkshireman and a country-boy. Setting myself up in the Eagle was intended as a demonstration of my maturity and seriousness and taste, then, and I duly shouted for my pub in the darts and domino league competitions – especially in the derby match against those Mitre whippersnappers. However, there is that third pub in the dale (near the Head), the Hilltop. It is too isolated for anybody except its immediate farmer neighbours to walk to, and its landlord and lady were widely regarded as rude and unfriendly, but a few people used to make the drive occasionally out of sense of duty to the struggling business, or for a darts match, or for old times' sake, or just for a change. One evening, when I was at the Eagle, Arthur and Agnes rolled in at twenty to eleven for a quick round of dominoes and a nightcap after spending the earlier part of the night in the Hilltop. Now, I knew that the Hilltop had not always been the pub's name. I had been told that years before it had been called the Haywain, and Arthur and Agnes, now in their sixties, were still in the habit of sometimes referring to it as the 'Wain. It had been the 'Wain when they had formed attachments to it in their youth, and it was the 'Wain now, whenever they and their friends remembered those past lifetimes and wanted to keep living them today. But when I marched up to Arthur, Agnes and friends at the domino table and asked pointedly how their time down the 'Wain had been, and when were they off down the 'Wain again because I might just tag along, they looked at me like the great pretender I was. After all, what sort of outsider, 'long-haired Arab', 'Hebrew desert-rat' (trailing away from his own proper home to pester other folk in theirs), or 'Herdwick' (imitating in his unkempt manner that shaggy breed of Lakeland sheep) would go so far as to usurp their words and claim knowledge he didn't share about their memories and relations, while simultaneously proclaiming his ignorance about what was up-dale from down-dale. It was 'up the Wain' at the very least!

On another occasion in the Eagle, Brian and I were leaning on the bar, sharing a pint and eyeing up the bevies of tourist women who frequently seemed to fill the pub on holiday weekends. Offcomers might be crowding him out on his own terrain, but at least sometimes there were compensations, Brian joked. But soon their men-folk turned up too and began partying, and Brian became more resentful: 'Why do all these people come here? Haven't they got pubs at home? Why don't they stay there with all their family and friends? Nay, you certainly can't fathom these offcomers', he concluded; and I agreed: 'No. There's no understanding the trailing bastards', and we gazed into the middle distance, nodding, until Brian stopped and looked at me askance – and I realised I had put my foot in it again.

After these mistakes, I saw that I would have to be more diplomatic in my approaches but initiating relationships quickly still seemed all-important, so I continued to eschew the admittedly tempting company of other urban newcomers and visitors, and, ignoring local reticence, tried to mix with everybody as if I had been doing so for years. Yet in local eyes I continued to be nothing but the mystery man. There I was, chatting up everything on two legs in a skirt – and, no doubt through shortsightedness, a few things that were not – all the while doing nothing that any self-respecting adult would call work. So, one evening Derek plonked his whisky down on the Eagle bar and invited me out the back for a fistfight. One reason his marriage was going through a particularly rocky patch was undoubtedly because, under the pretence of working together at Hattie's restaurant and playing badminton together at the club when he was at the quarry, his wife and I were having an affair. Fortunately, just then, my darts partner found more reason to step in against Derek, call him names and take the fight outside and off my hands. But there was another occasion when Sid cornered me behind a table in the Eagle, and told me he had made phone calls about me and saw through my lies, I was only in Wanet on sufferance, and when they had had enough of me, he, as self-appointed gatekeeper, would kick me out again. And as his friends glanced in on him and me from a respectful distance and grinned, he carried on:

SID: So tell me, Nigel. What's your aim in life? what right have you got to exist?

NIGEL: What do you mean, what 'right'?

SID: I mean don't you feel a parasite living off society? Living off the backs of other people, like me? I know I would.

NIGEL: Yes, I s'pose I do at the moment. It is rather parasitical. But after college I hope to pay it back by teaching.

SID: Don't worry Nigel. We're all parasites. We all live off society in some way. . . So, uh, where does your money come from then?

NIGEL: Well, there's some from a little teaching I've done already . . . and the rest is from a grant from the college.

SID: So mostly you live off grant money from someone else then.

NIGEL: Yes, at the moment.

SID: Don't worry. You'll pay it back by passing on what you've learnt to your pupils, right?

NIGEL: Yeah. That's how I hope to repay it.

SID: So are you gonna tell all those townies what you learn about country life then?

NIGEL: No, its just a project for college.

SID: But I bet there's lots of characters round here to interest you! Lots of real individuals, eh! Like where else could you find a character like me but in the country?

NIGEL: Well, we're all unique individuals aren't we, Sid? You, me, we're none of us like anyone else anywhere.

SID: But aren't you gonna go and write about your experiences here? Aren't you studying something like sociology?

NIGEL: Social history – like how local people's lives have changed round here since the 1800s, not just kings' and queens'.

SID: You know, Nige, you just gotta talk to the old men! Aye, you'll find there's far more real history from them than in all those bloody libraries and books.

NIGEL: I know.

SID: Like you missed some real history here tonight, you know . . . Arthur and me had an argument, about the site of the first Barclay Farm. You've probably never even heard of it, have you?

NIGEL: Isn't it up Riggdale?

SID: Aye, that's it. Now I was arguing that the original site of it was different to where it is now, by Willowbank Farm, and in the end you know I proved Arthur wrong . . . I like proving people wrong. And proving them right, if they are right. Like, I'd do everything I could to prove you wrong. Just like I would to prove you right . . . Like, recently I proved someone wrong by making love to his wife when he was about six feet away.

NIGEL: What? Really? . . . And did he know what was going on? Was he watching?

SID: No. But he said there was no one else for his wife but him, and she claimed the same, so I was happy to prove them both wrong! . . . Now then, Nigel: only three people know that . . . You, me and his wife. But if four people get to know, I'll know where to come looking. Okay?

NIGEL: Right. I'll remember.

SID: You see that you do lad . . . You could say I've got a warped sense of humour, but you need a sense of humour to get by, and the best humour is warped.

NIGEL: Right.

SID: You know my wife's got no sense of humour at all. I don't know how the bat gets by . . . Anyhow. Let's get a drink, lad. Come on. Fancy one?

NIGEL: Sure!

So, acquiescing to Sid's bullying, and half-apologising to Derek as women like Doris advised me to do for whatever advances I had made towards his wife, I started making a big effort to step on fewer people's toes. Gradually, I succeeded. 'Shave off your beard,' Doris suggested, 'to show you're not hiding anything beneath. No one local wears one of those things, and nowt but about 10 per cent of women find them sexually attractive anyway'. So I did. And I showed Sid I was no threat. He could beat me at darts or dominoes almost any time he chose, so surely some other newcomer would be more deserving to be the butt of his critical attention – then I could laugh at his wittiness together with the rest of his fans. By having enough local people criticise my behaviour, I learnt more about how I was being locally perceived and hence how these impressions could be more successfully managed. I gradually came to know not only how to avoid such situations in future but also how people were to be more properly approached, and then I tried to accede to their wishes. I had reached the stage where local people were prepared to consider negotiating some sort of regular relationship with me. If I was going to stick around Sid for a while, for example, then it would be in terms of not gainsaying him and realising my own naivety and youthfulness and relying on him to feed me snippets of more adult fare as he saw fit. And the same with others too. I tried to tailor myself to what I had discovered would be most likely to garner their favourable comments, to become what, as an outsider and a newcomer, they would least dislike me to be. And until I could see what that was, I would change my pushy joviality to a more retiring taciturnity and silence.

I also procured more local, 'real' work. I knew Doris and Fred Harvey owned the farm nearest my cottage, because I bought milk from them, and had spoken with them in the pubs when they came at weekends or for the darts and domino league matches. So after a few months in the dale, I offered Fred a hand on the farm for the following weekend. I explained I was getting bored with all my reading of history books and registers, and how I could fit that quota of work into a day at the library and some afternoon note-taking anyway. Fred admitted there was lots of work, but what could I do on a farm? If I was more trouble than I was worth, then he would soon throw me off. Fortunately the trial went well. I became a more regular helper, albeit with the simplest of tasks such as mucking-out the cow shippons, driving the tractors, feeding the sheep and digging all kinds of holes. And when Easter came, and Hattie wanted the cottage back for her tourists, Doris suggested I move into one of her caravans near the farmhouse. After that, most days found me working on Cedar High Farm, from eight in the morning (after Fred had finished milking and had had his breakfast) sometimes until nine or ten at night. Doris and Fred housed me as their farm lad, all the while teaching me how to differentiate hay from straw, and good hay from bad; how to hold a sheep by the horns without ripping them off, and a lamb by the forelegs whilst its testicles are nipped; how to pull a beef calf out of its birthing mother by timed yanks on a rope, and how to let the calf suckle my fingers to quieten it whilst it shares the back seat of the car on our way to market (and a morning in the Gapton crowds).

However, while working for Doris and Fred and thus, for reasons of loyalty as well as time, for no one else, I was still able to maintain a wide circle of friends to see after work or on days off. Eira still entertained me as someone middle class and a cut above the rest of the dross around her; and Bertha still suggested I seek employment as a local history teacher, and told me of her daughter's progress in Law. Mrs Smythe kept me informed about her thankless task of dating all the fine buildings in this backwater. Barbara came for tea and made her boyfriend a little jealous, so that they maybe delayed the time they ditched each other. Matthew always needed help running the youth club in the hall, when the lads preferred smoking and cycling in gangs outside and just beyond his domain. The Thurn Thespians still needed a curtain puller for their pantomimes. And Florence still welcomed a hand with Sunday School parties and carol singing – even if I excused myself when they sang in the Eagle so that I could nip round to the back door and hear Jack say he wouldn't give the sponging tosspots a penny for that singing, and when was I finally going to get on to a real man's drink like Tetley's bitter, and off that Gnats' Piss lager.

Moreover, in all this mixing with local friends, I always tried to direct conversation as little as possible, and to introduce few alien topics and thoughts. Also, staying silent greatly increased my ability, over the months, to memorise words and phrases for my notebooks. For my field-notes took the form of a chronological diary of all the interactions which I was part of or observed. Soon after a conversation, therefore, I would jot down on a piece of paper key words and phrases from which I tried to reconstruct the complete interaction later in the day, for example, who said what, stood and moved where, reacted how, and so on.

As time progressed, then, I came to enjoy a fair number of friendships with local people and share regular conversations with them. I was still a 'rum bugger', doing all my studying in the caravan, always being there at the public occasion, but I was *their* rum bugger. They knew they had my measure. What I had been and done before Wanet and my continuing relations with those places and times were of lessening relevance. It was only natural that once I began living and farming in Wanet the outside world would become distant and even a day per week swotting over dry books in a town library be a bind. Local details were the only interesting ones so when I got kicked in the head by a nervous young heifer as I was mucking out one morning on the farm, news of the event soon travelled around my circle, and in the Eagle that night there were rumours of claims for industrial accident on Cedar High, while Sid anxiously asked about the condition of the heifer's hoof.

Doris and Fred were eager to expand Cedar High Farm and join the few 'big leaguers' in the dale. Buying and renting fields whenever they could, they had land and stock dotted about almost from one end of Wanet to the other. Doris had inherited the farm at the death of her first husband, Richard. Some hard years had followed, but now she had Fred to care for the animals – 100 sheep and forty milk cows, which they hoped to increase to sixty and make the dale's largest milking herd – while she ran the milkround, and tutored her teenage daughter in the farmhouse, and improved the camping ground and caravan park (when the National Park was not blocking her plans).

Doris was always battling the National Park. Fred, however, was a quiet sort; moody and monosyllabic, he reserved his words for his dog and sheep and cows (like having bets with them about which would calve first, Bandy Legs or Flora). He would do his work in silence and alone if he could, and only grew really voluble in a temper. Doris was the talker on the farm. And as Cedar High belonged to her first too, she claimed more experience about just what the National Park was up to. In the shape of the warden and his pencil-pushing minions, she knew the Park was set on keeping her and her family pitiable, poor and dependent on hand-outs from bureaucrats.

Some years ago, there had been a retired doctor in Wanet who spoke the Park's language and whom Doris had engaged to write, on occasion, to the committees on her behalf, with the odd success. But then he had died and she had been left with no form of lobby to push through vital farm developments. Maybe I, the bookish offcomer on her farm, could use this penchant to similar good effect and act as a broker in her dealings with these alien structures and officials of the outside world. Helping Fred out round the farm like a young boy was all well and good, and he did need to relax a bit, but if I could champion her case for farm expansion, that would be even better. Unfortunately, my letter-writing career on behalf of Cedar High was a flop. Fred had scoffed at the idea from the start – after all, I was still a child. The test had been to see whether my hyperbole could convince the Daz soap company to send Doris the two free railway tickets for which she had been saving packet tops, faster than usual. With my letter accompanying the request what should have been a formality became a disaster – they never came at all! So Doris ended up agreeing that Fred was right, I was just a lad without skills. Certainly, I was an eager enough apprentice, and a pair of willing hands was not to be scoffed at but I would need constant supervision and careful tutoring if my offcomer's weaknesses and blindness were to be overcome.

While I was accepted on the farm, then, Doris came to treat me less and less as a grown-up guest, and more as just another youngster around her heels (she had four children, and only one had begun becoming independent). As such, I was transformed from someone she worried about pleasing and making comfortable, to a child she could regularly tell to shut up at the table when I offered an opinion on the hierarchy of a herd of cows. She would look at me as if I were cretinous when I playfully petted her favourite sheepdog as if it were a spoilt city dog and not a trained Wanet working dog, and threaten to knock me down when I drove a noisy tractor too close to the shippon where she was milking the cows, causing them, in consternation, to kick off the suction caps which she had just disinfected and applied to their teats. I knew nothing about farm management, she reminded me, so I had better not make a fool of myself, just keep quiet and learn – especially when she and Fred were talking. For really I was a nothing, a stray, with no talents, no prospects and no stamina, so of course people would ignore me. I was petted and spoilt and received too many letters from my parents. And I was also lazy and inept. She worked from six every morning, not lying-in till eight, so me getting bossy and ordering her around at haytime, and carrying more bales than her, was no good at all. She had worked Cedar High for years and she was not having me try to take over! And when she and Fred employed Sid Askrig for a few months on the farm, to help in the construction of a new cowshed to seat Fred's intended sixty milk-beasts, and I was delegated to serve as Sid's builder's mate, he agreed too. I was still a waste of space, an inherently weak and work-shy townie who had to leave the worksite to find a toilet, not just a wall, for the routine business of passing water, an effeminate student who liked to find frequent excuses to sit in his caravan and read and write. As his apprentice, Sid assured me, I was as useless as a chocolate fireguard, and as Doris and Fred's farm lad, he was positive I was as worthless as tits on a bull.

Sid did not always appear the happiest and most settled of people. He and his wife, Joanna, found it difficult to get on well together for any length of time, and his eldest son, now in his teens, did not give him the respect Sid felt he deserved – ever since Sid had blackened his mother's eye and threatened her with a shotgun when she wanted to leave Sid and all the flirting for good. Sid was a jack-of-all-trades, and both through the constant searching for work of his labourer father and his own peripatetic and miscellaneous jobbing, he had come into contact with many people outside Wanet. He had seen the way the world was turning, and he did not like it at all. For the artisan and his trade were losing out, in a country gone insane, to governments that gave free rides to parasites and lame ducks. It seemed the more you could scrounge, and the more you could fake experience with book-learning, and the longer you could escape from the real working world in school and college, the higher you were esteemed. The old world and its values needed protecting, and come the civil war, Sid would help the army and the police crush these hooligans, trouble-makers, radicals, Blacks and students. Until then, Sid was determined that he would at least be master in his own domain.

Once Sid had explained this to me, and I had watched him tell tourists to 'Bugger off home', and castigate walkers for crossing farm land ('What the hell did think they were doing? Next week he'd come and strip naked in their back gardens and see how they liked it'), I knew how to become more of an acceptable apprentice. So, over the months, Sid and I laboured together, him keeping up his tirades against a changing world, and reminding me what he would do to various parts of my anatomy if I gave him any more cement with bits of unmixed gravel in, me keeping quiet and following instructions. Slowly the shed was built.

I did not always enjoy my hours as Doris and Fred's farm lad and Sid's builder's mate. The cow-muck kept coming, and just when I thought I had finished brushing the yard cleaner than it had been for years. The mixing of cement was tedious, and it seemed the best excitement of the week was discovering a new way of opening a bag of cement with the blade of a shovel. Sometimes I still wished I was one of the tourists, blithely photographing a windswept Wanet Wold or a cobbled lane or a dour, seventeenth-century farmhouse, and then driving on again. However, I was determined to maintain the legitimacy I had achieved in my local relations, to maintain the silence of the unskilled identities they had given me, and to harvest the data they brought. So when Doris threatened me with another 'barney' if I did not start to 'shape' and follow her orders quickly and efficiently, and when Sid told me for the 'n'th time how with all my years of schooling and paper diplomas he could still teach me more in six months of watching him lay blocks and render walls, so much in fact that it would probably make my brain explode. When I had really had enough, I would head for the nearest toilet, punch the air and count to ten. My earlier mistakes showed me it was better to withdraw than to argue. In arguing and forgetting myself, I would soon return to what came naturally – being seen as an offcomer. Besides I remembered that the charge of adultery which Derek had levelled against me had not seemed ludicrous to his fellow-locals. He was regarded as generally hot-tempered and in that instance wrong but I had still been advised to apologise. This was an alien world, and in a contretemps with Sid or Doris I realised that their seniority and longevity in the dale would almost always assure them of the benefit of the doubt, at least as far as their friends were concerned. So, away from the public eye I reminded myself that the data were more important than immediate self-esteem. I was only here temporarily and when the job was done I would return to my world, my friends, my reference group which awaited me outside. Meanwhile, I had no need to flaunt my values in order to reassure myself of their 'absolute' validity; I was just to sit tight and watch others, in different worlds, expressing theirs. And meanwhile, this non-adult silence was how they had chosen to adopt me, and how we had agreed it would be appropriate for us to interact; this silence was what Doris and Sid now expected of me. It was my part in the *modus vivendi* we had developed with each other. For when it was not the silence of a child, lost in his own ignorant little world, or perhaps a well-mannered youth who has learnt to accept what he is given until offered more, Doris knew it was the 'underneath' side of a moody student, or the 'wrong side out' of a lad who has had too much 'pop' at the pub the night before and is too jiggered the next morning to speak. But whatever it was, Doris promised me, my silence would be reciprocated by theirs. She and Fred would never tell people off the farm of my failings, nor of their kindnesses in wasting time tutoring me. My secrets were safe on Cedar High, and it was the same with Sid. I could stay around him as long as I kept quiet. This was what was proper, for it was only the master-craftsman who had something worthwhile to say.

There was one night at the Eagle when the *modus vivendi* which Sid and I had reached was clearly demonstrated; and publicly too. Earlier in the evening, some men had returned from a day out at a football match in Manchester slightly the worse for wear. They had been drinking on the way back, some to celebrate Arsenal's victory and others to drown United's defeat. By the end of the evening they were ripe for action, so Foxy started shoving and taunting a bigger and more re-served Brian. However, 'Big Bri' didn't appreciate Foxy's sparring and told him so but Foxy was ready to chance his arm and carried on shoving, and the scene rapidly became more confrontational. The land-lord, Charlie, washing glasses behind the bar, began to look worried. At this point, Wilbur, their elder by a generation, who had been sitting on the window seat chatting with Fred and Joanna, thought it best to intervene, and called out: 'Hey, lads, lads. Cool it, okay?' Big Bri was well-riled by now, however, and not about to have Wilbur pull rank, so he rebuked him by reminding Wilbur that he himself had been spoiling for a fight earlier – all the way back in the car after United's drubbing, and even before he had had anything to drink! Wilbur was outmanoeu-vred. Okay, he relented, if the lads wanted a fight, then fine, but at least they should decide on the teams first so who was it to be? Wilbur suggested the nearby towns of Leyton versus Gapton – that way there would be no quarrels about who was Wanet – but Foxy's pal George countered with England versus Scotland which would be more signifi-cant. Then Sid stepped in, striding round from the other end of the bar. No, he had it: it would be England versus Wales. He was definite and would brook no counter-proposal, and that seemed settled. I began to feel a bit anxious. As far as I could see, I was the only Welshman in the room – good old Sid! I checked the positions of my opponents and braced myself at the bar. It looked like Foxy's and Big Bri's differences were going to be forgotten and it was me against the lot of them – the whole half-dozen or so. But then Sid did a funny thing. 'It's England versus Wales', he said, 'and I think I'm siding with Wales.' I exhaled with relief, not to mention pride. It was the work team – him and his apprentice against all comers. But Sid did not stop there. Stepping up to the original sparring pair, he politely asked Brian if he, Sid, could deal with Foxy first and then give Brian what was left over. Brian grinned and agreed, with equal politeness, and Foxy grinned too. The tone had changed. For Foxy had been Sid's apprentice a few years previously, before he had opened up his own account as a builder, and Sid was obviously about to remind him who was still boss. So with Foxy mouthing off about how much fun it would be mashing (a far shorter) Sid if only he would stand up, Sid put the barely resisting Foxy in a full-nelson and, wrestling him to the pub floor, playfully rubbed his nose in the carpet. Foxy kept a barrage of insults coming from the thick pile about 'short-arse Sid' and 'baldy Wilbur' and 'fatty Fred', but the show belonged to Sid and his laughing peers. So after Sid had given the 'cheeky bugger' a few more minutes of what he deserved, Wilbur and Fred pulled him off Foxy and out of the pub. We lads who were left commended Foxy on his brazenness and gall, but it had really been Sid's standing in local relationships that had been ostentatiously restated. And one of those had been with me.

7

The Ethics of the Research

From positions of anomaly, what I had achieved with Doris and with Sid were routine ways of behaving together which we regarded as legitimate, and which we regularly repeated. Our intercourse had become habitual, something to be expected, and yet it was based on a deliberate act of separation, of my separating feelings and beliefs from outside Wanet from those I exhibited in relation to Doris and Sid within the dale. Moreover, I had stopped using 'anthropology' as the explanatory label for my interests and activities and settled for something which seemed locally suited – local history. Before I go any further in describing our relationships, therefore, I want to explain this decision, or at least place it in its disciplinary, circumstantial and biographical contexts.

Considering, with the security and satisfaction of hindsight, his stock response to the Panare in the field that he had come to learn their language, Jean-Paul Dumont reflects that at the time this half-truth satisfied him completely (1978, pp 43–4). The objects of his doctoral thesis, he treated his Panare with 'a paradoxical blend of absolute good and bad faith'. He gave them an interpretable role, told himself he was not in the business of doing them harm and, thus, eagerly justified his presence to himself. The stakes, he recalls, were high after all – mistakes by him, rejection by them, and he could be out of anthropology and an academic career. That neither of these things happened is evidenced by his book but then having been introduced by the Venezuelan gendarmes, and a westerner to boot, the odds in the power game, he admits, were stacked rather in his favour from the start.

As I prepared myself for the field, I was similarly buoyed up by paradox, not to mention chauvinism. I was a scientist about to gain 'his' people, his fund of private data with which to address academic debate. After long years of what felt like impotent, neophytic reading of other anthropologists' empires – Firth's Tikopia, Fortes's Tallensi, Leach's Kachin – in which, ultimately, they were not to be gainsaid, I was at last to lay claim to an academic personality of my own. Mine, moreover, would be a British empire: an ethnographical fortress in England not in some remote and backward area of Africa or South East Asia. Studying the natives of Cumbria, I felt, was not the perpetration of a harmful act so much as a pilgrimage; or, at least, a chance for me to partake in a joint celebration of our Britishness. After three generations and a hundred years on British soil, a representative of the Jewish Rapport family would definitely have arrived. It was true I was going to Cumbria to gather information on them but my feelings were of friendship, modesty, respect, even longing. I had come through Clifton and Cambridge but now, at 24, it was they who were going to complete my education, complete me as a Briton. They were going to show me that my Anglophilic leanings and yearnings, and my dislike of ethnic (Jewish) isolationism were justified. In Wanet I was going to learn that English people of the soil were different from their Continental counterparts, as from their counterparts in the ethnographies of more distant tribes and peasants. For these were people of rampant individualism, who had long enjoyed that legal and political liberty which had freed them from an overbearing and over-determining society or social structure, long demanded that freedom of conscience which had unshackled them from the irrationalities of custom and religion, and long fostered those notions of solidarity, alongside eccentricity, which had culminated recently in the Welfare State. Mine then was to be a lucky sojourn, not in conditions of rudeness and superstition but at the heart of civilisation, among the descendants and peers of Britons I could thus better learn to appreciate, emulate and know: John Stuart Mill, Emily Bronte, Charles Darwin, Christina Rossetti, Edward Elgar, E. M. Forster, and so on. In short, my preparations were a pleasant time for I was readying myself for the fulfilment of a long process – if not two of them. By fieldworking in England I would be becoming more completely British and more fully an anthropologist at the same time.

From these jingoistic heights, however, my doctoral supervisor soon brought me down. Having decided upon the research location and gained accommodation, he counselled discretion and caution. It was a tourist area and yet I should tell no one where I was going. His experience in Shetland was that sudden visitors from another life could be most unsettling, particularly in terms of how local people had come to see you. Moreover, when I had moved in, I should be extremely careful about how I explained myself, and give little away before I had an idea about how the information was likely to be received. It was possible, for example, that my youth and apparent unemployment would count against me (a la Condry, 1979, p. 110), as may the taint of the newcomer. I should dissociate myself from the tourist, the visitor, the second-home owner, as far as possible. As stranger and academic, in short, I would receive little licence for naivety or idiosyncrasy. Fitting in was the important thing, and, at least initially, avoiding the accoutrements of formal sociological research: camera, note-books, tape-recorder for these smacked of the outsider – the tourist, the official, the bureaucrat, the busybody – and an intrusive one to boot.

When I moved into Wanet, I realised the appositeness of this advice. It was a terribly anxious time as I have explained, and I felt that all my efforts had to go into staying *in situ*, to remain in Wanet, to not being seen as a tourist or townie, and to getting close enough to local people to gather data on their behaviour. As Okely has observed, even if longing for another life and identity is often the unconscious compulsion to undergo an anthropological quest, the fantasies and romance are soon transformed by the act of fieldwork, by the concrete knowledge of another lived-in reality (1983, p. 46). It was very hard work. People did not seem so enlightened, so liberal, so happy, and nor were they particularly welcoming as indeed, with Sid, their eccentricities often seemed turned against me. The pettiness of local lives, the mundanity, depressed me, and how would I have felt, I reflected, if one of them had suddenly turned up on my doorstep and expected to be invited in. In fact, the academy seemed very far away, other ethnographic accounts of natives' lives pale, simplistic and unreal, and what I was up to felt rather like snooping. But I soon banished the latter thought – it was the only way to keep on. Besides, this was what was expected of me as an anthropologist after all. It was what all those eminent names had done before me. It was for the advance of understanding and the betterment of science (no alien categories introduced; only naturalistic observation; and so on). It was for my PhD., and when Sid began interrogating me, and Kevin threatened to silence anybody who reported on his mates to anyone in the outside world, it became a battle of stubbornness and wits which I wanted to win – my mates, my world, my class, my vision, my project, me, against them.

And here I was, back on familiar ground after all, for defining myself in opposition and dabbling with contradictions was what I was most wont to do. Before fieldwork, I had been a Welshman not an Englishman, Jewish and not Welsh, and yet an atheistic Briton and not a Jew. I had been a public schoolboy and not a state school gadabout, but someone who kept to his Cardiff vowels and eschewed a Home Counties' poshness; and yet someone for whom Cardiff schools were not considered good enough. I had been middle class not lower class, but from Jewish working-class origins, and yet I was now finally escaping the taint of commerce and trade. I had had a comfortable upbringing and had looked out over a large back lawn on to the cramped housing estates beyond but I espoused a deep empathy with the have-nots who had to achieve by struggling and did not inherit with grace, yet I did not want to give up the security of my material well-being. I had believed in social justice, been moved by '... to each according to his needs', but I feared the tyranny of the majority which might ensue outside a benevolent despotism, and yet did not want any bounds put upon the free development of individual personalities. I wanted to keep on improving myself – to be stronger, more well-read, more well-known – but I also wanted to lose myself in the anonymity of a group, and yet did not want to belong to any one social identity, category, situation and be robbed of my specialness, individuality and potential.

What these habitual feelings reveal, I suggest, is a character at once seeking the security of social stereotypes as a means of defining himself and others, and yet, once reached, fearful of how these definitions might encompass and 'explain' him completely. It could be a picture of someone hovering between achievement and belonging, while not feeling that any one set or type defines him, or that he lives up to it, adequately. Someone who constantly wavers between 'arriving' and achieving another identity which expresses him more completely for to feel complete rapport was to admit that I could achieve no better, and be no happier, and surely I was destined for greater things, and my climb of improvement would continue. Surely this experience would be just another learning one, and its relations sloughed off before the final me would emerge on to a social stage more suited to an appreciation of my complete array of gradually-fashioned but now commendable accomplishments, where I would not have to pretend to fit other people's expectations and adapt myself to their alien agendas. Furthermore, to feel complete rapport was to risk my individuality for if I fitted any one social category or sat content in any one social situation, then what was left of me which was visible and unique, which gave purpose and meaning to my individual life, and made a special biography calling for particular explanation? I would merely be an assimilating Jew, a middle-class Briton, an ex-public-schoolboy, one of the Cardiff Rapports, part of the professionalising nouveaux riches, and so on.

This was the persona whom the shock of fieldwork brought to the fore, highly insecure but determined to do whatever it took to survive the year in Wanet and retrieve from it what was needed in order to pass the next test, to climb the next rung. It became an experience in the construction of a better self, once I realised that here was somewhere else I did not want to stop, with people who might make 'friends of convenience' but who would never appreciate or esteem where I had come from or was going to. Besides, I had my real 'friend' in my own old persona. Faced by the fieldwork situation it was a comfort, like an old team or a stratagem which had won through before – getting me from exam to exam, prep school to public school, undergraduate to postgraduate – and now it would do so again. No doubt my anxiety and the sense of hostility was of my own making and the result of expecta-

tions (of how they would feel about a nosy outsider) fulfilling themselves. No doubt secreting notes about my person and writing up
my journal at night made me imagine threatening innuendo in Sid's
account of his shotgun, in Fred's monosyllables, in Doris's talk of
castrated tups, but I was alone, a fifth columnist, and felt deserving of
their dislike and rebuke. I was like one of those 'trailing Hebrews' they
kept complaining about, drag-rats who wandered in from nowhere and
disturbed local life before wandering away into the desert again. In
short, settling into Wanet entailed trading my fairy-tale hopes for more
customary expectations, not feeling at home with consociates because
my real place was in opposition and contrast.

The self-centredness, the selfishness, of this fieldwork persona seems
very bald now but I do not believe it is unique. Dumont, remember, only
felt encumbered to justify his behaviour when once again safely ensconced
in a senior combination room. As far as I was concerned, if I was to
remain in the field a debilitating conscience was a luxury I could not
afford. I felt uneasy that I could not explain my project in its own terms,
but then by the hours of free labour which I was providing my main
informants I was repaying something at least. (The gift of £100 which
Fred and Doris gave me as a going-away present – not before, they said,
because they reckoned I would just drink it away down the pub – went
some way to assuring me that I had not been a burden.) I was aware of
the basic inequality inherent in the whole exercise – I had not asked to
study them and they had not invited me – but by accepting their aggress-
ion, granting them daily superordination, and adopting uncomplain-
ingly whatever lowly statuses they chose to accord me, I tried to salve
the sore of my 'writing them up' later. Indeed, after I had been in Wanet
a number of months, felt more confident that I would pass the test (almost
imagine the feeling of its end), and had got to know my informants
better, I even allowed myself moments of thinking that perhaps they
were right. Their values and skills *were* superior to mine. Here *were* the
true descendants of renaissance man – wholly practical, able in so many
ways, and self-sufficient. As a few people were saying, maybe I should
find a nice local girl and a small farm for rent and settle down. . . .

Since leaving the field and returning to 'college', I have not kept up
ties but now it is over ten years later. My informants and their valley
homes appear in this book in disguised forms, and I feel that my
constructions of the people they were and the relations they shared one
year quite a while ago do not harm them now. If ethics come to be
described as situational 'work rules', as Vidich and Bensman prescribe
(1964, p. 347), the norms of proper practice by which specific relationships are structured and maintained and the terms by which they are to
be expressed, then I believe I give here a true, an 'ethical', account of

how I perceived my relations with Doris and Sid. In general, I would echo the sentiments of John Barnes that there is no immaculate praxis for fieldwork. Ethical and intellectual compromise are intrinsic characteristics of social research and whichever choice is made is unlikely to bring complete satisfaction. The competent fieldworker is he or she who learns to live with an uneasy conscience but continues to be worried by it (cited in Akeroyd, 1984, p. 154). But this still does not wholly justify research. This is still a rationalisation of my bringing Doris and Sid to print, whether I preserve the integrity of our relations and working practices or not. It still sounds as though I am having my cake and eating it so I want to offer a more constructive suggestion of how the ethical dilemma can be brought to good effect.

Just before I left the field, I remember phoning a good friend in Cardiff and telling her how fed up I was with fieldworking and the roles I had adopted in Wanet. 'Look on the bright side,' she said, 'Soon you'll be leaving all those country bumpkins behind, and what they think won't matter any more.' This made me more melancholy. I had a sudden vision of the plurality and relativity of values and versions in a complex society. In effect, now there was no way that I would escape from Doris and Sid and the rest on to some 'higher plane' of objective knowledge for even when I left Wanet, we would still all be living in Britain and I would merely be exchanging one set of talking-relationships and working practices for another. I might pretend superiority (my versions were more scientific, more artistic, more liberal etc.) but I would still be believing in those versions, in their moments of use, absolutely. Even if I had absolute faith in the sheer relativity of my position and views, in that absoluteness I would always be 'kissing-cousin' to Doris and 'brother' to Sid. In their prejudices, strategies, insecurities were clear counterparts to my own. In short, here was recognition that the complex society of today's 'creolising', 'inter-referencing', 'massificating' world is, in Tyler's image, a highly fragmentary and pluralistic one, a world without a single synthesising allegory or episteme and with an inexhaustible supply of them (1986, p. 132). In fact, there are almost as many epistemes to differentiate between as there are individuals, all jostling, rewriting, subverting, comparing, translating and parodying one another without consensus and without end (cf. Clifford, 1986, p. 22; and Hannerz, 1988, pp 552–5).

This also extends to systems of ethics. In a pluralistic world, ethical truths are multiple and contradictory. Each holds to account a different set of routine practices, each pertains to a particular group of interactants, each is exclusive and constituted in opposition, without there being any necessary overarching totalism, so that what is ethical to one party, and in one situation, may be heretical in the next. Moreover, this is something to which we in Britain have long been exposed; for it is evidenced in an ambiguity of the British class system that Strathern would place at its very heart – closed, introspective, caste-like groups between which, nevertheless, individuals routinely move (1982b, pp 270–1). That is, by all accounts British society has long been complex; composed of a plurality of distinct groups whose members are bound together and bounded against outsiders by working camaraderie, by shared knowledge of eccentricities, proclivities and skills, by common pride in distinct histories. Indeed, a maximisation of social group distinctions may be said to be a British fetish, with one's social life spent, in large measure, exploring and maintaining discriminatory practices and evaluations, and wending ways through social landscapes chock-a-block with the diversions of division. The English language, for instance, far from being an instrument of easy communication may be seen to serve as a vehicle of social exclusion, an emblem of exclusiveness in accent, terminology and subject-matter, a means of sifting that information which members of other groups may gain access to from that which should be restricted to one's own alone. Through English, group distinctions are maintained, with members of different groups only meeting in terms of more or less cliched and stereotypical settings, topics and occasions. The important truths, meanwhile, and the distinctive ways of talking about them, of elaborating upon them, are kept private to the group and become all the more valuable and significant for the dichotomy (see Rapport, 1990, pp 13–17). And yet, British society is also one of great process, however surreptitious and gradual, of regular movement of individuals from group to group. It is a society composed of individuals who act as autonomous units, continually breaching the boundaries of different groups in their independent progress from one to another. As individuals move, they change the histories, the proclivities, the eccentricities of the groups of which they become part, but they also come to adopt different working practices, different routines of interaction and different habitual community truths. They learn to espouse the ethics of their particular present situation and eschew prior ones. Hence, *in extremis*, if individuals in British society are always on the move, and always see each stop within a group as a possibly temporary one, then their modal working community, the 'group' to which they in effect consistently belong, is themselves alone. As they continually trade one set of ethical practices for another, the longest standing elaborations of meaning, and in this respect most true, remain private to themselves, so that as that arch-figure of transience, Oscar Wilde, quipped: 'A truth ceases to be true when more than one person believes in it' (1968 [1894], p. 434).

Sociologists also represent highly transient and marginal figures in this complex picture of plural groups and ethics but what differentiates them is that they boast their liminality and routinise it. They make a virtue out of their transience, and admit to the subversiveness of publishing the results of their incursions. As Becker summarises the case: 'a good [sociological] study will make somebody angry' (1964, p. 267). The reason given for critiquing informants' private self-images or public rhetoric is that since context- or value-free research that is not contaminated by the bias of someone's particular point of view is impossible, and since the sociologist has multiple and conflicting loyalties – to sponsors, funders, subjects, colleagues, publishers, the state, and so on – the only choice concerns whose side to be on, which becomes a matter of taking sides as personal sympathies and political circumstances dictate. Admit to the limitations of one's vantage-point then, the sociologists advise, but publish because the revelation of discrimination, of normative deviance, within groups boasting behavioural ideals, and the relativising, the putting into perspective, of rules, interests, beliefs and selves locally regarded as *a priori* and absolute is of scientific and moral gain (Becker, 1977, *passim*; also cf. Wallis, 1977, pp 149–50; and Bell and Newby, 1977, pp 9–10).

Social anthropologists, it seems to me, are often more self-doubting, less 'capital-P' political animals. Closer ties to informants, fieldwork in an environment where they feel more like guests, and among people who are less likely to be able to publish counter-reports, all militate against the brazenly revelatory, even antagonistic, stance above. However, I still believe there is something we can learn from this. Sociologists admit to the ethical dilemma, admit to bias, and make a choice – they take sides. As comparative sociologists, we too can allow for ethical dilemma, allow for a plurality of ethical positions – by juxtaposition. That is, as anthropologists, we journey between situations and communities, talking-relationships and selves, and consciously connect and compare these in order to garner information. We purposefully enter into different working practices, abide by diverse ethical relations, come to learn meanings and truths that are constructed in inevitable opposition. It is this contrast, of course, which has informed our theory. Without these differences and our construction of partial connexions between them, we would have no anthropological experiences; and it is this process which must be openly admitted into our reports. We must recognise that our research inevitably takes us from world to world, ethic to ethic, recognise that our behaviour from the standpoint of any one will seem inconstant, even hypocritical, and describe our journey and recount its ethical contradictions as a vital component of our data and analysis. Our reports become, in Boon's words (1982, pp 236–7), works of provocative intent, 'playfully' defamiliarising. They exorcise the spectre of uniformity in a world of increasing structural unity but do not privilege one world or another (our works should lack the final stasis and closure for that).

It is in this way that I would justify my writing this account. To succeed in the field was for me to join a new set of talking-relationships. I had my own self-oriented reasons for attempting this and wanting to succeed, but success depended upon me negotiating a number of very different selves which I then maintained for the year. Now I attempt to juxtapose those selves from inside the field and out, and shuttle between the routine social worlds of which they were part, so as to show how creative, manifold, and contrastive these different worlds are.

8

The Habits of Interaction

To return to Wanet, then, I have recounted how relations with Doris Harvey and Sid Askrig came to be mutually regarded as routine. Such routine entailed regular ways Sid and Doris spoke to me as we shared the day-to-day work of the farm and the building site, and regular ways in which I remained attentive yet quiet. We had come to expect that our paths would cross in these habitual fashions, and it was only apt and proper that they did.

Some months passed. Everyday interactions and everyday tasks. And the more I spoke with Doris or with Sid the more I recognised in these interactions not just something regular and repetitive – Sid berating me with long tirades against women, work, beer, sex, his feet, BBC Radio disc-jockeys and the general state of the nation, and Doris continually bemoaning the uncertain condition of her farm, its rabid enemies and fickle friends – but something actually cyclical. Sid and Doris would repeatedly use the same words to make their points, in the same order. So as I silently conferred with my talking-partner, I would recognise the same phrases, and then these regularly followed by one of a number of other phrases: phrase A being regularly followed by phrase B, or maybe phrase C, and then phrase B being followed by D, or phrase C by E, and so on. Talking to me as we worked on the farm, met in the pubs and suchlike, Sid and Doris seemed to construct their utterances from regular verbal building blocks, put together in a number of regular ways.

I became more interested and after spending all these hours with Doris and with Sid watched them when they spoke with each other. It was strange. For, sure enough, I could observe the same array of phrases as with me, and the same cyclicality, but the interactions had far more of a staccato quality. I got the impression of verbal skirmishes. It was as if compared with the luxury each had when expressing themselves before me as their demure conversational partner, when together each had to fight to get their phrases out in full and in the correct order. I could recognise the same verbal associations as when I spoke to each separately and I felt I could guess at what possible choice of phrases Sid or Doris had it in their minds to say next, but they never quite got the chance because the other would jump in with a phrase of their own and off the talk would go in another direction. What was also odd was the regularity of these skirmishes. Sid and Doris would regularly 'interrupt' each other's flow and the conversation would routinely zigzag from a snippet of one person's set of associated phrases to a snippet of the other's, an attenuation of Doris's grievances against the National Park, for example, being regularly followed by an attenuation of Sid's idyll about the happiness of their joint and secure childhood.

My feelings of oddness intensified as I followed Sid and Doris round the dale and they met others in the street, store, field and home, and I copied out my reconstructions of the interactions in my notebooks. I felt I knew what Sid or Doris intended to say because they had been rehearsing the complete script with me, day-in and day-out but in their other zigzagging conversations, I never felt they had the opportunity, never mind the desire, to understand each other in the same way. I felt like the sole member of an audience at an all-encompassing comedy of errors for compared with what I had heard each say later interactions seemed so superficial. The participants would keep seizing upon each other's words and keep relating them to superficially similar phrases of their own which, besides the overlapping word or two, were in fact very different from how the initial speaker would have carried on if given time, and so the conversation would continue, jumping from a fractured part of one person's string of verbal associations to a fractured part of another's. Beneath the routine surface of these repeated interactions, I felt I was witness to often gross disagreement and great misunderstanding.

I explored this further when I left the dale and began to analyse the interactional material I had collected. I discovered I could indeed describe sets of preferred phrasal associations, and that different speakers, like Sid and Doris, possessed different sets. But more than this, by carefully linking the snippets of phrases that speakers had been able to reveal in different conversations, including their more extended harangues before me, strings of associations became longer and longer. Associated words became great chains, which traversed a whole world of opinion and then returned the speaker to his or her starting point. That is, the strings of phrases came to form long closed loops, and travelling along one of these verbal paths eventually brought one back to the words one had started with, thus: phrase A – phrase B – C – N – (. . .) – O – H – A; or phrase A – M – E – (. . .) – B – S – A. I felt that the strings of verbal associations had revealed enclosed loops of thought which located their owner in a complete and self-contained world of people and events, of values, norms and constraints. Moreover, I did not consider this operation to be a decontextualisation of people's words so much as a *re*contextualisation of them. I was abstracting from interactional skirmishes which I had witnessed in the field and was returning words to the larger worlds of opinion which I felt speakers possessed and from which they had extracted the words for the rushed business of routine conversation in the first place. What I was doing was to suggest that beneath the messy and ambiguous reality of every-day conversational exchanges were a number of more private realities in which speakers cognitively lived; and that it was out of the complex meeting of these different individuals' different verbal worlds that the comedic conversations I had witnessed in the field derived.

I decided to call these loops of thought *world-views*. For, self-enclosed and complete, each was like a whole world of ideas around which its owner might cognitively travel. Moreover, one set of aggregated phrases often resulted in a loop of thought, a world-view, very different from that constructed from another set. Opinions would differ, expecta-tions of behaviour, and the people and events it was relevant (interest-ing, funny, proper. . .) to consider. Some world-views were more popu-lous, more general, more vague, more emotional than others. Alto-gether, from Doris's regularly associated phrases nine different world-views were revealed, and from Sid's seven, which I shall describe in the following two chapters. That is, I shall describe Doris and Sid as if they were living and talking in a number of different, bounded social environments at the same time. In one world-view, Doris, for example, will regularly associate the phrases: 'I am a local of Wanet'; 'I hate the National Park'; 'We were here on Cedar High Farm first'; 'This house was built in the 1600s'; 'Offcomers just bring pomp to religion'; 'Tour-ists come from poor urban breeding stock'; and 'There are lots of different kinds of intelligence but in farming you get the most'; while the phrasal association: 'People are jealous of us here on Cedar High Farm'; 'We don't do badly even if we are a big family'; 'Jon likes to find out more about people just to make fun of them'; 'Your kids should give you all you need in life'; will be representative of another world-view. For although the same words, even phrases, might occur in each loop, their meanings are different. For while words and phrases are always the building blocks from which loops of thought are constructed, mean-ing in each loop derives from how these blocks are specifically linked, how words are related and contrasted to each other as a cognitive set. In other words, meaning derives from the very particular association of words and phrases of which the loop is made up. Thus, the same words in different cognitive contexts, different world-views, when differently associated with other words, might act as different building blocks. Hence, in both of the extracts from Doris's world-views, above, the words 'Cedar High Farm' appear: in one they refer to an aspect of a local world in a traditional Wanet now being suffocated by outsiders' laws and tramped across by outsiders' boots; and in the other to a continuing haven for Doris and her family when fighting the nosey parents of other local families who would like nothing more than to find ways of besmirching her maternal reputation. As a component of different verbal sets, 'Cedar High Farm' has different meanings.

A further feature of these bounded verbal loops or world-views, I discovered, was that not only did Sid and Doris populate each of their worlds differently – different characters and norms, different relationships and happenings – they also assumed a different *persona*, that is, they defined themselves differently, when acting in each particular context. Inclusive of each world-view was an identity which Doris and Sid would enact, which, in accordance with the intercourse that was perceived to be taking place in that world, would hold certain values, think in a certain way, and speak with a certain voice. I found Sid and Doris to be a number of different people in different moments of expression.

In an important sense context had become, had been revealed as, something internal, something more private to the individual speaker than public and inherent in an interactional setting. Context was the way speakers were internalising words and relating them to others in their heads, and hence, the same cognitive context could reappear in any number of externally different situations. And so it was with the converse: the same interactional setting could be cognitively contextualised in any number of different ways. This is not to say that there was no regularity or consistency between cognitive definition and external setting. For example, Doris possessed a number of routine ways of behaving when talking with Sid in the kitchen on Cedar High Farm, but the decision to behave in a certain way was an internal one, seemingly not forced upon her by immanencies of the place or other partners in the interaction *per se*. It was the individual who decided upon the social identity of a particular setting, its links with other habitual settings, and the appropriate behavioural responses called for from him or herself and others. In sum, cognitive context had been revealed as something *prior* to interaction, something which individuals brought to interactions with others and then attempted to enunciate and express before them. Sid and Doris, then, would habitually meet and proclaim consistent opinions before one another, however attenuated particular utterances would be. What I was intent on doing was to re-aggregate these attenuated expressions, returning speakers' words to their regular cognitive contexts, and thereby reaching the logic behind the interactions. And it was their world-views, I discovered, which Doris and Sid used to construct, populate and antici-pate the social worlds around them, which furnished them with expectations before they met with other people in interaction, opinions during such meetings and conclusions afterwards. Hence it is these world-views with which I want to detail before bringing Doris and Sid together and showing what happens when they do meet.

It is to the personae of Doris and then Sid, and the worlds of opinion which each enunciates – including their opinions on each other – that I now turn. In Chapter 9, I describe the nine world-views which my diary of interaction revealed to me that Doris used during my time in the dale, and in Chapter 10, the seven I collected and collated from Sid.

9

Doris's Personae and World-Views

Doris Harvey is in her late thirties. She has lived in the dale of Wanet all her life, for the past seventeen years or so on Cedar High Farm. She inherited the farm at the death of her first husband, Richard, and now she runs it with her second, Fred (in his early forties). Doris has one son and one daughter from her first marriage, Keith (19) and Karen (15), and another son and daughter from her second, Craig (9) and Jessica (12). Her mother has been dead for a number of years but her father, Alfred (a retired farm manager), is still alive and lives in a council house opposite the Mitre pub, near his second daughter (Doris's younger sister) Joanna. Completing the immediate familial picture (Figure 9.1), three of Doris's in-laws have died (her first husband's father and Fred's parents) but her first mother-in-law, Polly, is still alive and owns a little cottage which faces on to the village green in a more secluded part of 'town'. And Fred's siblings now mean that Doris has a brother-in-law, Arthur, who runs a small farm with his wife in Thurn, and two sisters-in-law, Dorothy and Liz, married in Kendal:

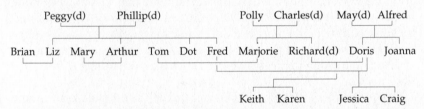

Figure 9.1: Doris Harvey's family.

For the sake of clarity I shall differentiate Doris's world-views and the persona she adopted when thinking and speaking in each by the following designations:

1. Doris as a farmer
2. Doris as English
3. Doris as a wife
4. Doris as a villager
5. Doris as middle class
6. Doris as a neighbour

    7. Doris as a friend
    8. Doris as aggrieved
    9. Doris as a mother

I will go through each of these in turn, reproducing in direct speech a few of the phrases which Doris would speak in each different persona and then summarising the rest of the verbal association, the routine behaviours, norms and opinions, people and events, of each world-view in reported speech. I include in this array a few of the opinions which Doris, in different personae, holds of some of her consociates in Wanet, such as Sid.

1. 'I love living and breathing things. Animals and nature. Nowt beats nature. Being out on the farm is the best life. And I get very involved in animals too. Happen too involved, but I can't help it . . . And they say farming is more intelligent than other jobs too, 'cause when you learn them it's in. But on the farm there's a hundred and one things that can go wrong, like on a cow, and you gotta look after them all.'

'I really think you should call Sid about that awful walling, Fred. Tell him to do it again on his own time. Or get Keith to redo it. That'd cap him. 'Cause we can't have the farm wall like that. People will come and think you did it!'

As a farmer, Doris finds she cannot overestimate the need to work hard. Hard work takes first priority. You must make sure you are fit to start no later than six in the morning, and then carry on till it gets dark. Even on Sunday you should do a few odd jobs. When you reach retirement is easily soon enough to pleasure yourself – to get soft and ill, to be petted and bored.

    Farming is the hardest of all jobs, the hardest work of all. So you find fewer lazy people in farming than in other professions, such as building, teaching, bureaucracy, the police, and so on – which often seem to be totally run by the lazy folk, in fact. Farming calls for more stamina and for keeping an even pace to the end, and more intelligence and common sense because you have such responsibility for other life and there is so much that can go awry. It also calls for more years of learning, and really you never stop because something new happens every day. So there is no short-cut to proficient farming. It can't just be found in books, like, say, medicine; and it can't just be taken from the imagination, like writing, for example.

    When you work hard you earn the respect of other industrious people – the harder you work the greater the respect. The sign of hardworking farmers is an effective farm, that is, where the man's sphere and the woman's sphere are each worked efficiently, and also work well together to form an integrated whole. And Doris will never be called lazy or inefficient, so she runs her farmhouse with meticulous care. She keeps it clean and suffers no mucked-up clothes or animals to cross the threshold. She paints and decorates, cooks and budgets precisely with her food allowance, keeping a pig and some hens and considering a goat too to use up all the scraps. She provides her farmer husband, Fred, with hot food on schedule, with hot water for him to wash in, and with clean, dry, mended clothes for him to change into. She revives him and keeps him rested so that he is always geared up to go outside again and work.

Outside, Fred looks after their farm and stock, and makes the money. He judges the weather and plans a work schedule. He feeds, cares for, breeds and sells their sheep and cattle, and also their working dogs. He builds farm walls and fences, renovates buildings as necessary, and keeps farm tools and machinery working smoothly. Doris helps him out when she can but really she does not have his skills, but she makes the offer all the same, and occasionally cleans out the milk pipeline after a milking. Then she reminds him to curb his temper and not be too rough with the cows, and tells him when she has seen their neighbours beginning siloing, and so on. She wants to make sure that Fred's work is always up to the mark. Generally, of course, this is not necessary and Fred manages to take care of it all by himself, and so he teases her about not leaving the farmhouse, and Doris will readily admit that she is hopeless outside, building or working the dogs or tractors, or whatever – as hopeless and funny, she guesses, as Fred is trying to find his own clothes in the house or his way around the larder. And that's as it should be. It is very seldom that Doris is so busy that she needs Fred to warm up some food or something, or to be reminded when other farm wives are going out to shop. Usually it's her boasting to Fred of some latest domestic bargain picked up, and her work never having stopped, and him boasting to her about another calf born and their milk output maybe soon reaching 100 gallons per day. Doris does not like to mention mistakes anyway, or to have her failings publicised, and, similarly, she does not remind Fred how, for instance, he is not best for whistling at dogs. It is only occasionally that mistakes make her so frustrated (such as spoiling the baking) that she exaggerates them instead, and has a good weep.

Doris knows that she and Fred are, on the whole, very good farmers. Their two spheres run well both separately and together, so she boasts any Cedar High Farm successes (for she will not have its reputation misconstrued) and she claims the respect that is her due. Meanwhile, she criticises the mistakes and inefficiencies of others: Neville is badly overstocked; Glover is always far too clean; and Tyler watches telly all day instead of muckspreading, and is pasty-faced because Meg underfeeds him. Doris easily sees through all their ploys and guises.

Sid Askrig is another good case in point. It is little wonder that Joanna, his wife, gives him some right good 'bollockings', for he is lazy and inconsistent and lacks learning. He always seems to be the last up of a morning, and then blames it on other noisy people partying late rather than on his own love for his bed – that's how he rolls to work with sleep still in his eyes. Once on the job, his heart is not in it and so he flits from task to task, completing few and taking full responsibility for none. It seems he would far rather booze all day, before coming to work in the evening and going at it crazily for half an hour or so, or else get others to run around for him while he sits back, moans, and spouts hare-brained ideas. He complains about Joanna's food ('stale crusts and a worm') instead of supporting her and keeping their difficulties private. The case with Joanna is that he is never home at regular times for long enough to appreciate her properly. He also tells lies and complains regularly about his new ailments – he cannot see well, or his back aches – but these have been the same for years. It looks like Sid will never really improve.

The trouble is that Sid never had a proper apprenticeship: so he cannot render or roughcast (but still blames it on too soft sand); he cannot measure straight levels (and blames it on his set-square); he walls so cock-eyed that it is painful to walk past his work; and he can't even pile up bags of cement neatly. What is more, Sid has little intelligence so everything comes hard to him – even for simple tasks he can't make do with materials at hand. Then to cap it all, he has the nerve to boast to people how he is a hard worker, and to call other people lazy, while conveniently forgetting that his odd half-hour here and there do not add up to even a single fair day's work!

Fred sometimes employs small farmers like Chris Noble and odd-job men like Sid to help him through a particularly busy period, and Doris does her bit and provides extra food for everybody at dinner. But she makes sure that people know which work is hers and Fred's and which is not for she certainly won't have her reputation sullied, or the efficiency and hard work of Fred and herself on Cedar High Farm go unnoticed.

2. 'Trouble is all the interbreeding we've got here now. Invasions from all over. Chinese, and lots of Arabs about. And Hebrews. And the curry-eaters that smell. And Blacks too . . . I've nowt against these tribes mind, but it can't be natural for them here, can it? And they breed too

fast, too. Like rats. And living twelve to a room: it's disgusting! Why do they let them? They should all go home and breed with their own kind . . . I mean no animal likes breeding with another kind does it? And they aren't really born to cities are they? Nor clothes. I mean they're more used to running round jungles naked.'

As English, Doris knows that national differences reflect natural ones. Thus each of the world's nations possesses a different breeding stock, as well as a different climate and way of life. Each nationality is naturally suited to its own nation, with its own habits, abilities, personal names, temperaments, problems and solutions. Fred can tell her about these things because in his Navy days he had to travel the world so Doris knows that: the Welsh are backward farmers who love singing; the French are poor peasants who grow onions; the Italians are weak and cowardly and always eat rice; the Pakistanis eat dogs, and curry and always smell; the Spaniards always wear moustaches to hide their funny teeth; the Arabs use human excreta to fertilise their crops (such as watermelon) because they have no cows; the Russians and the Poles are 'commies' who are put in internment in frozen wastes; and the 'Blackies' go around jungles in Africa with bones through their noses, eating each other like animals.

Fred can also explain foreign news items to Doris from the *Daily Express*, such as some troubles over Blacks in South Africa but Doris is not, in fact, all that interested. For what happens outside England is not really relevant to her and rarely comprehensible, and the more distant and weird the nation the truer this becomes. But that's only natural. Each nationality is happiest dealing with its own kind in its own nation. It would be a joke to suggest, then, that Doris was not suited to the England she was bred for, or could be happier somewhere else – as an 'Iti', for example. She is happy with English situations (like in the 'Fawlty Towers' serial on telly, or 'Coronation Street' or 'Emmerdale Farm'), and among her fellow-Englishmen.

The mixing of nationalities, moreover, is unnatural and leads to bad consequences. Habits meet which do not suit one another. Jews become property sharks and bleed their English tenants, and Blacks make ghettoes, get fat living off the dole and ruin the English economy while English children find these foreigners frightening. Doris remembers how scared she and Joanna were when they saw their first 'Darkie'. She'd never been as scared in her life – no spittle and her adrenalin pumping round. They ran home and their mother locked the door but she had nightmares about him catching her for his cooking-pot for ages after. And now children see them round the place all the time.

What is even worse is that mixing leads to the unnatural act of interbreeding. No species should breed with another, but in England it seems to be happening more and more, so that in the worst places, like Liverpool, orderliness is being replaced by a riotous bedlam. It's frightening to imagine these mixed breeds taking over in the end, all Englishmen going from white to black and becoming tribes with the rest of them. What is clear is that a successful nation is a separate nationality so Englishmen should be brought home and foreigners sent away. No foreigner can do an English job better than an Englishman anyway, even though it is easy to see why they should want to come here, breed half-castes, and try. What is less clear is why English people should want to travel, and suffer dangers and discomforts abroad. But then, when the defences are raised, they always rally round the flag and no doubt would do so again if a new wave of invaders, such as the Russians, were to chance their arm. But for a fully thriving England, the nation needs the support of all its people – English people naturally bred to an English way of life.

3. 'My conscience would prick me too much if I started asking for things now. I know Fred can't afford diamond bracelets and gold rings and that, yet . . . But he's got so much manly strength inside him still. He can carry on all day and keep it up . . . And he can get into such tempers – but he's hellishly handsome then. He can really fly at folk, you know. And he used to terrify people at darts in the Eagle. He used to shatter his opponents by the end.'

'It seems Lily's having a real affair with Tom, not just playing the field. They're very droll together, but they're getting quite a reputation . . . She said in the Eagle how she loved him and couldn't help it and always would, and she didn't mind who knew. But her Allen still doesn't act like *he* does. It needs talking about definitely. I mean I'd tell Fred straight off if something like that happened to me 'cause I reckon it's impossible to carry on the marriage to someone regardless . . . And Lily must be late forties at least so I s'pose she's lucky someone wanting her at all. But then like they say: you always end up finding your Number One in the end.'

As a wife, Doris feels that women are as different from men as Jersey cows are from Friesians. Indeed, rather like Jerseys, women are anxious and unpredictable creatures. They are emotional and weak, nervous and prone to worry: they need patient handling. Meanwhile, like Friesians, men are large, predictable beasts. Also, they are independent 'loners' who do not show their true feelings, and they do everything to extremes, from working to drinking to fighting. But however different the sexes are, they still need each other, just like a herd of cows is incomplete without both Jerseys and Friesians. So it is lucky the sexes are attracted to each other and prepared to put up with the other's differences.

Furthermore, each person is driven to find a single partner of the opposite sex, and you can no more dance without this partner than you can do anything else in life. So you find out how the other sex thinks, what is attractive to it, and you follow your nose until you catch the mate you want to settle down with. Men, then, get to know that women are looking for someone handsome and strong, and that less then 10 per cent like beards. Women get to know that men like pretty faces and good figures, and appreciate you in tight clothes, but dislike it if you get either too possessive or too flirtatious.

Once you have found your perfect mate you fight to keep him, and ward off other eligible, unattached or otherwise loose women who would steal his affections. A good tactic, for example, is to keep a man interested by keeping him jealous and uncertain, and you can always smell another woman on him to know if you are being successful. Men, on the other hand, should fight other men for their women, if a warning-off is not sufficient and apologies not forthcoming. They should also protect women from the insults and frustration of cissy-men who get aggressive with women because they are too pansy to challenge their own kind. Besides, the man should take the upper hand in the relationship (and keep a firm hold of the purse strings) while women should stay at home out of harm's way, work hard, respect their husband, and not wander round like scamps and squander what he earns. The fact that they are provided for shows that they are loved. Of course, men should also take their women out occasionally, to pubs and shows with other couples, and buy them little gifts but the men who get henpecked and become doormats ruin themselves, and the relationship as well.

However, if mutual affection between the woman and the man withers, then the relationship does too and ought to be halted. Marital vows are really only a formality and it is affect which really holds things together, along with mutual loyalty and joint pride in the relationship, and complete openness and respective give-and-take.

Doris knows she and Fred have a strong relationship. They enjoy each other's company as well as that of other couples who are successfully together like themselves. But Doris remains on her guard, because there are always singles and some couples around Wanet less happy than she and Fred, who could nevertheless spoil their relationship. She has seen it happen many a time. The married folk who go out alone, or who do not know one another's whereabouts and plans, and the bachelors and divorcees out to pick someone up in a bar. Unhappy in their own lives, these people will always be after partners of the opposite sex who they hope will alter their fate. So Doris avoids people like these when she possibly can.

Sid and Joanna Askrig are good examples of this type. They seem to go days without talking, while Sid claims to have women all over the place and Joanna is always on the look-out for another man. Then, when they do get back together, it is not long before Joanna is throwing temper tantrums again, and Sid is letting her have her own way. They really are a strange couple. At least they could admit it's over once and for all (like Lily Thompson seems to be doing) and people would know where they stood. Also, they would be giving themselves the chance to find true happiness somewhere else. At any rate, she and Fred try to have nothing to do with either of them or their marriage, and steer well clear.

4. 'You learn something new in the country every day. Farming isn't simple but city people have no idea. And it's impossible to explain so it's best just to steer well clear. Most of the public are so stupid and shortsighted. They just don't see past the end of their nose . . . People are too soft now. They're just eager to finish work and sit down and watch telly or go out driving. I hate how soft everyone's got, and they're getting softer and softer.'

'I pity town-dwellers; I'd go mad there. It's a different mentality . . . But why do they have to trail? I never have – more than a few hundred yards from one part of the dale to another. And they don't understand a village way of life but they always still try and change it. They say you gotta change with the times, but we're losing our character. Even the church has gone up the shit now – all pompous and fur coats 'cause of all these foreigners here.'

As a villager, Doris knows she belongs to a traditional way of life in Wanet which in the past amounted to something of a haven. To the outsider, the life may have looked old-fashioned but to those who grew up in it it was the best. It was hard too and bred hard people, but then they were suited to Wanet's harsh climate and sodden fells. They knew their land and had learnt to live with it: they could foretell when the dale was to be cut off by snow; when a morning moon meant late evening light; how best to use the walls which went straight up the fells, and the barns which lay just below the allotments; how to withstand the cold and the wet; how to speak Wanet dialect and repeat local sayings and customs – 'Never guess the number of lambs your ewes will give you or that brings bad luck', for instance. Schooling in Wanet was rough and ready, and strict, but it was good, and local children learnt how to be hardy and obedient and quiet. Two teachers in fact were enough to look after sixty pupils.

Work was hard in the past but there was always enough of it, and afterwards you would meet fellow-villagers in church – each family in its own pew – or informally at home or in the pub. Pub landlords were polite and smart, while shopkeepers kept prices down so that everyone prospered on the local diet of eggs, bacon, butter and bread. Everyone took part in local events, like galas and house auctions,and kept abreast of local news by reading it up in the parish magazine or the *Westmorland Gazette*.

Maybe the best thing about the traditional way of life in Wanet was that relations between villagers were so secure. You knew all about all the members of your family, and kept in close contact even as they moved round the dale from farm to farm. And you were sure to see them all together on Wanet Fair Day. In those days, families were so alike too: 'Apples fell never far from the tree', as they used to say. That is why Doris is ambitious – she's just like all Thwaites. And you could see all the same features in other families too: so John Beck walled as badly as his father; Jane Dyson put on weight like her mother; her Fred was a staunch Liberal like the Harveys all were; and the Hoovers from near Leyton dealt in scrap-metal like they always did. There were no gypsies in Wanet then, just local families who lived near one another and knew all about everyone's histories and plans, secrets and quirks. Villagers trusted each other in those days. They were friendly and you knew how they were going to behave.

Over the past ten years, however, Doris has found that all this has changed. There has been an invasion of offcomers, townies who have come to Wanet and brought their foreign habits and outsider ways of life with them, even though they have no real place in Wanet and no local names. They are from a different, poorer breeding stock, suited to the cities maybe, but here making them seem feeble and lazy, alcoholic and poor-sighted, and time-wasting. Even in the cities, in fact, where life is after all easy, they seem unskilled in what they do – whether it is building or jockeying horses – and prefer to depend on hand-outs and charity. They are ignorant of Wanet weather, animals and land, they have no respect for Wanet traditions, and seem intent on making Wanet just like the places they left. They steal local words and mispronounce them, or else replace them with ones of their own, just like they steal Wanet land and ruin it for farming. Wanet is now sadly changed. The church flounders under offcomer pomp. The shops are dirty and shop-keepers argumentative and impolite. The pubs are full of bearded, longhaired 'Arabs', while publicans charge more, close earlier and overheat the premises for their sickly clientele. Their bar staff look bored or anorexic and act like they're doing you a favour. The school is staffed by far too many offcomers, uninterested in local ways. School food is poor and the place just turns out weakly, disobedient children who are more likely to riot in the streets than survive the fells. Yet all this is, of course, condoned by the offcomer school governors. Nor is it just the children who are changing. Even adults, Wanet born and bred, are getting contaminated and becoming tired and soft. They act as if they were better than their fellows, quarrel with them, hide their real feelings (as if they were the Royal Family, or something), and even get at one another through offcomer solicitors. In the end they think they are too good for Wanet and leave the village all together.

Sid Askrig provides a fine example. Doris always thought that he, for one, was immune, but of late he too seems to have been struck down by the offcomer bug and is not the trusted villager he once was. Time was he would stand up to offcomers like he would the Wanet land (when offcomers were needing Tetanus injections, after some knee scrape, just to stop them dropping like flies). Sid would swindle them and 'borrow' tools they left lying around; for instance he once bought £100 worth of tractor tyres for £5, including, it seemed, some tyres still being used! He would call offcomers to account, challenging the new landlord in the Mitre, for example, as to why he had got rid of Courage ale and brought in some foreign stuff which was so sour that people had to move over and drink in the Eagle. He would stand up to offcomers, reminding those teachers and governors and parents, for instance, who were very smug and self-satisfied at having introduced an insurance policy against loss of life and limb at the primary school that no amount of insurance can compensate for injury (whatever they might feel), and since they were paid well enough to provide one hundred per cent safety in school, why didn't they get on and do it? In short, Sid was someone Doris felt she knew. She knew where he worked and who he was with. She knew his past, and how he earned his nickname, 'The Chief', because he used to joke at being terribly bossy when he worked as a joiner in Leyton. She knew all his rum qualities, such as having the guts to drive a JCB digger all the way from Gapton to Wanet in under ninety minutes, burning rubber like crazy from sliding down all the fell roads.

But now Sid has gone very weird. He hangs around with unknown people and copies their ways. Whenever Doris sees him he looks so white and soft that she feels sick. It is because he is up half the night and in bed for most of the day. Like the offcomers he has become competitive and overbearing too.

The only solution to the offcomer invasion, Doris believes, is to sit it out. Offcomers were not bred for Wanet and their intelligence has evolved to suit a home elsewhere. Eventually they must realise this and leave the village alone. In the meantime Doris would like nothing to do with them, to avoid them completely, do them no favours, tease them and be hostile if necessary, and just keep on with the traditional Wanet way of life.

It would also help if more money could be spent on the cities so that the poor people would not want to leave them. Doris already gives what clothes she can to Oxfam, but if the Royal Family were to spare some of their wealth, if taxes on beer and cigarettes were less, and if the free National Health services were extended (to spectacles, for example), maybe city people would again leave them alone.

5. 'These rioters in Liverpool are disgusting. And now it's London too. Why do they let them behave like that? They should lock them up with rats ... And I can't understand why the government is being so weak and soft. They just talk about an illness, and finding causes. There's no 'illness'. These rioters just need their wilfulness braying out of them.'

'I always vote Tory and I'd not vote at all before I voted Labour. It's been brayed into me. 'Cause only the Tories can give the country the harsh medicine it needs. It's too easy under Labour. I just hope they let the Tories have a real try ... It's 'cause so many people are uneducated and uninformed and naive to vote. Happen they shouldn't be allowed to ... Fred and me have sort of halfway tastes at the moment, anyway. But I saw a nice posh bank-manager at Lloyds last week about a loan.'

As middle class, Doris knows that people's behaviour divides them into three broad grades. At the top are the upper classes who always act poshly. They have clean, responsible jobs which call for long years of education and continued diligence, and earn them deservedly high salaries. They have good tastes in food and proper accents when they speak. They are considerate, with finely tuned consciences. They are well-mannered and good sports. They respect their neighbours, respect property and obey the law (they are never cruel and never commit murder), they rest on Sundays and go to church. Above all, they are consistent – they stick to their principles and they are realists, recognising that only stamina, sacrifice and deferred gratification bring rewards.

This is how everyone should try to behave, Doris believes, for this is the morally upright, the correct way, but not everyone has yet reached this level of improvement. Hence, below the upper classes are middle-class people who respect their brains and authority, and are busy trying to emulate them. Doris sees Fred and herself in this grade at the moment, and working hard to be better; so their tastes in food may be just middling but they are beginning to learn about rice and pasta. Their accents and clothes-sense may also be middling but they are starting to improve. Meanwhile, they avoid lying, cheating, smoking, committing adultery, and killing or being cruel to animals. They respect their MP and the National Park wardens and accept that they know best. They read the Bible when they can, and obey the Law. They try to be broad-minded in all they do, accepting for example that all races, even Blacks, are God's children and all have a right to exist. They act realistically, vote Conservative, and forgo immediate pleasuring for the sake of permanent improvement.

The upper classes should notice those who are trying to improve (even though they might still be hard at work themselves) and give encouragement where due, so Doris is pleased to count some posh people, such as County Councillors, among her friends. She also has great hopes for her children. Craig is doing well in primary school. His teachers are industrious and provide a good environment for learning posh behaviour. One day Craig too might become a teacher, and not have to work with his hands. Karen already has four CSEs and is going to start college with the aim of getting herself a job in hairdressing. Keith is now assured of becoming an army officer and Doris is already proud when he comes home in his uniform, reads the lesson in church and shows off all the new things he now knows. Her children will be thought of like others' of her middle-class friends who bettered their lot, like Andrew Laver who became a headmaster, and Clive Hoskins who went to America and mines gold.

Sad to say, however, there are some who do not try to better them-selves and behave as uprightly as the upper classes, but are content, instead, to lead easy lives in laziness and immorality. These are the lower classes. They are unskilled labourers, always in search of short-term gain, always selfishly after more pay for less work – that is if they have jobs at all. Thanks to the Labour Party they can now live on the dole, overspend and have no care for savings. They are vulgar, brash and cruel, and obviously without conscience. What they need, Doris feels, is to be made to work. Stop welfare payments to them as well as the free National Health services, and remove their right to vote, be-cause they need no sympathy until they remember what even a little effort at self-improvement can achieve.

Sid Askrig is in this grade, Doris can see. He is content to receive money for nothing from a Labour government or their local councils (for whom he probably votes), just like all these nationalised industries do. He works on Sundays, never sticking to any principles for long, and refusing to defer immediate cash until later, only to spend all he has on gaudy clothes and ostentatious pleasuring! Furthermore, he is highly ill-mannered and will always burst into other people's conversations, even when money and posh people are involved (who hate having financial matters discussed so openly). Sid just has no respect for those who have made it to the top. Even doctors – educated, paid and responsible enough to cut people open, operate on them, send samples to laboratories for testing, and diagnose all their bugs – Sid criticises. What he needs is to taught a lesson: a good serious illness, like lung cancer, would soon change Sid for the better.

Even Sid's kind is not the very worst, however. Unfortunately there are some members of the lower classes who not only do nothing to improve, but actually rebel against upright standards of behaviour and do wrong on purpose! And led by some left-wing Labour lunatics they are getting harder and harder to control. They demonstrate against the upper classes in the street, riot, destroy property, hospitalise the innocent and cause untold grief. They are inhuman. Nevertheless, since people are responsible for their own actions, these rebels must be made examples of. People must be reminded that all sins are paid for. If thieves were marked for life, or maimed, rioters tanned, and demonstrators for nuclear disarmament or whatever interned in camps like in Russia, then others of their mind would soon learn respect for the Law and the police, for the law-abiding middle classes who are innocently working hard, and for the upper classes who have made it already.

6. 'I worked for every stick on this farm. But you want to do all of a job properly, without anyone's help, don't you? And get your own benefits. It's every man for himself and I'm working for the farm. I could never work for "the nation", or for other people.'

'I've just realised how much more government control there is over us in the past few years. Before, we were separate but now we're ordered about by the National Park people and the District Council, and there's the Milk Marketing Board bulk tanker and the Government at every turn. We're controlled now . . . And the real shame is how the Government stops you working. I hate people coming to tell me what to do. They should give business and money interests priority. But this farm's almost nationalised; and that means small wages and everyone poor and everyone the same.'

As a neighbour, Doris knows that everyone has their own individual little lives to lead. The world is a market and everyone must have something to sell. They may not be destined to like what they have to sell, needless to say, but they can still hope to stand independent and proud, to have a successful business buffer them from the harsh market forces, helping them to forget that they are lonely and alone.

Doris's business is selling Cedar High Farm and she does it with quite some flair. She sells bottled milk, eggs, newspapers, and other dairy produce on a milkround and she sells camping space and caravan berths to tourists, carefully providing for their needs, from clean shower blocks to muck-free paths and cute ducklings scampering along them.

Buyers and sellers on a market are interdependent, however, and individuals who are considerate to each other's business enterprises sympathise with one another's worries and help them out. This is especially true for close neighbours, like in Wanet, where businesses are on connecting land and all face the same market conditions so Doris would expect neighbours in Wanet openly to reciprocate with one another. There is a Wanet Business Association, after all, and it should be flourishing, with news, problems and advice in constant circulation. Doris would like an open exchange of views on a quieter, cleaner village for tourists, for example, and advice on enlargening her milkround clientele, for more tourists at Cedar High Farm mean good takings for everyone. Then again, an Association could better link neighbours as employers and employees, and buyers and sellers; and better settle any disputes and thrash out compromises over prices and competition.

Sadly, however, Doris finds herself in a sick country where this is not how things work, where the powers-that-be want to kill off any chance of individual independence and pride and where, instead of being considerate, people deny each others' businesses the chance to survive. So instead of helping people and their businesses, for instance by providing tax relief, grants and incentives, and giving priority to business needs, governments seem intent on increased 'dictation'. They put up petrol prices, for example, which will keep tourists away. They change milk pasteurisation laws so as to make milk more expensive to bottle. Meanwhile, big businesses (farming suppliers, tool makers, soap companies) bleed the small people dry with exorbitant prices. Bureaucrats (from National Park committees and local councils and the RSPCA) act like little Hitlers, wasting people's time with confusing red tape, ignoring their cries for help, vetoing grants, and sitting around like carrion crows until individual businesses die. The legal system, meanwhile, is so uncertain that individuals dare not go there for redress.

Even within Wanet, where Doris might expect more appreciation of this sickness, and more attempts to form a cooperative stand against this dictation, since people are all in a similar boat, you find crazy, suicidal behaviour. Neighbours compete and try to sell each other dud products. They rebel, gossip, are spiteful and rude, and do their best to ruin each other's businesses. All Tom Glover seems to think about, for example, is how to undercut Doris's prices of milk and caravans. All Sid Askrig seems to do is to show contempt when his neighbours employ him, and pour scorn on their businesses. When Doris finds him some little jobs to do around Cedar High, for example, as a caring neighbour, and mindful of his need for a little backpocket-money, how does he reciprocate but by arriving late, leaving early, being choosy about what he will do, and accomplishing bugger-all besides driving round on a tractor and disturbing her tourists by his noise and by the 'scrow' of cigarette packets he leaves in his wake. And when the National Park officers come and complain to her about his mess, Sid will have only succeeded in harming his own business chances as well as hers. And that is typical. Instead of helping one another, neighbours in Wanet allow themselves to be divided. They assist governmental and other attempts to kill businesses off, each one hoping that they will be the only one left, and able to retire rich on the proceeds.

The situation frightens Doris for with businesses in such close proximity, neighbours can do anything against you. So she tries hard to antagonise no one, to say nothing that could be misconstrued, to state no opinions whatsoever, or else things could easily bounce back against her milkround. She keeps on finding Sid little jobs, for example, and buying off him the useless little secondhand articles he sometimes turns up with – she cannot afford him taking offence and bearing grudges. She tries to keep calm. Maybe one day her destiny will take her out of Wanet or into a less risky business all together – such as running a pub.

7. 'I don't like socialising with friends and having Father there too. He's become a real drag, always on the moan about his Mini 'cause he's too damn tight to get rid of it. He's boring. But it's not natural is it? You can't relax and enjoy yourself and do anything with y' father there watching, can you? 'Cause you're always having to watch y'self. Not that I'm burning the candle at both ends now like I was in my twenties, but even as an old woman, like, I wouldn't want to go out of an evening with him about, in the same social occasion.'

'Beer is the problem, I reckon. They shouldn't sell it to kids. I mean I hate to mention what they were all getting up to at that New Year's Eve disco. What a racket! Just noise. And kids smoking and drinking, and bottles everywhere . . . and them playing around on the floor. You know. I'd be embarrassed to do what they were doing . . . And even our Karen was lying there beneath someone with just her two fat little feet sticking out below her!'

As a friend, Doris really enjoys mixing with people of her own age. She finds that people can be broadly differentiated into three age bands: young people, mature people and old people. And age guides all – you should always be able to tell where to slot someone by the way they behave. Young people, then, do everything to excess. They: have no self-control, boozing, gambling, overspending, and ending up having to steal to recoup their losses; burn the candle down at both ends so that only youthful vigour keeps them going; can never stick to a decision and always vacillate; and cannot think straight and will not be told. Old people, on the other hand, should behave in opposite fashion, always leading sober and responsible lives as befit leaders of the community, elders of the church, chairmen of councils and committees. Somewhere in between these are the mature people, like Doris herself. They have learnt sense and self-control, and are just building up to being in the prime of life.

It is natural that these categories of people should want to stick together and keep to themselves. You cannot really enjoy being with someone of a different age who behaves so differently to you. It's obvious that you would be bored with one another, and how can you properly relax when you are constantly wondering how some older person is judging you? Doris, at any rate, does not feel comfortable around young people or old and always gravitates towards the group of peers she has known since school. It's a great group and they always seek each other out, arrange lifts, meet in a local pub, have suppers and parties together, keep tabs on each others' plans and movements and news, just as they have done for years. They have all reached a point where they are neither tight with money nor too easy-going, and they have all learnt to drink their share but not to excess. They also have their own darts and domino team which plays others in the local league, and everybody makes sure they are there to support and keep abreast of the team's progress.

Sid Askrig is a stalwart of this group and Doris always looks forward to seeing him out somewhere because he throws himself so wholeheartedly into the occasion. When they meet in the pubs or the restaurants around about, they have some excellent binges and Sid is usually on great form. Even on a week-day night these sessions can go on until half past four in the morning, Sid sometimes even sleeping at the pub. The next day they all suffer from the infectious hangovers and back aches of the group, but even then Sid is full of good tips – such as how a glass of water before bed stops your brain dehydrating and giving you a sore head. It's not that Sid wants to get you out boozing again straight away – like from lunchtime the next day! – it's just that he knows that mature people should stick together. So if you miss a group get-together, and stay in to recuperate instead, you end up just as tired because you keep wondering what your friends are getting up to all the time and what gossip and fun you are missing. And so even when Sid's been down himself, it never takes long before he bounces back.

Things would be perfect if only people of different ages would leave the mature people alone but they do not. For some reason, young people and old all try to spoil their enjoyment. Young people, for example, will not keep to themselves but insist on gatecrashing mature get-togethers and inflicting their wild excesses on Doris and her friends. The only thing to do, short of physically expelling them, seems to be to act as patronisingly as possible, to laugh at their feeble attempts at boozing and sex, and to tease them about their lack of self-control. Maybe in this way they will eventually get the message that their being there is not natural and their company not welcomed, and so learn to stay with their own kind.

But then when it's not young people making nuisances of themselves, it's the old, such as Doris's father, Alfred, and his horse-racing cronies. They behave so beneath themselves, gambling at two race-meets a day, drinking all night, yet penny-pinching and refusing to treat one another, and then moaning to the likes of Doris when they cannot get up the next day. Doris sometimes wonders whether some of them ever learnt self-control at all. The only thing that can be said about their antics is that they provide Doris and her friends with a good laugh: when it's not Alfred and his claims to famous gambling victories, it's Arthur Harvey and his watertight car, needed for when he next drives into the beck, pissed!

It is true that old people eventually get their come-uppance and suffer their heart attacks, strokes and gout, but it would still be nice if everybody could just act naturally for once, as their age demands, without depending on Doris and her mature friends, by laughter, criticism and sarcy hints, to sort them out.

8. 'Folk prefer to pity you than envy you. They dislike it if you try and get ahead and make a little money and improve yourself. And be a bit bigger and better than you were. They soon change their opinions . . . Aren't people horrible? I hate Wanet sometimes.'

'Someone's reported us. An inspector's coming tomorrow. They're making trouble for us. They never stop. They'll be trying to take over the farm. They must think us soft. And easy prey. And come here to scrounge and try and copy and steal everything we've got. Folks'll do anything against you and your farm if you give them so much as an inch.'

As aggrieved, Doris dislikes most people and the dump of a world in which she has to live with them. For it is a world in which misfortune always seems to befall the undeserving and in which other people are happy then to gloat. People are fickle. They pretend to pity you but they do not really want you to recover and get a bit better and richer than you were because they regard your gain as their loss, and then they will steal or kill what you have worked for and love so that you cannot enjoy it.

Doris has not had an easy life. She was certainly not born a capitalist: she began with nothing and has worked hard for all she owns. First she started with Richard and together they ran his parents' small farm of twenty-one acres, seventeen sheep and twenty-five cows (seven on milk). They started with nothing more than £100 each, but after five years or so of hard graft things began to pick up. Then, suddenly, Richard was taken ill. The doctor took ages to come and by the time the hospital diagnosed heart failure he was dead. For a year Doris was crazy with grief. All of Wanet seemed concerned and offered her money and gifts. But then, slowly, she came round, picked up the pieces, and with two young children, her trusty dog 'Black' and the help of Richard's mother Polly and sister Marjorie and good old friend Arthur Harvey, she began to make a go of Cedar High herself. She mucked-out, hay-timed, and looked forward to the spring when the pregnant stock changed shape almost every day. But the people around her soon changed too, and Doris saw what fairweather friends they had been from the start. They just wanted her in a pitiable state, and when she snapped out of it they soon began standing in her way. Henderson 'borrowed' her straw, for example, and Robert Baines from next door tried to give her hoggs a 'better home'.

Then Doris met Fred Harvey – through Arthur, Richard's friend – and in him found someone fired by an equal enthusiasm to make Cedar High Farm work. And it proved a good partnership. After just two years the farm was keeping them both and Fred could give up his previous job as a joiner. He had grown up on a farm after all, until Arthur inherited it and Fred joined the Navy. Now they own most of sixty acres, 100 sheep, eighty cows (forty on milk). Money is still hard to come by and they work very hard but slowly, they are improving themselves. Doris still weeps when, through sheer negligence, things go wrong, but she can now feel proud at having achieved something out of nothing. She has done it for Richard, and to show to the

Hendersons and the Baineses of this world that she can succeed despite
their hindrance and without their charity. And Doris swears that they
will not backslide, that, for instance, Fred will never again have to go
out to work. The farm is their joint project and it will see them both
through so they do everything together: working the dogs; hay-timing;
feeding the stock, checking its health and scheduling its movements;
budgeting and saving (so as to avoid loans and debts); dealing with
VAT men, correspondence and accounts; hiring labourers; planning
expenditures (feedstuffs, petrol, machinery), sales (cows, calves, lambs
and pups) and investments (another hay meadow, a new milking shed,
a new hopper for dairy nuts). Doris is determined to plough all the
profits back and keep on making Cedar High bigger and better.

Of course, she has become no more popular with her fickle neighbours. Indeed, the more she and Fred have prospered the more jealous
and opposed people have become, all the more eager to ruin them, take
over the farm and return her to her grieving state. So Frank Todd is
delirious to be able to rob them of a cheap £50 let they desperately
wanted for pasture, and David Boulding tries to offer more money for
land they are already renting for hay, so that they have to gather up the
bales extra quickly before he can count them and estimate their returns.
When they employ Sid Askrig to help with the farm improvements for a
while, he breaks the cement-mixer or the hay-raking tines on the tractor
or newly ordered building materials or something on the car as soon as
their backs are turned. In fact, Sid is a prime example of the dangers she
and Fred face. They hire him because he is one of the cheapest around
but this turns out just to be a ploy to get on to their land. Once there he
walks round the place as if he owned it and then tries to take over as if
he were the gaffer. He bosses their other labourers to do his bidding. He
orders materials, borrows tools and uses the phone unbidden, even
using their names. He exaggerates about what he knows how to do,
tries to cheat them by being paid for work not done and disrupts
whatever jobs he is involved with. Then, when the job *is* eventually
finished he will not go away but brings his children round to cause
more of a mess. Meanwhile he boasts off the farm how he is doing all
the work and how by themselves they are helpless.

But by now Doris knows this is normal fare. People wish her and
Fred ill. They will trespass on their land, or drive up and down outside
it, in order to spy out more weak spots, steal what good ideas they
cannot copy, and turn other people against them and yet, with each
other, Doris feels she and Fred can carry on. Cedar High, the farmhouse
and their bed – these are boundaries to their sanctuary. Inside these
walls she is able to ignore the world outside and its worries. This is her
land and she will never be cheated out of it. She will give as good as she

gets and do whatever is necessary to defend it, so as soon as Sid Askrig and Bill Fraser can be dispensed with, doing the odd jobs, she and Fred will get rid of them. Until then, they must show Sid, for example, who is boss: curse him for his mistakes and make him do any bad work again, on his own time; not let him fob off 'missing' goods onto them so that they get the blame; supervise him at all times and not let him rearrange their schedules; shut him up as soon as his scornful tongue starts wagging – (what he says off the farm now cannot be any worse than what he has said in the past); and lead him around in circles about their plans so that he ends up spouting such ridiculous notions that you have to laugh. Laughing at these fickle outsiders, at their debts, failures and stupidity, at least gives them a little touch of their own medicine.

Besides Fred, only for those who stood by her regardless – 'Gran', Marjorie, Arthur – does Doris have a care. It's not safe to give a hostage to fortune and show *how* she cares, but she chats and helps out when she can: when Gran's house needs new plastering, or Arthur is prey to some vindictiveness (someone castrates his bull), and they need her and Fred's support.

On Cedar High she is determined not to squander her and Fred's chance of being safe and secure.

9. 'Your kids should give you all you need in life. They should make you happy and I s'pose annoyed and make you cry sometimes too. But they still need pulling up on small matters 'cause little things grow to big ones. It's logical. And that reflects on the whole family . . . I don't know: I'd happen murder mine if they stole.'

'Karen's not earned a button yet for the farm, so why should it go on feeding her? . . . Come on, use your common sense. Today's kids don't help you at all or pay you back. They just get lazy and impudent, and sulk around doing nowt. But there's still a right and a wrong way to be learnt . . . And they say we just don't know all we'll have to answer for in the end.'

As a mother, Doris knows that a large, close and happy family can bring its members the greatest joy on earth – a complete life in which all the emotions are experienced and shared to the full. Achieving this is not easy, however, because every member has to behave as he or she should, and remember that they have a joint reputation to uphold, common finances and work to arrange and information to share. In particular there must be a certain give-and-take between parents and children; and yet this is within a parent's power to create and maintain, none the less. Doris very much hopes to succeed.

One of the difficulties is that everyone is born with certain fixed temperaments and abilities, likes and dislikes, which are hard to remove and impossible to hide – especially if you know what to look for. Most parents grow to be quite experienced in reading children's characters, and the signs of the Zodiac help too. So in Keith, for example, Doris can see a 'mummy's boy' who is clever but not brilliant, and no farmer. Karen, meanwhile, hides within herself and puts on a hard exterior. She is fat and bossy; and she hates eggs. Jessica is truculent, but also is deep and cunning. She has a brain, likes watching telly and reads comics galore. Craig, her baby, is soft and stupid but he is helpful, with a heart of gold, and he may one day be a farmer, even though he is a runt. Sometimes you can still read these characteristics in adults too, and parents certainly can get to know their own. Doris knows she is a born organiser, but stupid, while Fred she sees as greedy, with a foul temper, but a born farmer.

When you are a child, however, you are not so self-conscious. You tend to live in your own little world so it is parents who are responsible for leading children into the real world and telling them about themselves, albeit at a gradual pace, for children are weak and sensitive creatures and could be behaviourally damaged. Before this time, children are not responsible. Even if they are real tearaways, they do not know who they are or what they are doing. Telling children about themselves and about the world around them is a very necessary task, moreover, because sometimes their characteristics have to be curbed if family duties are to be carried through and happiness to ensue. Children have to made conscious of themselves so that they can control themselves for the greater familial good.

Doris feels she and Fred are good parents. They love all babies, they make sure their own are well-dressed and fed, and they never leave their responsibilities to others. They also work well together, Fred and her, supporting each other's decisions and caring for each other's comforts (such as tea in bed). With Craig, her baby, now nine, all of Doris's children have been told about themselves and instructed how parents and children must act towards each other if their family is to be a success. They know that children must respect their parents, learn from them and copy what they do, but be quiet and mannerly at the same time. They must give their parents first priority, and always be ready to help them out at work when the family savings are at stake. When they are away from home and in the company of other families, they must be loyal: spread no gossip and behave well, for they carry the familial reputation. When they get home they must freely report what they have done, holding nothing back and telling no lies. This is how Doris remembers behaving as a girl. She played quietly outside or else she helped her mother clean and cook, and was always on hand to accept the blame if something went wrong.

Sadly, Doris finds that her children still do not behave quite as they should. Karen is still too selfish and lazy, unwilling to concentrate on the job at hand until it is finished. Jessica is too often 'underneath', and miserable at her chores. Craig has been stupid around the stock for too long, and is still unable to channel his energy. Nonetheless, it is part of the parental lot to discipline children – and no one else should have to discipline your own – and Doris tries to do so and not be too soft. She picks them up on their faults all the time, teases them or curses them or threatens them with Fred's belt. When this still does not bring respect, she passes them on to Fred himself.

On the whole, however, Doris thinks she and Fred have not done too badly. They provide a warm, comfortable and loving home, full of familial togetherness. They get all the children out on the farm helping, like at hay-timing, and slip in new skills to be picked up all the time. If the children get ill Doris always has her medicine cupboard, and all the while, she and Fred are making the farm a success so as to give the children pocket-money, a good start in life, and as much security as possible.

However, there are other dangers to be countered, because unfortunately her family is not the only one in the world. There are always other children around dying to teach yours their bad habits, and there are always other parents who forget their own failures (such as the Desmonds who are all liars, or the Squires who all wet their beds) and try to mar their neighbours' parental reputations by casting aspersions on them and digging up dirt. It was especially trying recently when a shortage of teachers meant that Dorothy Brown, Mary Cowper and Sarah Wells were with Craig and Jessica at the primary school all day. Doris had to give repeated warnings to her two to divulge nothing, no matter into what business, financial and other, these mothers might nose.

Then again, Sid and Joanna Askrig seem to come snooping round far too often, trying to get to the bottom of things, and there is another reason for strict discretion. What a failure their family is! For a start, they do not support each other and in addition they do not know how to command the loyalty, respect and obedience of their children. They do not read their characters correctly (such as Dennis's, their eldest's, habit of constantly switching interests), so they cannot properly call them into line. Now Dennis has ended up hating Sid. He refuses to admit his father has taught him anything, stays out late, and will reveal nothing about his whereabouts. Christopher, even at thirteen, smokes in the carpark toilets, and runs away and hides when called to work. Meanwhile, Helen (fifteen) puts on hideous make-up and is not nearly contrite enough when told to clean it off; she might even be on drugs as well. Yet when you try and tell Joanna or Sid about their horrid, unmanageable children, they praise their errors and start prying into your own life instead!

Privacy for your family is not easy to come by, Doris knows. But if someone were to insult their children or be cruel, then Fred would not stand idly by; because what is levelled against one reflects on all. It all makes it harder for a parent to secure a happy family, but Doris will never give up trying.

These, then, are the nine world-views which I found Doris using during my time in Wanet and the different identities which she would assume and allocate to others: the nine ways in which I recorded her aggregating words and phrases into habitual loops of thoughts in my diary of interaction. Now I turn to Sid Askrig and recount the regular terms in which I heard him speak.

10

Sid's Personae and World-Views

Sid Askrig, like his wife Joanna, is in his mid thirties. He and Joanna have two sons (Figure 9.1), Dennis (16) and Christopher (13), and one daughter, Helen (15), and they live in a leased cottage on Wanet Main Street. Joanna has always lived in Wanet, in one part of the dale or another, but Sid (although born there) spent a number of years as an adolescent moving around the Wanet–Gapton–Leyton area as his father sought increasingly scarce work as a cowman. His father has retired now and he and Sid's mother live with a married daughter (Jane) on a council estate in Leyton; Sid's other sister is married in Gapton. Meanwhile, Sid and Joanna have lived in Wanet Town and in their little cottage (next door to Joanna's father) all their married life. Sid served an apprenticeship as a builder but is really a jack-of-all-trades. Joanna earns a few extra pounds of housekeeping money per week by working the odd hour or two as a daily maid, cleaning some of the larger houses in Wanet Town (such as the impressive Victorian vicarage) and their eldest son Dennis has recently left school and acquired work as farm lad on a large local farm, the Baineses' (next to Cedar High).

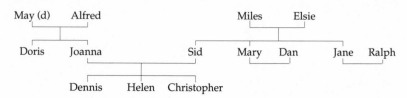

Figure 10.1: Sid Askrig's family.

From Sid I collected seven long strings of words and phrases that he habitually associated together, seven worlds of opinion, which I differentiate by entitling as follows:

1. Sid as a craftsman
2. Sid as a local
3. Sid as a husband
4. Sid as a pal

5. Sid as a father
6. Sid as a man
7. Sid as English

1. 'Walling's yet another of my skills, thou knows. And I'm looking forward to starting here. I like this work. It either gets you fit or fucked. And you'll need a pair of gloves, lad, if you're gonna keep up with me. 'Cause you'll be lifting a few! I'm certainly gonna learn you something: you'll be seeing stones in front of your eyes before we're finished . . . Good stones though, these are. Nicely dressed.'

'I was called out the bath yesterday to help calve that cow. So what with one thing and another I got bugger-all done on the rendering . . . Nay, but Wyman's men must have done this coat here. It's so uneven it's just like they tipped the render on!'

As a craftsman, Sid sees the world divided up between those who stand on their own two feet due to skill and stamina and hard work, and those who are lazy and do not try, preferring to live like parasites off the backs of other people's taxes, dependent on dole money or grants. For the latter Sid has nothing but contempt. In fact, it hardly seems natural not to want to work, not to want to earn your independence and become freelance. This, at least, has always been Sid's aim and one which he has pursued with some success for now he is a fast and experienced master-craftsman, qualified in numerous trades and proficient in his practice of each. He is skilled in laying blocks and bricks, roofing, hedging and dry-stone walling, plastering and rendering; can drive heavy goods vehicles, tractors and JCB earth movers; can manage a farm and work with dogs, cows and sheep; and can act as a haulage contractor, a barman, even a grave-digger. In addition he is also gradually achieving mastery in decorating, welding and joining.

Being a master-craftsman deserves the highest respect, because mastery only comes after long years of practice and apprenticeship. There is no short-cut, whatever all these college kids with their paper diplomas might now say. They are all claiming mastery over something they rightly have no idea about. Sid reserves his respect for real craftsmen, and he knows quite a few. Whether in trades he himself now tackles or learns, or ones like gardening and engineering which he probably never will, he knows masters from the Wanet area right down to London and the south, and it's gratifying to know they return his respect.

By rights, master-craftsmen should be rich as well as respected. Their skills should be highly sought after on the open market, and rewarded, enabling them to maintain themselves handsomely. Sid's skills should have brought him more money than he knew what to do with, while people should be queuing up to watch him work, and for the honour of buying what he crafts. But sadly the world today does not work like that. In fact, the world today seems to be run more as a charity for the lazy and unskilled, by pups with just the little and dangerous know-ledge of a few years' book-learning. In their hands true craftsmen get to be treated as if lower than a snake's navel, their experience earning them no respect and no money. Meanwhile, punters pay for rubbishy work, and the ignorant and incapable are enabled to lead comfortable lives until they retire, paid handsomely for shoddy work or even for not working at all. Sometimes they are paid simply to stay in college and get more and more useless education all their so-called 'working lives'! Then those few who actually use their learning, like scientists, end up inventing machines which cut back the jobs a man can do and the ways open to earning a respectable wage.

All around him Sid sees these contemptible, narrow-backed ignora-muses making gains. Wanet, for example, is choking on them – rich, rowdy, boozed-up, work-shy, hypochondriacal time-wasters. No one seems to expect or respect real mastery any more. Even when Sid lends a hand to an old customer like Doris Harvey and applies himself to some problem of hers on Cedar High Farm, she expects him to carry straw bales on his back (instead of using the mechanical elevator) or barrow gravel to the cement mixer all day (instead of one trip with the tractor bucket) – as if he were a common labourer with a back to bend, and to sweat, but with no skills or brain. She even makes tea for the other labourers, such as David Feather, before she gets round to him!

Sid's course is clear. If he is not appreciated by customers like the Harveys then he must take his skills elsewhere. When they see the difference between his work and others' he can't believe that they won't beg him to return, and pay properly for his expertise. He should remind them that for a true craftsman it's still a seller's market. The long-term solution, however, is that the genuine working man should refuse to pay for the lazy and the unskilled for one day more. If there were no grants and no hand-outs (and therefore no taxes either) then everyone would be forced to work and all this unhealthy dependency would die. And if people still did not want to make the effort and work, it would simply mean that they did not want to live; and since only sick, unnatu-ral animals do not want to live, these people could be rounded up and put out of their misery – burned, shot, done away with – now.

2. 'It's these outsiders who are to blame. Everything worked better before they stuck their stumps in everywhere . . . Us locals should get rid of them all. We shouldn't mix with them or co-operate or tell 'em

what we think even. 'Cause these people can argue anything. And get you saying anything. And they always answer your question with another.'

'Probably what the National Park does on farms, and that, is illegal. I mean they aren't an elected body so why not take 'em to the Strasbourg International Court or something! They're really hated up Gapton way as well, you know . . . I think you need to be harder with them because then they seem to back down. They got less money and power now by all accounts.'

As a local, Sid is proud to count himself part of a community which truly is as old as the hills that surround it. Wanet is so traditional and true, it even has a Biblical feel to it. It is so close and friendly and open a community that all its members know the same things about their fellows (both living and dead), about traditional skills and customs (from farm management to bartering and bargaining to pubbing), about local happenings (such as the kids' youth club and the grown-ups' sports day and communal suppers), and about the local land. In fact if Sid travels too far away from Wanet he is likely to get an attack of agoraphobia!

In recent years, however, Wanet has been invaded by outsiders. First the offcomers sent their spies in to reconnoitre. Then these went and brought more. Now they all wander round Wanet as if they owned it, ignoring the locals, – not even acknowledging them when they bump into them. They get busy buying up all the houses and land, then they begin sticking their oars into all parts of local life, swamping the pubs, even usurping local Wanet committees.

The more Sid gets to know about offcomers, the less he likes them. They are immoral drug-addicts, winoes, homosexuals – and all the time they try to deceive you about their true selves by hiding behind glasses and beards. They are spoilt and bad sports, they are selfish and weak, they are lazy and live off charity, they are stupid and unable to learn. Why even their medicine is cock-eyed, with doctors causing more pain not less, and surgeons sewing up people with their instruments still inside, and nurses inducing childbirth and making women need more stitches and help.

The only reason offcomers seem to survive is that they are also cliquey. They stick together and help each other out. That's why offcomers in Wanet are always favoured by all these outside bodies – the National Park, the police, the hospitals, the RSPCA, the electricity boards, the local councils, Whitehall – while local people are passed over. Not only are offcomers invading but they're also bringing double standards, and it's all being funded out of local taxes and rates.

The counter-offensive, towards the goals of booting offcomers off local committees and land, out of Wanet Town, and finally out of the dale completely, must be on two fronts. Firstly, locals must stand united and help one another. Secondly, locals must ignore offcomers whenever possible – and when not, be rude: curse them to their faces and wish them a speedy departure, if not death. On the first front, locals should maintain as close and varied links with one another as possible, keep up to date on all local news and take part in local events, such as pub suppers and darts matches. They must keep up local ways and skills (not copy offcomers) and take pride in them too, boasting both their knowledge of local people and events, and their involvement in continuing local sagas, because no one else will help locals if they don't help themselves. And this means showing no favouritism either. All local people must be treated fairly and the same, and it's no good trying to gain at another's expense.

On the second front, offcomers should be cheated as often as possible. Moreover, locals must learn to beat them at their own games: if they are silver-tongued in committee, then locals must refrain from saying anything at all until the committees simply collapse; if their doctors are quacks then locals must learn to diagnose themselves right in front of them; if their lawyers and policemen spout jargon then locals must find the terminological loopholes and recite them back; if their shopkeepers mark up extortionate prices then they must be bartered down; and if their building and farming inspectors start snooping then they must be physically chucked off the land.

In these difficult times, Sid feels he does his best to maintain his traditional home and fight the invaders. He is strong, a loyal local. He has a great deal of local knowledge and he uses it wisely. He reminds fellow-locals about a united opposition, and he reminds offcomers that they are here on sufferance, that their every action is observed and that here at least they have to justify their continued existence. Indeed, Sid likes to think of himself as something of a local spokesman, responsible for threatening offcomers when their behaviour oversteps the line of the guest, and warning them that next time they might just find themselves out on their arses. He sometimes says it to them like a joke, but the serious implications are always clear.

In this role, Sid feels he earns local respect, and fortunately the job is not thankless and he is not alone. His wife Joanna is a great support, and there are other women too, like Peg Foley, Mary Cowper, and Doris Harvey who will always be there to build up the youth club and provide the local kids with some traditional enjoyment when offcomer organisation has collapsed. In fact, both the Harveys, Doris and Fred, are good locals. They take part in some great old boozing sessions, dominoing and darting until the early hours and then providing shoulders to stagger home on, even giving your car a tow when the keyhole to the ignition seems to have mysteriously closed up of its own accord! Doris and Fred always seem ready to participate, with few promptings from Sid. Sometimes, of course, they get the pubs mixed up, or go to the wrong one first, but they always drink somewhere local – you know you'll meet up with them somewhere in the end. Moreover, the Harveys often seem to provide Wanet with good talking points, since they are usually party to one ongoing saga or another. At the moment it is their new cowshed over which they are battling the National Park and keeping local skills alive. Wanet needs new things happening, needs interesting events that local people can get involved with and discuss, or the community will not be the same. And with the assistance of people like the Harveys, Sid helps provide them.

The fight against the offcomers is not easy. They are many and strong but Sid stays tricky and hard to catch, and maybe one day Wanet will win.

3. 'If I get disturbed on the nest again by these late-night boozers, then someone's gonna hear about it! . . . No animal likes being disturbed like that after all. And if one of them so much as touches the new van then they'll get two barrels-full of my shotgun in the gut. I got it laying by the window ready.'

'Well I'd better get back and see what the old bat's got for my tea tonight. Two mouldy crusts and a worm most likely, if she's the wrong side out again like yesterday . . . But if she's not too twined, we'll see you both for a jar at the Eagle later.'

As a husband, Sid finds himself caught up in a turbulent marriage with a history of conflict. For many years he's struggled to keep it going, sometimes even having to threaten Jóanna with his shotgun to stop her walking out on him. Now they've developed a routine which cuts down the disputes and awkward silences. This involves them not seeing each other during the day or telling each other what they'll be doing or even expecting the other to be interested. Instead they try to maintain a strict separation, in this way depending on each other for news in the evening, each having to take on trust what the other tells. Sid finds that this voluntary silence stimulates interest, even jealousy, again. If they do happen to bump into one another, then it can be a bit embarrassing, and mutual teasing usually results so that each gets reminded of the arrangement and retreats to a proper distance. Sid teases Joanna about the time it takes her to do the shopping, and how the only really safe place for her is at home. If she catches him up on some building site then he reminds her of the ever-present dangers of falling masonry while she always bugs him by saying how he can't be working very hard if he has time for all this gabbing to women. So they part, and are forced to wait till the evening or the gossip of somebody else or, in Joanna's case, until the binoculars are retrieved – Sid knows they are always trying to focus on him – in order to find out how the other has been getting on.

Sid teases Joanna when she is not there too. He calls her 'butch' and nicknames her 'Boris': he says she's lazy and frigid and keeps hissing at him like a snake! He's only joking, of course, but if she does have her feelers out after gossip then serves her right what she hears. It also reminds other folks not to get too close. It's his prerogative to say the nastiest things, and a measure of the strength of his and Joanna's relationship (even if it's quirky too, and the things he says sometimes air genuine frustrations which he might wish different). But only he has the right to say them, and woe betide anyone who seriously tries to comment or otherwise interfere.

But then his and Joanna's workaday separation is not so peculiar. It's normal enough for her to be at home, making the house a clean, warm and comfortable place for him to rest in, and he's right to expect her to buy and cook his food and serve it on time, to clean his clothes, to tend him when he's sick and urge him not to overwork, to sleep with him and pleasure him at night. Meanwhile, there he is, out making the money and bringing it back for them both to spend. He drives her to the shops, chaperones her to the pubs and warms her through the night.

Indeed, marriages that do not run along such lines Sid finds a mystery, if not downright odd. Like old George Weston having his wife out with him tending to the stock – no doubt he also has other men coming round to service her at night! Then there's Doris Harvey – what an old battle-axe she's becoming! She'll be henpecking poor old Fred to death in no time. In fact, last time Sid was round their place, helping Fred back-rake the silage, Doris even came out of the house to tell him how to do it! Obviously not content with her own work, the little busybody had to come and stick her snout into his. It was all Sid could do to stop himself really telling her where she could put her time-wasting 'advice'.

On the whole, Sid finds that his and Joanna's marriage, with its secrets, teasing and dividing of labour, now works pretty well, certainly better than it has in the past. They try to show more of an interest in each other's views, to listen more to each other's worries and fears, to change their bad habits (such as Sid's agoraphobia, which he knows can make him impossible to live with), and generally to get to know each other again. They both now seem to be making a real effort to make a go of it. Sometimes the familiarity of the house can make it quite a cosy, not to say passionate, nesting place. Going out in the evenings can be fun too. Occasionally he even takes Joanna out to inspect a job he has just completed and then they discuss his next one – or what outlay their budget can now afford on a new van. Often they are out together for a drink or a meal of an evening, at the pub and after in some other couple's house. Sometimes they even have other couples back to their spot for nightcaps or a late supper. Of course, the tantrums still break out, when Joanna wants to go somewhere and he won't take her, or when he's arranged an evening out with friends from work and she wants to stay home. Then she shouts and fights and sulks. But nowadays these are outnumbered by the nights they go out together in harmony, showing themselves off as a couple and able to criticise those who are not. Joanna makes sure they both look nice - her own preparations can take hours – and that makes Sid feel good. And even if Joanna starts flirting because she feels he's been ignoring her or something, he jokily threatens to see to her at home, and then sets to pulling the head off whoever has been chatting her up. He defends what they have together and that feels good too.

4. 'When Doris, Joanna and me were kids by Millwood Farm, we used to have great fun. Even the weather was better in them days. And we lacked nowt . . . People were different and all. Thoughtful, not spiteful and gossiping and laughing at each other.'

'God, Frederick is one for changing his mind! He's had some teeth out so he's probably still sitting in the house, sore, not feeling like doing a spot of blocking. But I don't know. You get a great vantage point on the whole farm from here and now the silly fucker wants the window put over there! . . . Cedar High's being badly organised and I'm getting just a bit sick of it.'

As a pal, Sid remembers his childhood as a perfect time. Life was really worth living then, not like now. Now people are so vicious and selfish and uncaring that no one is popular with anyone else. Now Sid finds himself alone in an increasingly hostile world.

What made childhood so great was the gang of pals Sid had around him and always seemed to be with. The core was made up of him and Doris Harvey and her sister Joanna who lived on a nearby farm, and then John Beck and the twins Tony and Phil Wells not far away either. Every summer seemed to be hot and just made for playing in the fields or in the amazing gardens of the big house and estate close by. Then there was haytiming and they would watch and help and learn a bit more each year. Even school was fun, with teachers who were strict but fair and knew their stuff. Most of all, Sid felt cared for at home. Times were hard and food was scarce but his parents always fed him and kept him warm. His father could only afford one night out at the pub per week, but every time he went there would be a packet of crisps for Sid to share with his sisters. When Sid was flat on his back for a month, coughing away with pneumonia, his parents waited on him hand and foot. People were thoughtful then, and generous.

Adolescence was a more miserable time because his father lost his job as cowman at the Todds' big farm and had to move the family to Leyton. There he got temporary farm-labouring jobs until he retired, and there, separated from his pals, Sid felt picked on and vulnerable. Beforehand, enemies always seemed to get their come-uppance (the worst of them even committing suicide) but now they escaped their due. Leaving school, Sid started working as a farmhand, sometimes having to walk miles through the dark and the storms between different hill-farms and his home, and always afraid in the pitch black that the winds would blow him right off the fells. Around Leyton, Sid always seemed to be harassed by the police. They called him a mischief, and gave him a clout whenever they saw him, and when it was not them, he found he was still being hounded by lads from enemy gangs.

As soon as he could, therefore, Sid moved back to Wanet, and things looked up immediately. John had left the dale, and Tony and Phil had got very caught up with their elderly father and their farm, but the rest of his old gang of childhood pals soon reconvened. Sid married Joanna (always his childhood sweetheart) and helped out behind the bar in the Eagle pub where her father had become the landlord. Doris had married Richard, a young farmer, and soon they were all living across the road from one another, rearing young families. Again it was a gay good time, a time of plenty, when a whole family could live comfortably off £15 a week. Beside the pub, Sid got work driving earth-moving equipment on the construction of the new road out past Leyton, and no farmers' wives you would come across ever let you go without a feed, roasts and all. Meanwhile, money seemed to stretch for ever. £38 per week felt like a millionaire, and there was easily enough for food and clothes and a good boozing session on Friday night to boot, with Doris and Richard and Joanna and him at the Eagle or in one of their homes. In fact, Cedar High came to feel just the same as home. Sid helped the work there in his spare time, building the farm up and then relaxing in the warm farmhouse afterwards. They would gossip, share news and swap strategies and opinions on 'outsiders' in other gangs. Of course, then there was the tragedy of Richard's death, but Fred moved in and things soon carried on as before. The gang worked together and protected its members' interests, with Cedar High as its base.

But recently Doris and Fred have become distant and unfriendly – with him even more so than with Joanna. They suddenly have no time, no interest in sharing news, no wish to be emotionally or professionally supportive, almost ignoring him, in fact. Sid feels hurt, and what's more, this change of heart couldn't have come at a worse time for it seems the world around him is now again full of horrible people, nasty pieces of work bent on causing harm to others. Indeed, the world itself sometimes seems to be in physical decay, with the pubs filthy, and even those immaculate estate gardens of his childhood now unkempt. Meanwhile, his parents' generation, while full of lively memories, is really a spent force, and no longer able to give constructive help. Sid loves listening to all the old tales but they won't bring back the past. So, now more than ever his peer-group of close pals needs to stay together – if only Doris and Fred would realise it! This is a time when they and Joanna and him must truly stick up for each other. For example, if properly worked – if Fred's lazy work schedule was improved – Cedar High could be comfortably providing for them all. There could be work and profits enough for the whole gang and more.

But Doris and Fred seem blind, both to the dangers and the way out. Sid reminds them, of course, whenever he can. He stresses the lines of division between their gang and their enemies (in case they can have forgotten), drops hints about loyalty, and keeps reasserting his own. He reminisces about their warm childhood together, the fun they had, the secrets shared, and how he somehow misses this togetherness now. He mentions the importance of old friends. More specifically, he visits Cedar High and helps as often as he can, always showing an interest in farm news, big or small. How many calves and lambs born and what, if any, complications? When was Nobby the bull finally caught and how many of the Baineses' heifers had he 'lined' in the meantime? Did Fred notice that sick Leicester ewe on the far side of Douggie's Paddock, and has he returned from burying that old Rough that died in the snow – because it can't have taken him that long to catch! And is the next job on the list to order the gravel, move the new static caravan, or dip the sheep at Arthur's place? In short, Sid gives unstintingly of his time, is always on hand for emergencies (such as when Fred's dog Jet is run over and has to be rushed to the vet in Leyton), and always shows excitement and pride in the latest farm improvements, in the new cowshed, or the gleaming new silo-forager, looking huge and impressive even as far away as the opposite fell. Finally, Sid makes sure he and Joanna are on hand whenever farm successes are to be celebrated, whether in the pub or over a meal. Because, like birthdays, these are occasions which should be special to the whole group – and to the group alone.

In this way Sid does his best to recreate the gang of pals of his childhood and, in a menacingly cold world, rekindle its warmth. He certainly boasts of these attachments before his enemies, warning them of his gang identity and of the security it gives him. And if Doris and Fred would only see reason and include him openly in farm planning and management like before, then their best asset would soon start paying dividends to them all.

5. 'Kids today are just too cute by half. They'll argue with you that black is white and yellow's no colour at all. They're spoilt and always think you can get something for nothing. They don't respect you. They're just bread-grabbing buggers . . . I mean, I was a bit mischievous as a lad but not hard to handle like kids today. Everything's a hassle to them. They know bugger-all, but they think they're so intelligent that they won't be told. They got no time for owt. All they want is some aggro . . . Like these soccer hooligans trying to look tough, with their boots on and jeans rolled up: if I found them on my plate I'd think they were a meal of spare ribs! . . . No, what they need is discipline. Or else just shooting with sawn-off shotguns and burying in shit-heaps.'

'Nay but you're an idle lad. Now just stop y' chittering or you'll get a slap round the lug and a gob-full of this calf-shit . . . I wish your tongue 'd get *rigor mortis*! I do that. Now no more of your impudence. You don't even know enough not to argue do you? Here. You'll get 25p if you sweep the new silo clean. So keep smiling, lad . . . Gay clean, mind. I want to see no bits of concrete there when the grass arrives.'

As a father, Sid finds himself wholly occupied with his children, Dennis, Helen and Christopher. Indeed, he takes great pleasure in dealing with children in general, knowing their names, noting their childish interests and ways. He feels a great responsibility as a father because children are inherently naive, with no self-control, whether over their own bladders, or a box of matches and a fire. So they have to be watched at all times. Also, as they slowly leave their childish worlds, children look up to adults as models. Therefore, the adults that children meet should be in control of themselves, educated and able. Sadly, however, some adults are not like this, and can dangerously threaten a child's gradual development into correct maturity. In fact, children have to be carefully protected from the bad influence of some adults – radical teachers, mean employers, sadistic policemen – to whom they can so easily fall prey.

Sid believes that, together with their mother, he has always provided well for his children – taught them and guided them. The boys got their arses kicked when necessary and all got their noisy, public tellings-off but all also got left alone in their childish worlds and not rushed out of them at an unnatural pace. So, for instance, the fact of death was hidden from them until they were ready, while money and sex were spoken about in their presence but not *to* them, so that they could slowly pick up what details they were able to (as long as their short concentration spans lasted). Sid also sometimes took the boys to work with him, setting them little chores and financially rewarding their efforts. As with adult realities and gossip, so he gradually introduced them into the world of adult work too. Indeed, Sid carefully protected all of his children's interests, physical, social and economic. They were rushed to doctors and hospital for further advice when necessary, and allowed to pleasure themselves, like by watching television, when the whim took them.

Sid's older two are now reaching full maturity, when they have more of a sense of public embarrassment and when their guidance ought to be left to hints and quiet reminders. Also they are starting to earn their own money, Dennis as a farm-labourer and Helen from some cleaning of local houses and shops. Sid's advice ought now to restrict itself to how Dennis can ensure he is properly paid or can seek better employment, and how Helen can better herself through a course in nursing. But over the years (and as he is still in the middle of doing with his youngest, Christopher), Sid knows he always reminded them how to behave properly – to respect adults, copy their parents (their skills, interests and enjoyments) obediently and in silence, be grateful for attention, time and money spent on them, and to repay all of this when their parents get old.

But sadly, Sid finds today's world full of bad influences on the young. The world is easier then ever, and kids' lives more comfortable, and yet generally they're turning out far worse. Most of the school-age children Sid meets are too impudent, and when they leave school they will not work, or, at least, will not learn to work slowly and well. Everything is a hassle to them, and they have no time. They will not hear adult advice or see adult example and just jabber away, like idiot-children, still living in their childish 'punk' worlds. They show no love for their parents, merely seeming to want to bleed them dry of their money. Then they get bored and start strutting around, showing off, as if their spindly bodies, their dirtiness and their ridiculous fashions were something any self-respecting adult could take seriously or want to see. They really make Sid want to laugh.

However, the situation is really no laughing matter, and even his own children are getting affected. It used to be that Sid could feel proud about the way they were following on, copying him and learning proper adult behaviour. Now they show less respect and are all mischief, even denying how he helped them in the past. They're going the way of Billy Cowper, Jessica Harvey, Johnnie Wells and the rest of that bunch.

It is probably modern-day schooling that is largely responsible for all this. Teachers have become soft, and their new-fangled and expensive teaching methods seem just crazy. Instead of being aimed at turning out adults at 15 or 16, able, like Sid, to take their place in a grown-up world and earn a living, education now seems to entail spending ridiculous sums on keeping people immature and irresponsible right into their thirties and beyond! What is called for is a return to the sanity and discipline of traditional schooling – give the long-haired layabouts, rioters, hooligans and punks, a good bashing.

What is worst, of course, is seeing your own children going the same way. When Sid thinks about that he just feels like giving up, sitting back and watching the world explode. He, for one, wouldn't even piss on the fires to put them out.

6. 'I hate work and everything to do with it. It's got nothing on sex, eh? . . . And you know what I could just see to now? An older woman. Like Sara's mum. 'Cause I quite like a bit of middle-age spread. Not Dorothy Brown, mind. She's just too big. Nay, nor Lily Thompson come to that. But Liza Hood – now she is a tidy woman. I could shaft her all right. Or Lorraine from the Mitre. I'd get my leg over that and give it a length right sharpish! God, her tits were sticking out like dog bollocks last night. And I reckon you'd need a dog too to round up that pair if they got loose.'

'God, I'd like to do Robbie Baines. I would that. I wish he'd cross me in public then I'd have an excuse to drop him. If I was as ugly as him I reckon I'd cut off my own head . . . And Eddie Milden's another: narrow-backed, snout-nosed bastard. He just won't be told. Mean and arrogant and stupid. And if you say owt to him he goes crazy and opens his great gob and shouts hisself hoarse. Great twined bugger. Well he's got a surprise coming next time I pass him on a public road 'cause I'm gonna fill his gob with a bunch of fives. For free!'

As a man, Sid knows that it is your sex which determines how you behave and really make you what you are. So, to be a man is to be heavy, big and strong, have a fierce temper and be able to withstand pain. Men like using their bodies and developing their physiques. They go after sex, sport, booze and fights, and are keen to improve their fitness in each. Men also like being handsome and attractive to women, so they take care how they dress and how they look. Only if the man is a homosexual or an eunuch, or his nature has been forcibly suppressed (as in a concentration camp) do his male behaviours not blatantly stand out.

Women are by nature just the opposite, and this always makes them seem to behave contrarily. In this respect women were the worst animal ever created, and relations with them are always hazardous. For example, when men want to 'get their end away', women want to refuse them; when men want to rest, women are all geared up to find the world's best lover; when men want children, women 'drop' as soon as they've been 'tupped'. Also there's a mystery about them which can render men impotent and cause their ruin. In fact, women are so temperamental and insincere that Sid sometimes jokes how mixing and having sex with them should be banned.

Worse even than the difficulties of relating to women, however, is the damage they do to relations between men. Since men are of the same kind and able to understand what's going on inside one another, there is the possibility of developing real closeness, and masculine relations which are long-lasting, rewarding and mutually supportive. Sadly, this does not often work out, and the reason is that women get in the way. Competition over temperamental women ends up turning men against their true friends. It is in men's nature, after all, to want to prove their masculinity, boast their abilities and demonstrate their prowess, and their various dealings with women are their best means of achieving this. But success with women can never be counted on, and another man's gain ends up feeling like your loss; so hurt pride, the laying of bets and fierce fights often follow.

Sid does his best to maintain close relations with good men-friends like Fred and Doug, and Wilbur from Leyton. When he and they get together they can have some real times, boozing and playing sport, and what a difference it is to the gaggle of geese you find when a few women get together. When Joanna and Doris and Marjorie meet up, for example, it's all gossip and nowt besides.

Nevertheless, when these women *are* by themselves Sid can't help himself from chasing after them. A quick cuddle, a telephone number, a one-night stand and Sid feels like he should. Then it's off to the pub, to beat his mates out of sight at darts and boast about his conquests, his dreams of women, his boxing, boozing and sporting abilities, and a sexual shaft which he can almost tie in a knot! Nobody else comes close when he's feeling his oats – compared with his best, they're no better than queers.

7. 'I know what I'll appreciate: when there's a civil war in this country between the police and all these agitators and demonstrators and half-

caste types and Blacks. That's what this country needs and I know which side I'll be on. I just hope the police will call on me to help restore law and order . . . Aye! That'll be the day.'

'We should send the troops into Brixton and send all the Blacks home. I mean Amin threw out all those Whites from Uganda didn't he? And English people should come home . . . And in Ireland the same. They should give the army more of a free hand to sort them out. Either kill the lot of them or pull the troops out and let them sort themselves out . . . Trouble is, the English must be the least violent race around. If this was America, that SAS lot would've got busy and shot up everything by now and it'd all be done with.'

As English, Sid knows that he is part of a unique way of life which is the most civilised in the world, and that this is something to be protected and to be rightly proud of. The English way of life, shared by all those who were born truly English, is characterised by typical ways of behaving, such as: by working hard; by typical temperaments and eccentricities, such as those displayed by Terry Wogan and Jimmy Young, Sid's favourite disc-jockeys on BBC Radio 2; and also by a typical way of speaking – the Queen's English.

In all these characteristics England is different from the rest. The Welsh, for example, are mostly all coal miners – ignorant, devious and sly. The Irish, of course, are idiots and always back-to-front. The Germans are killers and well-nigh inhuman in their cruelty. The Swiss are cowards. The Pakistanis are always dirty. Indians are squanderers. Blacks are lazy loafers who just breed like crazy. The Americans are short-tempered and violent: they flare up and shoot one another at the slightest provocation.

It is obvious that the English way of life is best, and it should be the duty of every English person to celebrate his or her heritage and be prepared to take concerted action to preserve it when necessary. He should get to know his land, its cities and shops, and be interested in all its conditions. He should have friends the length and breadth of the land, always buy English produce, and always support English sports teams playing abroad.

The trouble is, of course, that more and more other races now also realise that English is best, and in their jealousy would like nothing better th.   ` bleed the way of life dry and thus rob Englishmen of their birthright. Sc `nglishmen must act fast. First off, England should leave the EEC. Then Englishmen should all live in England, and keep their island pure; they don't need to become part of the travelling circus of foreigners. For holidays, there is plenty to see in England itself; and for living and working, Englishmen should be showing foreigners that they are always on hand to defend their land, united and proud. (In his own agoraphobia Sid can see his body subconsciously warning him against un-English acts).

Once home again, Englishmen should support the police against enemies already within, from Vanessa Redgrave and her Socialist Workers' Party or whatever, to the Blacks. Even at the expense of a civil war, these conspirators should be shot, and the streets again made safe and free of rioters and demonstrators. All the non-English should be expelled.

Similarly, Englishmen should support the army and take an interest in its modern equipment and a pride in its heroes (like its anti-terrorist squad, the SAS). There should be a general acceptance that in today's unstable world, attack is the only defence so when dealing with terrorists, from the Baader-Meinhof gang to the IRA, shoot to kill. When threatened by Russia, be prepared to use nuclear weapons.

Finally, Englishmen should have a thought for their allies, those in lesser races who are prepared to admire the English way of life from a distance, and recognise how England needs preserving and defending. For example, there is Hong Kong, willing to sell England products cheaply, and America, willing to ally its power (sporting and military) with England's so as to defeat common enemies.

The English way of life is a real wealth, and even as foreigners and conspirators seem to be overrunning his home more and more, it is something that Sid is determined not to lose.

11

A Routine Conversation

In the previous two chapters I have been reporting the ways in which I found Doris and Sid's daily utterances to consist of different sets of phrases, regularly repeated, and how I found these sets to be cyclical. Travelling along one of their strings of verbal associations eventually brought me back to the phrase I had started from, and thus I have described these sets of associated phrases as amounting to closed loops. What also struck me about the phrasal loops was how entire and complete each was. Each loop seemed to represent a whole world, a world replete with relevant people and events, manners and mores, institutions and relations, evaluations and expectations. No doubt this impression of entirety, of each phrasal loop describable independently of the others, was brought about in part by what I felt to be the often great differences between one verbal aggregation and another. At different moments, Doris and Sid seemed to be living in quite distinct environments, social and otherwise, speaking with quite different voices for each and assuming different identities. Hence, I have interpreted these habitual and cyclical sets of phrases as Doris possessing nine personae and world-views and Sid seven. In describing Doris or Sid from what my field-notes revealed that they said over the year, I would not have been able to paint just one picture, one neat and consistent account of the way they populated Wanet Town and the world beyond with people, objects and events and then reacted to their depictions. Rather the converse: the ways in which Doris and Sid spoke about the social landscapes they construed around them and the landmarks, physical and other, of which the latter were constructed, revealed sets of thoughts which were very diverse. Poring over my notebooks and collating conversations, I found this diversity quite chaotic, and the inconsistency remarkable. But I had coped with it in the field as only a minor irritation. My immediate reaction of 'How can Doris (or Sid) act like this, and say such a thing? Don't they remember what they said only this morning (or the other day, or last week, or in the kitchen a moment before)? How can they be so brazen about contradicting themselves in such a duplicitous (or rather multiplicitous) fashion?' was soon overtaken and replaced by the business of getting on with the routine interaction at hand. In everyday situations, that is, diversity and inconstancy of opinion was swallowed up by the regularity of moving from one habitual interactional routine to another, and the habituality once one was ensconced in each.

I have explained how I achieved talking-relationships with Doris and with Sid, regular ways of talking and acting together which we regarded as legitimate, and how they routinely enacted talking-relationships with each other. But consistency between these, sameness from one talking-relationship to another was not, I realised, socially necessary or, it seemed, cognitively important. Only the stranger, socially dislocated and placing habit in question (and, more precisely, annotating conversations and then juxtaposing these records in alien ways) would possibly have to deal with what Schutz has described as the incoherence, partiality and contradictoriness inherent in the assumptions of people's everyday commonsensical knowledge (1944, *passim*). But then again, I did not feel I was discovering and describing for Doris and Sid mere membership in a set of community-wide perspectives, a Schutzian system of commonsensical definitions by which a common cultural world was regulated and, at least situationally, brought to order (1953, *passim*). For one thing, there were obviously large differences between some of the assumptions held by Doris and those held by Sid. Not only were their own loops of opinion highly diverse but between Doris's loops and Sid's there was only partial overlapping – they could not easily be said to be always living within the same commonsensical worlds. For another thing, as I mentioned before, I did not find I could tie Doris's or Sid's different selves and opinions to seemingly objectively or overtly different situations. Their diversity could not be explained in terms of regular work-roles as opposed to play, for example, or kitchen as opposed to building-site, or insider-interaction as opposed to that with strangers, or talk between peers as opposed to that between those of unequal status. The logic behind their diversity seemed to be far more subjective and particular. Moreover, this was a logic which I was most keen to understand and recount, and by no means corrupt. I did not want to impose a spurious unity upon Doris or Sid, to say, for example, that 'Doris seemed to mistrust many people and dislike many of the situations she found herself in, and fear much for the future' for this would be to rob my data of much of its precision and deny the validity of its intricacy and detail. This would seem to be a reduction of Doris's and Sid's diversity for the sake of a dubious leap of abstraction; to posit singularity, for example, because of an *a priori* belief that personalities must comprise integrated attitudinal wholes. Whereas it seemed far more pertinent to me to aspire to internal judgements and definitions, and to record, for instance, that Doris sometimes described National Park officers as the bane of her existence in Wanet and representative of much that was evil, as they paved the way for offcomers to usurp local heritage while keeping village people subservient and weak – (and she may have been speaking on the farm or in the pub, to someone I might otherwise have described as an outsider or a local, having just said something I took as indicative of her being emotional or stoic, friendly or distant) – while at other times Doris saw the 'same' National Park officers as representative members of a polite and cultured middle class that she was anxious to prosper within and whose tastes and manners she was eager to imitate and enjoin. Therefore I wanted to escape the hegemony of seemingly shared and singular objective events in favour of my definition of context as the way an individual perceives a situation when he or she acts and speaks, or hears others doing so. I wanted to maintain the notion that an appreciation of context was basic to an understanding of what Doris or Sid meant by their words and actions, but add the caveat that the logic behind their behaviour, its wider reference, might be a definition of context which was special and private to them, so that their behaviour might be seen as the result of their recognition in particular events or as a particular situation a further enactment of a particular social context in which they feel that the words and actions of a particular persona would be apposite.

Similarly, I did not want to say simply that Doris and Sid's conversation with one another often seemed to consist of joint sessions of complaint, bemoaning present difficulties, and comparing which of their neighbours' personalities were more hateful and which ill-fated circumstance they most deserved, for this seeming agreement in views would be to negate all aspects of social intercourse but the most superficial – as we shall see. Hence, I would keep the nine Dorises and the seven Sids which I have described as just that – a variety of voices speaking in a variety of social worlds, the 'same' individuals but perceiving themselves in a number of different cognitive contexts simultaneously, operating a number of personae and a number of worldviews. Moving from talking-relationship to talking-relationship, Doris and Sid were not perturbed by this diversity – or even seemingly cognisant. There were no attempts to rationalise their objectively inconsistent statements, few occasions when talking-partners would question contradictions, and no need, it seemed, to be rid of cognitive dissonance in aid of singular ways of speaking and behaving. If they *were* reminded of their inconstancy, and it was not done by a (cheeky) child who was to be told to mind his manners and shut-up, then it was the case of what they said before having been misheard or misunderstood. In fact what they had meant was the same as what they had just said. Therefore from the verbal loop of regularly associated phrases I have imagined a cognitive one – a loop of thought around which Doris or Sid might mentally travel, not ordinarily troubled by phrasal journeys they might make on other occasions. So, sometimes, to return to the above instance, Doris spoke about the National Park officers as a 'villager' and sometimes as 'middle class', and that is how I have wished to record her words in my ethnography.

The key to this diversity is, of course, verbal: in the reductive generalisations I have eschewed above, it is a precise association of words in Doris's and Sid's ordinary daily usage which would be lost. 'National Park officers' come to mean something for Doris in different worldviews because they are part of different verbal arrays. The words are differently compared and contrasted, differently juxtaposed against other words, so as to form distinct cognitive sets. That is, the building blocks from which I have argued that Doris and Sid construct their world-views, their loops of thought, are verbal. The meaning of each loop derives from them choosing to use particular words as blocks and then relating these to others in particular ways so as to make certain shapes. Hence, words in different loops, 'National Park officers' as parts of different cognitive contexts become different building blocks, with different meanings.

This is the key to diversity not only within Doris or Sid, to the many distinct meanings they possessed for the 'same' words, but also to the diversity between them, and it is to this that I now want to turn. Although regular and almost daily occurrences, I have described interaction between Doris and Sid, in a brief reference, as akin to verbal skirmishes in which conversation would zigzag from a snippet extracted from a phrasal loop of one speaker to a snippet from the other, as each interpreted the other's words in terms of world-views of their own. That is, whenever Doris or Sid sought oral confirmation from their conversational partner that they agreed or understood or were at least still listening, I had the sense that not only a verbal flow but also a cognitive one was being interrupted as their talking-partner took off from their words in another direction as a result of seeming overlaps with phrasal aggregations of his or her own. So, while none the less orderly and routine, I found their intercourse superficial and distorted because each would achieve only partial expression of their loops of thought before having their words recontextualised in terms of the other's alien verbal associations. This distortion I can now describe as arising out of the 'same' words, informed by different world-views and housed in different cognitive contexts, coming to mean different things to the two speakers. In this way, conversation could possess both an apparent order and a proper sequentiality of protagonists' statements and yet also what I felt to be miscommunication and superficiality of often farcical proportions.

Let me show what I mean by the following conversation, where Doris encounters Sid in her farmhouse kitchen one Saturday evening in July. It is quarter to eight in the evening and the end of a hard working day taken up with laying the concrete floor of Cedar High Farm's large new cowshed and grass silo (which will eventually mean that Doris and Fred's expanding herd of cows-in-milk will not need to be dispersed in different barns around Wanet Town, and will be able to be fed in winter on a nutritious silage as well as hay). Doris and Fred have had a professional firm of builders come for a few days and erect the steel girder shell and aluminium roof, and now they have the task of completing the walls and floor themselves and deciding on the internal layout of cattle stalls, feeding passages and pens. They have already driven around the dale comparing the structural solutions of the other large farmers who have invested in a modern cowshed, and have drawn up their own plans. They have also hired Sid to lay most of the concrete blocks for the walls and allocated Nigel, their farmhand, as his temporary builder's mate. Now the building is finally taking shape.

Today Fred and Doris decided to make a big push with the barn floor. That meant Doris doing some of Fred's work, while Fred helped Sid and Nigel. Doris and Fred also hired Lesley for the day as an extra pair of hands. Lesley usually drives a lorry for a Prongten firm of haulage contractors but he does not mind a weekend job every now and then for an extra bit of pocket-money. He is in his mid forties but still a bachelor, so he has no real weekend familial duties, and much of his weekly pay seems to go to his mother for rent. So, while he and Sid worked the cement-mixer all day, Nigel drove the wet concrete into the barn in the tractor bucket where Fred laid it and smoothed it out to his and young Craig's satisfaction. Meanwhile, Doris, Karen and Jessica were busy keeping all the men fed and checking up on their progress in the tea-breaks, as well as seeing to Fred's usual routine with the milk-beasts (fetching them from pasture, milking, feeding and mucking them out) and their own jobs looking after the tourists in the caravans and campsite.

At half past seven the day's work was finally judged complete. A fair start had been made on the barn floor, Lesley had been paid his cash, and he and Sid had left for their homes. Nigel had been allowed to slip away five minutes earlier, when there were only the cement mixer and the shovels left to clean, so that he could shower and dress for his Saturday night out with the other local young bloods down the pub. Doris had done the milking and was just finishing refrigerating the bottled milk for the morning milkround when Karen had stuck her head out of the backdoor of the farmhouse and shouted that the chips were ready and to come and get them if people wanted them hot.

Now, Doris is serving up the food to a kitchen table consisting of Fred, Craig, Karen and Jessica, and a washed and changed Nigel. He, in fact, is the only one already refreshed, as Doris complains:

DORIS: Nay, I'm really stored tonight.

NIGEL: Yeah? How about you, Fred?

FRED: I'm too jiggered to be stored.

DORIS: You know Lesley is so thin! It's because they have a bad table up at Wenvoe Farm. I think his father's got an ulcer so there can't be much meat that they have up there. But that's what Lesley needs for this sort of hard work ... Aye, there's a bad table up at Wenvoe definitely ... You know, Lesley I don't mind, but Sid's tongue – that's really something a lot worse. He's really scornful, you know, Fred. I hate that ... Like he asked me this afternoon if I'd come to see if you'd all done it right in the shed! That's really nasty. All I was doing was coming to see what was going on. That was all. And then Sid said something nasty later too. Uuh ... Oh yes. When I was paying Lesley he said: 'Oh. Pay as well as food!' or something like that. Just being nasty that is, and scornful.

FRED: He didn't mean owt.

NIGEL: I thought he was just making fun of what Lesley was worth.

DORIS: So I thought happen you had said something to him about our set-up, Nigel?

NIGEL: No ... Not a word. I don't say anything about the farm.

DORIS: Well don't, will you! And make sure. Be careful of Sid 'cause last night in the pub he asked me what I thought of you, and I said you were deep, and how you said nowt about anything unless you were asked. I said you had little to say and didn't think much about anything – and that's true, isn't it Nigel?

NIGEL: Well, yes ... I keep quiet ....

DORIS: But Sid said he could find out anything he wanted from you! He just told you a whole load of lies and then he found out whatever it was he wanted to know ... So you haven't told him owt have you, Nigel?

NIGEL: No. All we talk about at work is women.

DORIS, FRED, KAREN: Ha! Ha! Ha!

FRED: That's Sid! Ha! Ha! Typical.

DORIS: Ooh. Ha! Ha! Yes, he's mad about women. He's always on about women ... But just be careful what you do tell him, Nigel. Okay?

[Sid walks in]

SID: Nay, no wonder Tom and David get into so much trouble! They were already in the Hilltop as I went past just now.

DORIS: Marjorie and Tom always set off for the pub at half past seven. Every Wednesday and Saturday without fail, they're at the Hilltop by then. And that's the way to do it really. That's better than going 10 till 2 . . . Mind you! It doesn't always work like that, going early and leaving early too, like!

SID: No way! Going to the pub at half past seven! I'd be awful sick by eleven o'clock . . . I'd be terrible sick by before eleven!

DORIS: I'd get poisoned if I drank from half seven right through! I feel bad enough the next day as it is! . . . But I s'pose darts players have to go in early, like, 'cause people are already getting fit for the winter league, it seems. I don't know.

SID: Darts! I've not played darts since I was in the Hilltop with you. I mean it's not worth it if you're awful, is it? No point at all . . . Well I'm off clay-pigeon shooting tomorrow, at Doug Ridley's.

DORIS: Oh! You play clay-pigeon shooting Sid, do you?

KAREN: Mum! . . . It's not 'playing' . . . It's 'a pastime' . . . .

DORIS: Well? . . . It's still a game and 'playing'. Isn't it? . . . Isn't that terribly expensive though Sid? I heard it was.

SID: Well, it's not too bad. Like you can buy ammo by the thousand, and that costs seventy quid odd – and Doug and me share that. Then there's the trap for about fifty quid, and that's Doug's . . . So it's not too bad, if there's a few of you doing it, like . . . And then someone's there releasing the clays.

DORIS: Oh. And who does that?

SID: Well, anyone. Anyone can release clays. Doug and me sometimes take turns and have a competition. 10p a hit, like . . . Ha! It was funny last night. I just couldn't hit owt at all. Not a thing! Awful I was. And then I went and hit the roughcast off the house wall! And that was at least a foot below where I'd been aiming. So in the end we re-did the sights, and it should be better now. 'Least it better be! Ha! . . . But you know who's a great shot? Wilbur Cowper. From Leyton. Postman, you know. Now he *can* shoot. I remember once there was just him and me out shooting foxes up on Black Fell. In a line, maybe sixty yards apart. And he got two, Bang! Bang! Just like that . . . And they weren't even together weren't them buggers. And both way beyond my distance. But he got them both. No hesitation . . . Aye, a great shot is old Wilb and no mistake.

FRED: Well now. Are we going out for a small drink then?

DORIS: I've still got too many jobs to do, I don't know. I've not even had time to start the washing yet!

KAREN: Auntie Joanna said *she* was going to the Eagle tonight, mum. And she said as how she'd better put in her curlers to face all the posh competition from you down there.

DORIS: Ooh she didn't, did she? Ha! Ha! Really? . . . Well, I dunno then. Happen we better go . . . So I better get these supper things cleared away at least. Well come on then woman. Side by! Side by! . . . Nay, I don't know, Karen. What a lump you are.

SID: I just drove our Helen up to her disco in Gapton, and the cheek of these kids! It's just something else . . . And they're all the same. From fifteen or sixteen till about – thirty. Bread-grabbing buggers! . . . I don't know. You just seem to get cheek from these kids and nowt besides.

DORIS: Till thirty! Ooh, how about that Nigel? . . . He's teasing you again . . . .

SID: Are you out again tonight then, Nigel? I reckoned you might be . . . Your hair is certainly shining.

NIGEL: Yes. I thought I'd go out for a while.

DORIS: Oh yes. Likes his beer does Nigel. You can't keep him in . . . But why not after a hard day? That's okay.

FRED: So it's off to the Eagle then, is it? . . .

NIGEL: Right then. I'll leave you to it. Thanks for supper.

DORIS: Right you are then, Nigel. Bye.

[Nigel exits]

Returning to my caravan in the back garden after leaving the farmhouse, I recorded this interaction in my diary. What I now intend is a more telling contextualisation of these behaviours. That is, I want to extrapolate from the words and actions I recorded to the meanings which I feel their perpetrators – and especially Sid and Doris – had imparted to them. This entails describing the fuller cognitive backgrounds to the utterances, the sets of views, the worlds of opinion, which I feel Sid and Doris had in mind when they spoke, so that their utterances are seen to be merely partial expressions of longer verbal aggregations, and their behaviours ambiguous abbreviations mediated by loops of thought which remain immanent but unseen. I call this procedure 'contextualisation' because, as I have said, although I might seem to be removing words from the objective context of the dinner table, I see it rather as returning elliptical behaviours to their true cognitive homes. It is to people and events, mores and manners in these latter cognitive contexts that their words are more completely seen to refer and their meanings to derive. . . .

Walking round from the new shed to the farmyard, Fred explains to Craig how when you're doing a spot of dry-stone walling you always put the old, mossy side of any stone that you have picked up outermost because you trust that the old wallers knew their stones better than you, and you want to follow their lead. Craig looks up and nods. Then they hear old 'fatso' Karen at the back porch calling them in and Fred jokes that they better jump to it and do as the big lump said before she sits on them. Doris, waiting for them by the cold-store room just ahead, laughs, and puts her arm around Craig, her baby. Women are always bossy, she explains. He'll have to learn that. Either they're bossy or else they're doormats, and without any gumption at all. That's why Karen is always bossing everybody, and always thinks she's right, even though she's still soft as muck beneath her hard shell.

Reaching the house porch, they take off their wellington boots and go inside. Nigel walks in a few seconds later and finds Fred seating himself at the head of the table, suddenly looking exhausted and in no mood to be trifled with. He's had a sodding hard day after all. Still, they really shaped, and made good time. First thing Fred knew, he was asking Craig (a gormless little bugger if ever there was one, just about able to read his timepiece) what the time did say, and it was evening. Now it would be nice to get a little praise or at least sympathy for the long day he has put in.

Doris, however, sitting down beside him does not oblige. She ignores Fred's pained expressions and lays claim to her own right to be com- forted and complimented: she has had a long day too. *'Nay, I'm really stored tonight'*, she says. It's no good Fred sitting there all high and mighty, looking grumpy and sorry for himself. She is as fed up as anyone, so she gets in ahead of him and says it. After all, she and him were working hand in hand, near enough, today, bettering the farm together, and striking another blow for their independence from nosy neighbours, both of the loutish newcomer variety and the fickle local. What's more, she is giving early warning to her kids that she will suffer none of their wilfulness or contrariness tonight. Neither she nor, by his looks, Fred are in any mood for anything but straightforward obedience and quiet.

Karen busies herself with getting the hot food to everyone's plate as Jessica and Craig flinch, and then seem as busy as they can eating, while waiting to see what happens next. Nigel, however, decides to step in and take the offensive rather than sit through another bolshy meal and be waiting for Doris to find some behaviour of his to call to task. It's Saturday night and tomorrow he's free to go to another Demolition Derby with a mate who works in a garage in Leyton. So, good-humouredly he says: *'Yeah? How about you, Fred?'* He gives Fred the opportunity he was seeking to have someone who noticed his temper ask how he feels. Besides, it's better to enlist Fred's participation in the conversation now rather than have him brought in by Doris later, possibly on her side and all the more annoyed because only her griev-ances had been getting an airing. Furthermore, Nigel decides this is the time to differentiate himself from the cowering kids. He may have been ordered around all day as if he were one of them but he is off work now and changed, and wants this to be recognised. He is not going to be cowed into more silence.

'I'm too jiggered to be stored', Fred tersely replies. He does not forgive Doris her self-centredness. Instead of complaining about how fed up she is and off-loading more of her anxieties. She should be sympathetic to him when he comes into the house to be revived, and complimentary of his efforts outside. Just let someone else do his work for one sole day and see how they feel at the end of it. All his problems would soon cap theirs! And then maybe he'd get left alone in peace a little more. As it is he is even too tired to be fed up, and certainly too tired to have to face whatever it is that is eating Doris now. After a day like he's put in he deserves more than to come in and hear tones like hers.

But Doris is not to be deviated from her course and she continues with her view of the day: *'You know Lesley is so thin! It's because they have a bad table up at Wenvoe Farm. I think his father's got an ulcer so there can't be much meat that they have up there. But that's what Lesley needs for this sort of hard work . . . Aye, there's a bad table up at Wenvoe definitely. . . .'* Doris pauses. Of course she knows that days like today mean hard work for the men and they have to be fit to cope, but she doesn't criticise Fred for his portly girth, does she? Nor hinder his love of food and suggest he might be less tired if he were carrying round less extra weight, however manly his size might be. Far from it. She feeds him up and keeps him big and happy. So he should remember how hard she works and compare this place with Wenvoe Farm! Lesley's father must be so anxious about the inefficient way everything seems to be done up there, and their failures in trying to keep afloat in this hardest of occupations, that he's worked himself into an ulcer. And he's tight, with it. Just like all them Payteys: his mother (Lesley's grandmother) especially. She used to be very mean in her food and housekeeping, even when her lads'd blow up at her to straighten her. And that says something in itself because men don't usually even realise what they're being fed, and just eat without complaint. So it must have got really bad up at Wenvoe in them days. But she just wouldn't be properly broken in and learn to keep to a happy medium, and now her son's the same and can't afford meat for the table. It's not Lesley's mother's fault of course. Doris knows that she is a fine cook and keeps an extensive vegetable garden. But it's meat that men need to keep them out at work, and potatoes and bacon and bread – whatever these offcomers and their scientists say about everything being bad for you nowadays. What do they know after all? If you listened to them you'd end up eating nowt. Whereas traditionally they'd eat everything here, men and women, and live long, robust lives – so this is what Doris provides at dinner everyday. She cannot be accused of budgeting badly or starving *her* family. They all work well and eat well. None of *them* looks white or weak and today was no exception. So now, at the end of the day, they should come together as a family, not retreat like diversome individuals into private grumpiness, comfort each other and stand united against the world outside. And talking about outsiders (while her point about Lesley sinks in), Sid is something else again. Doris explains: '*You know, Lesley I don't mind, but Sid's tongue – that's really something a lot worse. He's really scornful, you know, Fred. I hate that. . .Like he asked me this afternoon if I'd come to see if you'd all done it right in the shed! That's really nasty. All I was doing was coming to see what was going on. That was all. And then Sid said something nasty later too. Uuh . . . Oh yes. When I was paying Lesley he said: "Oh. Pay as well as food!" or something like that. Just being nasty that is, and scornful.*' The way Sid behaved was one of the main reasons she had had such a difficult day and was so stored now. Having outsiders coming in and tramping across her land, her home, was bad enough but having rude and nasty outsiders like Sid is beyond the pale. And now she's reminded Fred about what they have at Cedar High compared to other places, he should be more receptive to her point. All day Sid was scornfully trying to drive a wedge between Fred and her as if the farm were not their joint marital enterprise and it was not her right, not to say duty, to come and see how business was progressing at the work site and if she could be of any help. And he was trying to catch them out and make her feel small just like he always does. Today he was even hinting that they still depended on their neighbours' charity on Cedar High, as in the days she was rebuilding it by herself after Richard's death, and needed to pay for labour in food and services not cash. There's been a lot of water under the bridge since then, she's worked hard, brought up four local children, but Sid and folks like him are eaten by jealousy and won't forget. Sid's a nothing himself, really, but there he was, still scratting around in the dirt all day for more ways to turn people against them at Cedar High. He'd just love them to be poor and pitiable again because then he'd have even more of an excuse to come in and try and run their lives for them. And she's sure around the village he'd not be short of a welcome ear. What's more, didn't she and Fred decide not to hire Sid any more than was absolutely necessary? Wasn't it only last week Fred was complaining that his walling was so uneven and cock-eyed that it hurt him just to walk past it? These big firms may be able to pay a labourer for doing nothing every hour of the day, but Cedar High certainly could not. And in what other country could you expect to be hired for a week's work and do nowt at all? So hasn't she a perfect right to lose her rag with Sid? It's high time Fred put his foot down and cursed him to his face for his sloppy work. Fred's still got a tongue in his head, it seems, when it suits him to be grumpy.

'*He didn't mean owt.*' Fred says this as consolation but it's hard not to sound dismissive. He's tired, and it does get boring, seeing Doris throwing her weight around like this. And she wonders at him getting fed up with her sometimes. It's not as if they don't already know what Sid can be like as they've discussed it a thousand times. It's just that "beggars can't be choosers". Ok, Sid is a queer little fellow, lazy and nosy and unreliable. He's like the cow's tail – he'll always come home last. And yes, he lacks a few top-stones so you need to watch he's not making a balls-up of everything all the time but he's cheap, and right now they can't afford better. Besides, he's bloody started the blocking so he can finish it. They're not going to pay someone else to go round after him cleaning up his scrow. He can sodding well do it himself.

Nigel tries to reassure Doris too: '*I thought he was just making fun of what Lesley was worth*'. He was there when Sid made his remark and he finds her interpretation wide of the mark, well wide, his tone tells her. Far from being hostile, Sid's joke had intended to highlight the contrast between casual helpers of Cedar High such as Lesley, who are paid for their contributions immediately, and regular supporters like himself who go home without a murmur, ready to accept payment whenever it best suits the farm's cash-flow situation, even when it's men like Sid not wimps like Lesley who are doing the real work about the place.

Doris does not like having her judgement questioned and her concerns poohpoohed. What's more, Fred not taking her call for sympathy and satisfaction seriously is one thing but her farmhand Nigel talking down to her, and in front of the rest of the family too, is quite another. Especially since, as an adult, trying to have a serious talk with Fred, 'father', and someone long acquainted with suffering at the hands of her fellow-locals, she obviously knows best. So she curtly reminds Nigel about his status in their relationship: '*So I thought happen you had said something to him about* our *set-up Nigel?*' Maybe he's been telling folks how she and Fred've got him working for no pay and forgotten to

mention the food, care, accommodation and tuition he's getting free in
return. She wouldn't put it past him if he's been blabbering on like this,
in his childish way, forgetting that she and Fred, the grown-ups, can do
all the talking that needs doing about Cedar High. Nigel's still weak
and far too bookish: sort of 'academic' and without the natural bloom of
a farm-child. And then it would be just like Sid too to take advantage of
garrulous youngsters to sniff out family secrets so that he could hold
their parents hostage to his foul tongue. And he doesn't miss a thing,
always asking questions to find out more about everyone like a right
devious Nosy Parker, just like he has been since their schooldays. He's
the same Sid Askrig, not happy unless he's teasing someone or laughing at them, and unless everything's going his way. (In school he'd sit
down and refuse to play if he didn't like the teams.) He always was a
bad sport and a cheat and he's no different now. But then it's probably
always the same in a village. The gossip is awful. It seems folks have to
try to get to the bottom of everything, especially local people. They just
can't let you be in your own family or business; always bitching about
your cows or sheep or cowmuck or milk or silage. It's like you can't do
owt without someone hearing and then making a fuss and rebelling
and trying to get back at you and your business; or reporting you to the
National Park. They just don't realise how short life is, and how they
shouldn't waste time on arguing but be nice to one another. Like the
Bible says: 'Love Thy Neighbour'. But most people forget the Ten
Commandments too, and Sid, especially, is a real black soul.

Nigel is taken aback and, reddening, replies: *'No. . . Not a word. I don't
say anything about the farm.'* Doris bringing the subject of his position on
the farm out into the open like this is really rather infra dig. He thought
they had reached agreement, adult and unspoken, that he was on the
farm to help, providing freely of his time and energy for reasons best
known to him, and that she and Fred would gratefully accept what he
was able to give for as long as it lasted, without probing too deeply into
the whys and wherefores. That was what she kept intimating anyway.
But now here she is really hitting below the belt. Serve him right for
opening his mouth in the first place. Anyhow, he has a quick think.
Sid's always been a bullying bastard, but no, Nigel's sure he's kept his
back covered so Sid couldn't have learnt anything incriminating.

Doris can see how fearful and embarrassed Nigel is looking, and
that's what she'd expect. Children always wilt under adult interroga-
tion which is exactly why Sid is so dangerous. However, there's no
point getting angry about it. Children can't help themselves, and Nigel
seems to be learning his lesson. So she'll just remind him how to behave
off the farm where he is seen as a representative of her and Fred, as his
surrogate parents, and how to ward off other parents' nosiness without

either being bad mannered or besmirching the family reputation after all the good this farm is doing him. So she says: *'Well don't, will you! And make sure. Be careful of Sid 'cause last night in the pub he asked me what I thought of you, and I said you were deep, and how you said nowt about anything unless you were asked. I said you had little to say and didn't think much about anything – and that's true, isn't it Nigel?'* As a parent she can easily read Nigel's ascriptions even if he can't. It's clear to see he was born deep and silent, a dreamer. And this is all right, at least for the time being. She tells him how he is because this is how he can act not to get the family into trouble – use his natural defences of taciturnity and Sid will be foiled in his attempts to get at them all through him. They have to stick up for one another, like she did for him. Only if they stand together will their private lives on the family farm be safe.

Nigel starts to feel better again. It's suspicion of Sid not of him that's still really behind Doris's probing, and he can almost afford himself the affluent feeling of finding the situation amusing. On the one hand Doris is so paranoid that she can't see people like Sid might be trying to get at *him* and not at her at all. Indeed Sid could be trying the opposite, trying to win her over, and using him (Nigel), a perfectly apposite outsider, as a pawn in the process. Just think, her paranoia is actually coming to his aid! On the other hand it's quite funny, not to mention sociologically significant, to see how his reticence, the reticence of an observing participant trying not to lead situations, is legitimatised by her as the simplicity of a child. *'Well, yes . . . I keep quiet . . .'*, he says. He's not actually going to admit to being an 'airhead' and not thinking a lot about anything, but he can certainly agree to being quiet. But he's also wary – Doris's tone tells him there's more to come and when Sid's involved it's probably nothing good. Will the hateful creep never stop trying to undermine the relationships he has worked so hard to attain? And after all this time too; Sid's perseverance really is shocking, not to mention his insecurity and possessiveness whenever someone gets within a mile of one of the people he regards as *his* special friends.

Doris presses her point home: *'But Sid said he could find out anything he wanted from you! He just told you a whole load of lies and then he found out whatever it was he wanted to know . . . So you haven't told him owt have you, Nigel?'* This may be embarrassing Nigel, keeping him the centre of attention like this at the dinner table, and she could have brought the matter up more privately at some other time, when 'father' didn't have to be there, but Nigel did decide to enter into the grown-ups' discussion in the first place as if he knew what he was talking about, so he now has to put up with the consequences even if they aren't to his liking. And he obviously needs to be shown that dealing with Sid is no joking matter. it is just lucky for Nigel that Sid picked her to blabber to, not someone who didn't have a special set-up with him and wouldn't have remained loyal to it, and wouldn't have come straight home and warned him instead before it became too late. It's not that she's annoyed with Nigel. After all, this is just what she would expect. No doubt if Sid had not been gossiping about him to her then he would have been off badmouthing about her somewhere else. He's tricky and dangerous and that's why parents are there, to keep a level head and protect children from the pitfalls of a prying and hypocritical adult world while they are too immature to protect themselves or even realise their own weaknesses and their child's grasp on the reality of things. All she would ask in return is a little appreciation for this care and attention. Some children after all are not so lucky and find themselves living in institutions or out on the streets or even dying of starvation. So it would be nice if her children kept civil tongues in their heads and answered her honestly and directly at all times, without holding anything back or being argumentative and rude, whatever truths they had to report.

Nigel is really shocked. All those hours working together on the building site and Sid is still plotting against him. Nigel was right always to half-suspect Sid of duplicity. And how clean is Doris coming with him now? Did she really ignore Sid's promptings when he told her (as he must have) how much of a suspicious snooping outsider he found Nigel? Nigel is also annoyed with himself. Doris led him on and he just walked straight into it. Acting calm and cocky, deriding her anxieties, until she bowls him over with this punchline so that her crazy fears become his own. Anyway, get a grip! This is just more of Sid's bluffing before Doris, just to stir up matters and prove his loyalty. Sid hasn't really found anything out. It is high time he put a stop to this line of questioning from Doris, so why not tell them what kind of monotonous drivel Sid really does spout all day at the site: '*No. All we talk about at work is women*', Nigel says with certainty and some surprise. He hopes the ingenuousness of his tone will finally convince them of the innocence of his and Sid's relations and of his self-control.

Doris and Fred laugh. Of course Nigel is such an innocent that it's possible even Sid hasn't been able to worm anything juicy out of him, even if Nigel knew what he was about in the first place! And it's good to be reminded of another side of Sid (the failed Romeo who still doesn't know his powder's sopping wet) and have a good laugh. And Karen laughs too because she's just finding out about sex now and wants to show she can imagine what Uncle Sid might try to get up to when it came to courting a lass.

Then, still laughing, Fred adds: '*That's Sid! Typical.*' It's a relief to have a change of tone and a joke after the heavy weather Doris makes of her interrogations. And this is the Sid Fred prefers to keep in view, the one he knows best from working together, the bungler, the frustrated lecher, the bigmouth always out for a lark. Laughable Sid, always full of hot air and not to be taken too seriously.

Doris is also relieved to remember another thing Sid is interested in and could be spending time on instead of spying on them at Cedar High. So she adds, laughing: *'Ooh. Yes, he's mad about women. He's always on about women . . . '* But then it's a bit embarrassing and not quite proper to be talking about this at the dinner table, men and women, adults and children together. It's terrible the things and the language you hear on a farm (and here she was, brought up to be a modest woman, and never use bad words or curse or swear), and she doesn't really want to hear what these men and their rude mouths get up to outside the farmhouse, so she brings the subject back to the serious and polite one they started with. A joke's a joke and she'd be the last one to stop children laughing but they mustn't lose sight of serious matters in the process. So she adds: *'But just be careful what you do tell him, Nigel. Ok?'* She can only make herself sound half-serious now, because she's not worried about farm secrets so much as wondering about the state of her sister's marriage. Joanna said they were getting on better together but Sid obviously hasn't stopped all the lewd talk, and probably mouthing off still about being unable to resist female wiles, or however he says it. If only a fraction of what he said were true it wouldn't bode all that well for what domestic life must be like in his home . . . .

Just at that moment Sid strides into the kitchen, unannounced, but giving no indication that he was listening at the door or heard anything amiss. Now his work clothes have been changed for a Saturday night pair of trousers and shirt. *'Nay, no wonder Tom and David get into so much trouble! They were already in the Hilltop as I went past just now'*, he says as he goes and leans on the Aga kitchen range, takes out and lights a cigarette, and casually watches the others eat. Not only has he found time to go home and get supped and washed but also to race updale on an errand, past the Hilltop pub, and back, in the same time it has taken his friends to sit down at their supper table! There's just no stopping him when he's got the bit between his teeth. And what should he see in passing but Tom Mason's car and David Feather's van. Tom Mason is married to Marjorie Smith, and hence is Doris's one-time brother-in-law, whom she still sees alot of and calls a good friend. David Feather is often hired by Doris and Fred for odd-jobs (like walling and tractor work) that Sid could do way better. So where were they today when Cedar High was calling on its trusty helpers? Where are they now when he has come back to find out how they are coping on the farm and lend his support to planning the future? Oh he knows very well what those two get up to. Very good they are at exercising their mouths instead of putting in decent hours of work for decent earnings, and very good at exercising their tongues and contributing to the hate and intrigue that has turned Wanet into such a horrid place. If only Doris and Fred could be made to see straight and differentiate between real friends and hypocrites. Tom Mason, especially, is a tight-arsed little bastard. And his wife's nothing but a petted whore who's not even worth a tupping. Sid has seen more life in a dead snake skin. Mason thinks nowt but money – he lives for it. His land is terribly overstocked and all his sheep are dirty-arsed buggers but if he had only 200 sheep up on his allotments instead of 400, he'd lose fewer lambs, use the land better and still get the same cash. And like they say, sometimes he feeds them and sometimes he's out feeding his great beer-gut instead. Sid certainly wouldn't turn down a penny for all the pints gone into making that belly! A few nights' work there, all right. And no doubt many of them were drunk alongside David Feather. Now *he* has got such an enormous gob on him that you wish his tongue 'd get rigor mortis. He should really have got a job as a chapel preacher, or more likely, they'll call him up to act as a loudhailer after the nuclear war. And he just explodes and gets in a right wrath as soon as you give him a piece of your mind, but then, like all Feathers, he soon reverses rapidly when you stand up to him. Aye, he's somebody Sid could happily strangle if someone put him up to it – even a hundred quid'd do. And if Sid ever did decide to murder someone like that, he'd do it so he'd never be found out.

Doris doesn't like Sid's tone. All day he was sarcastic about her and Fred's efforts on Cedar High to become a bit more independent and middle class, and now here he is again, marching in as if he owned the place and criticising her longtime friends Tom and Marjorie Mason, as if they couldn't teach him a thing or two about good manners. Well, for his information, she knows their habits slightly better than him, and their being out now is not whimsy but part of their regular work pattern, regularity which would be light-years from anything he could ever understand. '*Marjorie and Tom always set off for the pub at half past seven. Every Wednesday and Saturday without fail, they're at the Hilltop at seven thirty. And that's the way to do it really. That's better than going 10 till 2 . . . Mind you! It doesn't always work like that, going early and leaving early too, like!*' Doris concludes with a laugh. Imagine someone like Sid Askrig leaving a pub before closing time! In fact him and his lower-class cronies probably rebel when the landlord tries to throw them all out at two in the morning, and then they take their lax behaviour and wantonness out into the Wanet streets. But with middle-class folks like the Masons it's very different. They can control themselves when they go drinking. They arrive on time and then leave in good time so as to be fit for the next day's work. You can count on the Masons. They are as reliable and steady as when they stuck by her after Richard's death, and Tom let Marjorie get away regularly to come and help Doris during that awful first year. Not like Sid and the rest of her fickle neighbours – here to gloat one minute and then gone the next. What's more, the Masons make a really nice couple. Tom can be a real card. And he's a real farmer too, not like those others up Thurn way, 'gentlemen-farmers' whom you never see dirty and just drive around all day visiting someone. The Masons may not be posh but it's not only posh people who've got all the brains and there's nothing wrong with being common. Not all brainy folks are upper class, and everyone loves a trier anyway, trying to move up a bit and make a go of it. What's more, Tom chaperones Marjorie so that they can relax together as husband and wife with other couples while escaping the attentions of both the younger generation and the elderly for a bit of peace. She and Fred have had some great evenings out with the Masons. They can be very droll together and at least for a few hours they can all end up forgetting their troubles all together. What's more, it's good to occupy the pubs to make sure the tourists who crowd you out all summer don't get it all their own way; so at least some traditional local pastimes carry on.

Sid realises that Doris can be a bit slow sometimes, but if she thinks that Tom and David will leave off their drinking early, on a Saturday night, because they arrived early, then she must have only just hatched! But then again, women don't really understand what men are about when they have a drinking session and vie with each other for the championship over the bitter. Not that what Tom and David are up to is exactly manly, sipping their way through a shandy or two, no doubt, like a couple of wimps, before the real men arrive and start putting it away. Because not even a healthy man, never mind a pair of prize pillocks, could take in 'liquid refreshment' at a normal pace from half past seven right through. And he tells Doris as much: *'No way! Going to the pub at half seven! I'd be awful sick by eleven o'clock – I'd be terrible sick by before eleven!'* It's not just that Doris can be slow, Sid knows. When she gets the wrong side out she can be right contrary. So it's always best to tread warily at first. Agree with her, go along with her train of thought, and then put in your own example of what you mean to say. So if he agrees that going to the pub early doesn't mean leaving early, and that he could never do it then what does that say about Tom and David's manliness? If *he* admits to an inability, to limits to his power to kill a pint of beer, then what kind of men must they be pretending to be! And doesn't that just prove what he was saying before about the differences between a true hardworking crew like Fred, Doris and him, and fakes like Tom and David, already off gallivanting and probably by now pissed as newts?

But Doris doesn't want to let Sid off the hook so easily. She is quite aware how adept Sid and others of his ilk are at boozing, and if he wants to claim that a bout from half past seven till eleven o'clock would make him sick, and merely make him sick, then to someone of her sensibilities it would prove positively poisonous! As it is, when Fred escorts her to meet other middle-class couples for a pleasant enough get-together, she can still feel the after-effects the next day. Of course being a woman doesn't help either because she will feel so much more than a man, and something silly is always likely to happen to her unless Fred remembers to keep a really close eye on her intake and the length of time they are out. So she says: *'I'd get poisoned the next day as it is! . . . But I s'pose darts players have to go in early, like, 'cause people are already getting fit for the winter league, it seems. I don't know.'* Of course it's different for Marjorie. Her going in early doesn't mean she's a scamp or unladylike or anything of that sort. On the contrary, she and Tom are such stalwarts of the Hilltop darts team that however ailing it has been in recent seasons, they don't give up, but dutifully go in and start practising again as early as the confident members of more proficient teams. They are determined to uphold the reputation of their pub and the group of mature friends who they can conveniently meet there in peace. And what a far cry the Masons' loyalty to local friends and local custom is from the things Sid Askrig gets up to and the sort he does them with.

'Darts!', says Sid. The way the female mind works is really something else, the things Doris dreams up. He just brings her round to seeing the reality about Tom and David's boozing – if you leave work early and start on the beer before half past seven then even a real man is going to be useless for work the next day too – when she goes off on some wild trail after darts. Tom and David, the great Thurn darts champions! Who is she trying to kid? The fact is, it just proves they have no manly honour and no shame. Ok, you want to compete with other men and take them for what you can get. And, granted, it's hard to restrain yourself when the whiff of combat gets in your nose, but only a right pair of fools keep playing when they are laughing stocks, in a joke team which keeps losing. That's the time to hide your shame and practise in private. Even Sid has his occasional fallow periods, as he explains: *'I've not played darts since I was in the Hilltop with you. I mean it's not worth it if you're awful, is it? No point at all.'* Of course comparing him with Tom or David is really a joke and Fred will have got the point and seen through the false modesty at least. Sid may not be a he-man when it comes to darts, or even up to Fred's standard, but he's no slouch either. Everyone knows he still loves to compete, and they can guess it wouldn't take much to get him in training again, and then, watch out!

And isn't it significant how the last time he took up the 'spears' was that fine evening they all had out together not so very long ago in the very same pub where Tom and David are now getting legless without a thought to Cedar High. Sid looks over to Fred and he nods in agreement but keeps his eyes on his plate, mopping up the last of his egg yolk with a slice of buttered bread. Fred and Doris must now remember what a great darts spot the Hilltop *used* to be when they'd all go there together. And they can't have forgotten the time Sid beat the great Len Scruton of Leyton in singles, man-to-man, when the Crown came to play. He really punished him that night with some amazing 'arrows' on a night never to be forgotten. So as that point really hits home, Sid changes topic: *'Well I'm off clay-pigeon shooting tomorrow, at Doug Ridley's'*. He wouldn't want people to think he'd forgotten how to play hard as well as work hard, and today he has earned his relaxation. But even when he plays he chooses a natural male pursuit like guns. His plumb eye which is so indispensable to his craft, enabling him to judge the straightest of lines in a row of blocks or a coat of render, is put to equal good effect behind gunsights. And in Doug Ridley he has an excellent mate. They compete with each other and, even though surrounded by deadly temptations, still manage to stay friends.

Doris is pleased for a change of subject matter. And when Sid starts talking about himself like this (instead of attacking her and her friends and trying to drag them all down to his level), it's amazing the things you can get him to say. He's always trying to show he knows more about everything but if you lead him on he can end up spouting something gay foolish – it gets to be a right comical carry-on. Fred can do it to him something cruel. He tells Sid half a tale so Sid thinks he's got him – you can just see him trying to work it all out – and then he'll come out with something really half-baked! Fred's got that knack, and it just shows how much less intelligent Sid is. So Doris says encouragingly: *'Oh! You play clay-pigeon shooting Sid, do you?'* There's Sid off playing when decent, hard-working farmers like her and Fred are finding ways of becoming even more efficient. Even on a Sunday there are Sunday jobs; like being up in the hills with the beasts. They change shape every day after all and you wouldn't want to miss that. That's the way you learn something new every day; and you get to feel that animals are human, with feelings, 'cause you talk to them and they understand the tone of your voice. You get to think like them and then you can understand and care for them, and they don't run off or leave you till they die. And then there's new life around all the time too which is what really makes the work rewarding. But then Doris wouldn't expect Sid to understand any of that. Even now he works fewer hours than Fred, and there's Fred eight years his senior. At Sid's age Fred must have been twice the man. There's not much you miss about a man as a wife and you can just see the strength Fred's got bred in him. You can't get out what's not been bred in in the first place, that's for sure. But then there are some people who are just born lazy and won't even try to improve and make themselves a bit more respectable.

Then Karen interrupts. '*Mum! . . . It's not "playing" . . . It's a pastime . . .*', she hints. Sometimes mum does make silly mistakes in English. As she says, it was her particular fate to be born stupid at spelling and at finding the right word so Karen quietly helps her so that she doesn't embarrass herself in front of Uncle Sid. Inside the family it can be funny, and everyone sort of expects it, but what would Uncle Sid make of it otherwise? And now Karen is grown-up enough to see the differences between being an adult and being a child. And playing just isn't something adults do.

Doris is annoyed at being sidetracked and warns her daughter by her tone against offering any further opinions: '*Well? . . . It's still a game and "playing". Isn't it?*', she says. She needs no lessons from a cheeky child in the middle of an adult conversation, especially when one of the adults is a nosy outsider who would just love some evidence of family disagreement or tension in their orderly relations. So she snubs Karen and shows Sid just who is still in command here, whatever might be the case in his own menagerie of a family. She is never too preoccupied to bring Karen up properly, to 'call' her when necessary, and show her there's a right and a wrong to be learnt in all things. It's just wilfulness after all and it is not even in Karen's nature. She does it out of spite, just competing, daring you to see who's in control. Besides, the last thing Doris needs tonight is any more aggravation coming her way, or she'll soon start dishing it out. Karen will get more than she bargained for and they'll just see who cracks first because it's no good spoiling children like her, or any children for that matter. If they live it all already when they're young, without discipline, then they seem to turn out all the worse as adults, or even die young before they get there. So, with Karen dealt with, Doris returns to the interesting topic of Sid's game-playing: '*Isn't that terribly expensive though Sid? I heard it was.*' Here are she and Fred, not having taken time off for years, while Sid, not exactly a model businessman – nor ever likely to be – seems to be throwing what little money he has away! What a way to behave; and in a recession too, when all decent people are working their hardest not to go under and to retain their independence and their pride. Young Douglas Ridley might know no better, but, of all things, Sid Askrig shouldn't be leading him further astray. This is just the bitter fruit of all those Labour governments giving out money to useless cases, propping up all those lame ducks and showing people they can go out and have a spending spree.

People always had too much money in their pockets, more than the country could afford, so they never learnt its value or how it should be earned not by playing or striking but by a fair day's work. So now you get poor people like Sid taking time off, overdressing, and spending way beyond their means. And what a husband he is! There he is, off spending *their* housekeeping with his cronies. The only consolation, Doris knows, is that things always come and pay you back in the end. In fact she's heard it said that you just don't know all you'll have to answer for in the end, more than you ever thought possible.

Sid is pleased with Doris's attention, pleased he can tell her more about his manly pursuits. So he explains: '*Well, it's not too bad. Like you can buy ammo by the thousand, and that costs seventy quid odd – and Doug and me share that. Then there's the trap for about fifty quid, and that's Doug's. . .So it's not too bad if there's a few of you doing it, like. . .And then someone's there releasing the clays.*' Doug and him and the rest of the boys have got it all worked out. It might seem pricey but they've got the finances nicely sussed so they have their fun, get in their bit of violence, compete with each other, and still manage to pool their resources. Besides, isn't this exactly what Sid deserves? As a master of his trade, hasn't he earned the freedom and independence to take time off and spend the fruits of his skilled labour when and where he chooses. It might seem expensive to some, but this is where his clients' respect and the fine lolly they are prepared to fork out for his craftsmanship get him.

It is as Doris thought – a shocking waste of money, immoral even, for someone in Sid's position. And what must Joanna think about all of this? She hasn't mentioned anything to Doris so far. Maybe he softens her up by pretending it is for the kids and taking them along as she slaves away at home. Maybe he ropes them into releasing the clays for him? It would be typical of Sid to drag his children further down his own disreputable path, as if giving them his biology wasn't burden enough! So Doris asks as if innocently interested: '*Oh. And who does that?*' Sid can be very weird when it comes to finding the worst layabouts and scamps to party with, and he can disappear into some very wild country to meet them, to different territory out past Leyton way, which Doris doesn't even know how to name and Sid is very fishy about. Lost places and lost people.

Sid is delighted with Doris's continued interest and decides to reward her with just a glimpse of 'the other side', the manly world that she should be associating him with. He'll let her into some of the excitement of the sport, the fight and the chase, even though she might find at the end the detail was too much for her and she wishes she'd never asked. These women are all the same. Their curiosity gets the better of them and they go beyond their depth. Joanna's always doing it and he gets a right laugh teasing her back home again. So he says, grinning at the thought and eyes bright: *'Well, anyone. Anyone can release clays. Doug and me sometimes take turns and have a competition. 10p a hit, like . . . It was funny last night. I just couldn't hit owt at all. Not a thing! Awful I was. And then I went and hit the roughcast off the house wall! And that was at least a foot below where I'd been aiming. So in the end we re-did the sights, and it should be better now. 'Least it better be! . . . But you know who's a great shot? Wilbur Cowper. From Leyton. Postman, you know. Now he can shoot. I remember once there was just him and me out shooting foxes up on Black Fell. In a line, maybe sixty yards apart. And he got two, Bang! Bang! Just like that. . .And they weren't even together weren't them buggers. And both way beyond my distance. But he got them both. No hesitation. . .Aye a great shot is old Wilb and no mistake.'* Sid finds himself almost getting carried away at the idea of all this manly fun, but catching Fred's eye he can see that he's enjoying it as well. Fred knows the great times you can have when you get a little friendly competition going away from the distraction of all these women. Because that's what Sid gets from his guns, a time to himself, and, in men like Doug and Wilb, mates who know not to spoil a good thing. They can all share an appreciation of physique, of technical ability (so that faulty gunsights can easily be remedied), of honour (so the sights aren't fixed in the middle of a game), of a world precisely regulated into straight lines and exact distances, of noise and the hunt, and of true worth. And this is a world which women had better stay inside the house and avoid because you never know what a stray bullet might hit, or how a man might decide to get his own back on their prying eyes! Of course Sid sometimes takes young Christopher along with him to work the trap, but that's different. You want your son to be proud of you and eager to copy what you do as far as he is capable. So Chris doesn't cramp anybody's style, and releasing the clays is child's play anyway.

Fred puts an end to Sid's reminiscence in authoritative tones: *'Well now. Are we going out for a small drink then?'* He's heard quite enough from Sid for one day, especially about these bow and spear people over Leyton way, shooting foxes to bits when they're trying to just crease them so the dogs can catch up. He's even heard tell of some small farms out that way that still muckspread by horse and cart and won't have owt to do with machines – at least those shops that haven't been so-called modernised, and now run by 'managers'. Anyway, it's obvious what Sid's come back for – he kept on about his drink all day – and equally obvious that Sid won't shut up or leave without one being arranged. And they have to be careful not to offend him so he goes blathering about how them on Cedar High are breeding moths in their wallets and staying home to count their money, or being too mean or unfriendly or tired or slow to go for a drink with their employees after work. For the time being they have to keep Sid sweet, at least till the shed is nearer completion. Besides, after that meal Fred can feel himself returning to reasonable form so, a short drink, and then peace from Sid, and bed.

Doris has her own views on that, however. All this talk about darts and shooting and hunting and drinking is all very well but she's not having these men forgetting just who it is that nourishes them and revives them so they can gad about after work. It's their wives. Sid may be totally wayward and lacking in any self-respect but she expects more from Fred. Not only did she help him out with his work today, but now she's has to see to her own. Even on a Saturday night she's not the sort of scampish wife who goes out and leaves a dirty house with a clean conscience. So she says: *'I've still got too many jobs to do, I don't know. I've not even had time to start the washing yet!'* After Sid's sarcasm today, it's good to show him just how seriously she takes her responsibilities inside the house too. And Fred will stand by her too. He'd never go out alone now and they'll just show Sid how they're in this together.

Then Karen pipes up again. *'Auntie Joanna said she was going to the Eagle tonight, mum. And she said as how she'd better put in her curlers to face all the posh competition from you down there.'* Even if mum sometimes treats her as if she were still a child, Auntie Joanna doesn't. She tells Karen all her plans and how she's anxious to look nice for a Saturday night out, and since this is a compliment to mum after all, maybe it'll make up for how she took what Karen said before. And she can show she remembers all the things mum's said about enjoying dressing up and keeping up with the fashions, and how Auntie Joanna was always playfully trying to outdo her in public, even as a little girl. That was just the way she was born.

Doris is surprised and, laughing, exclaims: *'Ooh she didn't, did she? Really?'* She's not sure whether to feel more pleased or embarrassed. It's a bit embarrassing having these womanly anxieties and wiles brought out so baldly in front of the men, but on the other hand it's exciting that her dress sense and attempts to improve her taste are being noticed and mentioned and even copied by other people, like Joanna, who would also like to act and appear a little more posh. Now she feels she is almost duty-bound to tidy herself up a bit and show her face, not to disappoint her fellow-wifely admirers. It wasn't her idea after all. She's made her protest and now she's really only obeying her husband's wishes and accepting his invitation. So she says: *'Well, I dunno then. Happen we better go. . . So I better get these supper things cleared away at least. Well come on then woman. Side by! Side by! . . . Nay, I don't know, Karen. What a lump you*

are.' Suddenly Doris finds herself in a happy rush and in the mood for a
Saturday night drink after all but there's still the table to clear, and if
Karen were as adult as she likes to think she is, then she would know
when to start tidying up without having to be told. She should know
Doris will need time to get ready and won't want to keep her husbandly
escort waiting too long, but of course Karen doesn't know and needs
constant reminding. And her puppy fat gives her away. It just proves
how lazy she still is when it comes to family chores. Today was typical.
She hardly did anything except vanish very cleverly as soon as she'd
seen to the breakfasts, and lock the door behind her so that the campsite
lost goodness knows how many possible customers. Doris has a good
mind to make her pay for those lost earnings from her own pocket. It's
the only way these kids will start to learn to mend their mistakes and
give back to the farm because it's not a charity, and you never get owt
for nowt in this world. Besides, children need criticism to spur them on
to doing better. No one is as much harmed by their continuing mistakes
as they are themselves after all. So even in the midst of her happy rush
Doris does not neglect her familial duties; and no doubt Sid will have
seen this too.

Sid is brought to mind of his own daughter, about the same age as
Karen, whom he has just run up to a crowd of her rowdy friends in
Gapton. He can't help but act the lenient father when she needs ferrying
somewhere, but does he get any thanks or even respect in return? Does
he buggery! Admittedly it was nice to have an excuse to get out of the
house quickly and leave Joanna to her primping – it always takes the
old bat hours of faffing about – but that's beside the point. Kids today
are just not what they were, but always pushy, never listening and
keeping quiet unless they're in a sulk. Then they laze around as
adolescents, having it too easy and expecting their parents to do
everything for them. The lads all idle around with their big boots on
and their trousers rolled halfway up their arse, trying to look tough, or
else they become students and do nothing useful besides wasting
taxpayers' money. None of them would survive a minute if they really
had to earn their daily bread, like in the Thirties. They couldn't even
imagine how hard life was then, men walking aimlessly up and down
the streets all day in all weathers, gales blowing and doors banging,
looking for work, and lots of murders and rough-housing, and men
getting blind drunk on home brew. Even after the war there was the
rationing and families having to share an egg for breakfast between
them. Kids today just don't know they're alive. They don't know what
hard graft is, just expecting society to keep them instead. Sid'd keep
them all right! Down the mines, or in the army, until they learnt a
proper trade and proper respect. And look at Nigel, sitting at the

supper table so clean and smug. In his twenties and still a student, he has wandered in from outside and is now sponging off some of the best folks in Wanet. What an example he's setting local kids too. They'll be wanting to be pampered and then kept by the state till they 'retire' next too. So he says: '*I just drove our Helen over to her disco in Gapton, and the cheek of these kids! It's just something else. . . And they're all the same. From fifteen or sixteen to about – thirty. Bread-grabbing buggers! . . . I don't know. You just seem to get cheek from these kids and nowt besides.*' Don't Doris and Fred remember the great times *they* had together as kids? When kids acted as kids? So why the hell do they forget their real friends and put up with parasites like Nigel now?

Doris giggles and looks pointedly at Nigel. You have to laugh at the younger generation, the things they get up to, unrestrainedly running after this fashion then that, desperately wanting money for one immature craze after another. And teasing them about their antics is just about the only way mature people like her and Fred and Sid seem to be able to get away from their nagging and have some time to relax among themselves – as it's only natural they should. On the other hand, Doris does not want Nigel going into one of his sulks. These youngsters, in the process of finding themselves and their adult identities, can be very sensitive and take offence at the slightest provocation. Nigel used to do it all the time before he got to know her and Fred's ways and how she didn't mean owt by anything she says. So she wants to assure him now that Sid only meant what he said as a joke. Especially since here Nigel is sitting at her table, after being so neighbourly as to help out her and Fred's businesses on the farm. He might just go off in a huff and not come again, and she wouldn't want to risk that. So she says: '*Till thirty! Ooh, how about that Nigel? . . . He's teasing you again.*' What's more, Doris doesn't want to get embroiled with Sid again as she would have to if she thought he was including her Karen or even her Keith in his criticism of teenagers. However he might be bringing up Helen, and whatever he thinks about Nigel, she warns him that she's not having *her* fifteen-year-old maligned in this house so she didn't hear that phrase. . . .

Sid is annoyed that Doris has decided to treat his point so lightly. Doesn't she and Fred see what they're encouraging? 'Teasing Nigel'! He'd tease Nigel all right. Five minutes alone with him in a calf hull and he'd soon wipe that grin off his face. Look at him sitting there at the Cedar High table, eating Wanet food, with his smush clothes and his washed hair and his city manners, just off to tickle some local girl's snatch and set her squawking, no doubt, as if he belonged in the place. How can Doris and Fred put up with it? Why do they waste time and money on him? It's not as if everyone else in Wanet was doing just fine and dandy. Offcomers have got some of them still living in council houses, struggling to make ends meet! Thirty years ago it wasn't so easy to just walk in here. They used to throw sods and stones at outsiders then – you couldn't just expect to waltz in. The only way in then was the two 'F's, as they used to say: fucking and fighting. Nay, and you can bet it'll be colour here next. They already say Bradford is worse than the Punjab. Hell, what'll Wanet be like in thirty more years? Will it be worth living then? Will they still be alive! Christ! They're running hard now just to stay in the same spot as it is while these lazy offcomers live off government hand-outs and grants and go round pretending they're working – until the pubs open. That's where you'll find Nigel most nights: supping away with the rest of them suspicious-looking outsiders – the teddy boys, and the hired assassins, and the hippies, and the rest of the crowd – taking up space so the Eagle's always heaving. Well, if Nigel *is* off out again tonight it's certainly not going to be with him and his pals. Whatever plans he, Doris and Fred have just been making they don't include an invitation to Nigel to join them. So he says: *'Are you out again tonight then, Nigel? I reckoned you might be. . . Your hair is certainly shining.'* You can poke fun at these effeminate offcomers all you like and they're none of them man enough to retaliate. Sid's seen more life in a fag-end. He wouldn't spit on Nigel's sort if he was dying of thirst. They're like spoilt, overgrown kids, the lot of them.

Nigel tries to stay calm. This is the pain-in-the-neck who's still suspicious and won't just let him be in Wanet. But Nigel won't be caught off his guard by Sid again, nor will he rise to this idiotic bait as if Sid's silly descriptions and parochial machinations were anything to him. So in as casual and detached a way as he can Nigel says: *'Yes. I thought I'd go out for a while.'* Saturday nights at the pubs are too busy to miss as you see people then you don't meet any other time. And he can't lie about it because then Doris might ask him to babysit, and he'll probably see them down the Eagle later anyway. But he doesn't want them to think he's a real boozer, or that his nightly trips are just automatic. It's really that a quick drink might be nice to wet the palate, after consideration, but he could take it or leave it.

Doris smiles knowingly. She can see just how Nigel's mind works. It's as transparent as all these youngsters'. They just can't keep themselves from excess and drinking all their money away but at least when he's with his cronies in the Mitre, he doesn't get too rowdy, or rile her by gatecrashing on her and her mature friends' parties. He's not like these lower-class youths, running riot after a couple of swigs of cheap scrumpy (and underage some of them too), the sort that could do with rounding up by the bobbies and locking in a concrete bunker overnight to cool off. No, Nigel put in a good day's work today so let him enjoy himself in his own little way afterwards. Like they say, it takes all sorts and living in a village you better get on with them all. So she says: *'Oh yes. Likes his beer does Nigel. You can't keep him in. . .But why not after a hard day? That's okay.'*

Fred pushes himself backwards away from the table and stands up, his chest and stomach looming large over those still sitting. He's had enough of this idle bantering. At this rate they'll still be here at closing time, and he's seen enough of Karen's blubber slowly shaking to and fro. It's the same at dinner. If he didn't get up at half past twelve and go for his wellies again, nobody would shift and the grass would be growing faster than the cowshed. *'So it's off to the Eagle then, is it?'*, he says. It's time for his bath to be run, then Sid can remove himself and they can get down the pub before his friends are wondering if him and Doris haven't got sleeping sickness, or all this extra work hasn't killed them!

Nigel is pleased to take the cue. It's been a tense meal, however informative. It'll be a relief to get out to the caravan, capture the interaction in his diary, and at least have a breather before it starts up again at the pub. *'Right then. I'll leave you to it. Thanks for supper'*, he says and leaves the table.

'Right you are then, Nigel. Bye', Doris says distractedly as Nigel goes out. Karen's at last cleared the dishes, Craig and Jennifer have eaten up and are about to scuttle off to watch telly. She'll just load the dishwasher and then she can think about the Eagle, the evening to come and what to wear – something casual but smart – which hopefully one of these offcomers won't be wearing too . . . .

12

The Conversation Analysed

I

I have been recontextualising a conversation on Cedar High Farm in terms of the different personae and world-views which animated it. Now I want to alter idiom and consider the conversation in terms of the sociolinguistics of speech communities and the social psychology of interpersonal exchange.

Successful communication, Gumperz and Tannen explain, is a matter of a subtle and complex coordination of conversational elements: turn-taking, direction of gaze, establishment of verbal rhythm, cooperation to produce identifiable lines of thematic progression, and recognition of and participation in formulaic routines (1979, p. 307). All these features of what might be called (after Brown and Levinson, 1978, p. 256) a culture's interactional systematics or ethos or predominant style, appear to be represented in the conversation just looked at. Doris and Sid, Fred, Karen and I (as well as the less verbal Christopher and Jessica) come together and partake of a 'speech event' with methodical character, with coordinated entry and orderly sequencing.

The signalling and interpretation of meaning within such a formulaic routine, Gumperz and Tannen continue (1979, pp 307–22), derive from an understanding of semantic content combined with an appreciation of cues of contextualisation. Participants in an interaction identify familiar and conventional types of activity and styles of speech which 'frame' the words they hear and enable them to define habitual 'speech situations'. The shared rules of conversational conduct thus entail common techniques of interpretation, and a constellation of features of conversational form (lexical choice, phonology, prosody, idiomatic and formulaic usage, interjections and so on) are said to direct fellow-interactants into interpreting one another's words in the same way. The definition of the speech situation becomes a joint activity, whose performance replicates part of the coherent and 'corporate' structure of everyday life (Schegloff, 1972, p. 350; Garfinkel, 1967, p. 11; and cf. Searle, 1971, p. 7). For the sociolinguists as for the ethnomethodologists, in short, the successful communication of meaning within a speech community is based on common expectations concerning conventionalised co-occurrence between potentialities of words' semantic content and aspects of discourses' surface style. As Hymes puts it, shared rules for the conduct and interpretation of speech represent the primary determination by a community of the competence and belonging of its members (1972, pp 54–8).

However, in another place (1973, pp 22–6) Hymes also urges a focus on the *single* communicative event, an emphasis less on the abstract linguistic code than the individual speech act, and he is mindful that what counts as a communicative event cannot be identified in advance since its status 'is entirely a question of [its] construal by a receiver'. Criteria of identity, that is, and judgements of sameness and difference are matters of what Winch would call 'internal relations' within a system of ideas (1970, p. 107). This is an emphasis I prefer, which is to say that I am loath at this juncture to follow the former hypothesis and simply extrapolate from the orderly nature of the above conversation and its superficial systematics to the character of the culture of sharing in a Wanet community of which the conversation forms part. For the social level at which one sees the Winchian ideational system and acts of construal and definition properly working is a moot point.

II

In differentiating social life from the refinements of the laboratory (linguistic or other), it is an immeasurably greater complexity which Louch argues we must recognise, a complexity which he sees as a condition of any social life which people would consider worth living (1969, p. 239). Certainly, in Doris and Sid's accounts of themselves and their appearances in the above conversation, as I have interpreted them, complexity if not complication has played a significant part in their lives. They have placed themselves at the centres of dense social environments. Indeed, the first analytical point I would want to make is that in this conversation we can see Doris and Sid constructing ongoing identities for themselves by maintaining relations to a host of other people, objects and events.

The mind, we understand from Bateson, operates in terms of relationships, 'things' being epiphenomena and knowledge of external events derived from perceiving the changing of relations between them. The mind operates with and upon differences, the unit of information being a difference, with the word 'idea' synonymous with 'difference'. Hence the mind may be conceived of as an aggregation of differences construed between *ego* and *alter* (Bateson and Ruesch, 1951, p. 173; 1973, pp 427, 457–8). In other words, things are defined by construing their relations of sameness and difference to other things – the more the relations, the more precise and manifold the definition becomes. Thus, to define oneself is to conceive of specific links with a myriad of others. The denser the relations, the more the evidence of one's existence, the greater the significance of that existence, the more exact the nature of that existence is made. The self becomes the hub, the anchoring point, of a constellation of things which it holds within its comparative field (cf. Miyamoto, 1970, p. 282; Adams-Webber, 1981, p. 187). Hence, in this conversation we find Sid and Doris defining themselves in relation to a wide array of *alters*: Doris and the poor table at Wenvoe Farm, the paying-off of Lesley, the set-up with Nigel, the fashion repartee with Joanna, the scornful tongue of Sid in the cowshed and his prying in the pub; Sid and the boozing of Tom and David, the bread-grabbing of Helen, the laziness of Nigel, clay pigeon shooting at the Ridleys', fox hunting with Wilbur Cowper, and Saturday night relaxing with Fred and Doris. They claim significance for themselves as regards other people and events, and provide contexts for themselves to act. The actions of many others have potential implications for them and the converse. Surrounded by gossiping, scrounging, spying, relaxing and competing *alters*, Doris and Sid construct identities for themselves at the centres of dense and highly meaningful social worlds. In satisfyingly full, rich and varied social lives, they can construe broad relevance and importance for their own thoughts and actions (cf. Schutz, 1944, p. 500).

Moreover, not only do we find Doris and Sid maintaining intricate personae and complex world-views as they converse with each other in this fashion but also, I would argue, *realising* them. In expressing and displaying their selves, in boasting the relevance which a host of other things have for them (and vice versa), Doris and Sid make these selves real. To talk through a self, that is, is to bring it to life, for saying is doing; and to use the created self in a populous social environment is to become cognisant of the multitude of real actions which that self could, if desired, effect. Hence, talking as a wife and a mother, as a friend and as aggrieved, or as a man and a pal, as a local and a father, Doris and Sid become assured of their definite existence. To give names to things is to give them shape and stability, to impose order upon an otherwise entropic universe, to create information as Bateson reminds us, and the validity of the names is a function of the user's belief in them. Moreover, this information is in no way inevitable: it is not necessarily or automatically constituted from external conditions. Rather, it derives from individuals defining their own stimuli in a social situation and constructing their own responses. Through language, individuals become origins of action upon the universe and centres of experience within it (1973, pp 249-50; also cf. Wiener, 1949, p. 18). Hence, giving names to selves and to worlds, and acting upon their assumptions in the course of their conversation, we see Doris and Sid boasting views made real.

However, to realise one pattern of things, to configure one order of people, objects and events, is to exclude and eschew others: 'pour faire des omelettes, il faut casser des oeufs' ('you cannot make omelettes without breaking eggs'). Every concept and organisation of information represents a type of taboo against other potential meanings, so Mannheim writes (1952, p. 2). Thus, we see Doris and Sid not only realising themselves in the above conversation, but also negating other identities they might have assumed, other opinions they might have held. In fact, we find them seeing what they expect to see – reaffirming people, objects and events which their world-views have led them to expect all along, their world-views acting as self-fulfilling prophecies whose meanings are self-sustaining. In other words, familiar things are perceived from the perspectives of previous orientations, with the re-sult that Doris's and Sid's conceptions of these things come to be reinforced and their hypotheses about the landscapes in which they live reconfirmed. Produced in compliance with prior expectations, the fea-tures of the worlds which Doris and Sid 'discover' around them seem not only obvious but inevitable, and as they interpret their experiences and 'uncover' meaning so their world-views are reaffirmed (cf. Shibutani, 1961, p. 136; Garfinkel, 1967, p. 53). Hence, Doris finds Lesley thin because, as she expected, he is underfed at home. Similarly, Wendy and Tom are at the pub early because they are habitually loyal to team-mates and consistent in their routines. Sid makes jokes about Lesley's pay because he is always nosing around for more ammunition for his nastiness and scorn while Sid's poor reputation as a husband is only exacerbated by his playing at shooting rather than spending time at home and money on his wife. Sid, on the other hand, sees more reasons for the trouble Tom and David 'always' get into if they booze away all hours of the afternoon and waste more time on darts. Meanwhile, Helen fails to appreciate the kindness of his driving her around and is as rude and grasping as usual. Nigel, as ever, is washed and groomed at the supper table before anyone else, ready to escape work and join other low-life as soon as he can; and, of course, Fed and Doris are eager to have a relaxing evening with him and Joanna, after a little reminder about who their best pals are. In this fashion, Doris's and Sid's world-views act as cognitive toothing-stones which precede their experiences by providing the foundation and extension from which the patterning and understanding of their experiences are built. Doris and Sid realise social orderings of people, objects and events which pre-existing sensibilities had led them to expect all along.

Furthermore, I suggest that Doris and Sid *want* to find what their world-views lead them to expect. They want their expectations of the world to be fulfilled For to achieve the security of habitual meanings is to avoid uncertainty and the highly aversive state of entropy. To find in new situations echoes and reflections of old is to have one's prior assumptions and evaluations vindicated, and to reaffirm that the world around one is governed by principles which are consistent, and amenable to one's reason and comprehension. Thus, in this conversation Doris and Sid are to be seen happily making habitual interpretations. And these are creative acts. On to the inherently meaningless universe they impose information, habitual codifications of expectable people and events. Of course, fulfilled expectations do not necessarily mean pleasant ones and, hence, in what Doris defines as Sid's nosiness, scorn and irresponsibility, and what Sid defines as Helen's impudence, we can see the occasioning of anxiety with Doris and Sid writing themselves into tense situations. Even in recounting Tom and David's effeminacy, Sid finds only a vicarious thrill, and yet the 'discovery' of worrying scenarios brings with it a kind of relief notwithstanding, because this behaviour is expectable and represents a kind of disorder with which they know how to deal. Doris and Sid might prefer each other, and Karen and Nigel and Tom and David and Helen *et al.*, to act differently but at least their behaviour is codifiable and not random. In short, there is comfort in successfully fulfilled expectations; or as Young and Wilmott phrase it: 'familiarity breeds content' (1974, p. 116).

<h1 style="text-align:center">III</h1>

Conversation, Berger and Luckmann assert, is the most important vehicle of reality maintenance. In conversation the contours of the social world are continuously firmed up (1969, p. 140) and conversation, we have heard, involves intentioned action, by speakers employing conventional verbal and non-verbal devices, in accordance with shared sets of interactional rules. In constructing and realising complex worldviews, and achieving the fulfilment of their expectations through routine acts of codification, Doris and Sid have been found regularly exchanging words and phrases in a fashion which both regard as legitimate combined with actions and in a setting which both find appropriate. They share notions of conversational propriety, notions of turn-taking, of use of kitchen space, of the politenesses due in someone's home, of the place of adults to expound upon the social world and make examples of its miscreants. Hence the conversation above may be described as a flowing sequence of mutual interpretings and, moreover, an oft-repeated occurrence, Doris and Sid may be found regularly interacting in this way as it represents part of an habitual talking-relationship which they maintain. Yet the contours of reality which their conversation replicates were seen to be far from shared or even necessarily compatible. Doris and Sid write themselves into often very different worlds for they use the conventional devices of expression in different ways. The words they exchange prove ambiguous enough for each to impart to them their own meanings, for each to aggregate them together as part of different associational sets to form different cognitive contexts. That is, Doris and Sid produce habitual social objects and events by conversing together via common forms for the pursuit of idiosyncratic ends. They validate what might be called a common linguistic surface by coming together and indicating, designating, appraising – construing objects at the same time and place (or at least in a time and place which, in physical space, overlap). Their discourse possesses an inherent duality, then, a commonly structured surface and a concurrent flow of private consciousness beneath. As Steiner summarises (1975, p. 46), behind every speech-act lies the uniqueness of a personal 'association-net', a private lexicon, and behind any community of habitual interactants lies an 'inexhaustibly multiple aggregate' of 'finally irreducible personal meanings'. But then *before* any meaning stands the relatively stable form which breaks down distances of time and place, affords ambiguity, and enables those routine meetings at which diversity can flourish. In this way, Doris and Sid's linguistic exchange is both an organising, uniformitising factor, and a primary force in the construction of individuality (cf. Sapir, 1956, p. 19; also Rapport, 1987, *passim*). Through language, the many lines of thought and action of their multiple personae meet (and keep on meeting through similar repeated occasions when they come together) and simultaneously confer different meanings on the world. Moreover, in my reconstruction of Doris and Sid's conversation this duality appears to go unnoticed. They do not recognise the diversity of their worldviews and the repeated misconstruing which results. Hence I have likened my feelings in attending upon such communicational distortion to sitting through a comedy of errors.

Now I suggest we are in a better position to account for what is taking place. Firstly I say that Doris and Sid expect to understand each other. They see each other around the dale and talk on almost a daily basis, and these interactions possess a calm or at least coherent linguistic surface as each finds the other obeying similar interactional systematics. Moreover, both occupy significant places in social landscapes which the other constructs. Both represent 'things' which the other uses to identify his or her selves, 'things' which each expects to be able to interact with and whose behaviour each should be able to affect. In other words, 'Sid' and 'Doris' are habitually made parts of events through which Doris and Sid fulfil their expectations. 'Sid' and 'Doris' are symbolic constructs through which Doris and Sid regularly realise their own selves but as we have discovered, the landscapes in which each locates the other are often at odds and thus, despite the frequency of their interaction and the overlaps, the nominal similarities, between the landmarks each uses, they never see themselves or the other as the other does, and they never meet in a singular social world. Furthermore, these differences do not come to the surface because each is so intent upon their own act of fulfilment, on their own definitions coming to fruition. That is, their mutual confidence in their world-views removes the need for experimentation. Here are assumptions which have allowed them to make sense of the universe in the past and from whose predictions they have every expectation of being able to do so again. While their desire for the security of the habitual, for knowable and known social worlds, and their pleasure at successfully achieving this, banishes the burden of doubt, there is no cause to question if the new and potentially alien can be understood and routinely dealt with as before. Thus, in conversation, each feels that they know what the other intends to say, interprets their words and actions as if they were the issue of characters and motives they were all too familiar with, and routinely interrupts when the other is speaking before their words have been properly or all-but-superficially contextualised. The result is a conversation of snippets, as we have seen, zigzagging from the worlds of one to those of the other, Doris and Sid talking past each other, and no closer to fully understanding one another at the end of their exchange than at the start. Their effect on each other is tangential and indirect, each occasioning the other to traverse in rapid succession a number of private worlds, producing an intricate collage of partially expressed scripts.

The question of why Doris and Sid should be so engrossed in their particular definitions of order and so intent on getting them expressed, endemically warding off uncertainty of the new, is harder to answer. Without going too deeply into the niceties of the psychology of 'cognitive style', of individuals being more or less rigid in their thought, more or less open to difference and comfortable with change (cf. Goldstein and Blackman, 1981, pp 121–2; Krech, Crutchfield and Ballachey, 1962, pp 45–6), of individuals having different proclivities for dealing with events either as *a priori* reproductions of 'value' or as *ex post facto* productions of 'information' (Paine, 1989, pp 6, 27–8), I can say that these definitions are what Doris and Sid take to be the grounds and evidence of their existence. They are the natural facts of their lives, the bases of that Schutzian (moral, normal, familiar, commonsensical) order from which all else may be measured. Here are two individuals at home in the centres of their social worlds, determined that they *will* take these facts for granted (1953, p. 29). Hence we find Doris definite in her interpretation of Sid's nosiness and scorn, and assured of Wendy and

Tom's loyalty as darts-team members and of the advantages of their regular hours in the Hilltop, while Sid is equally definite in his interpretation of Tom and David's weakness, and of the cheekiness of today's youth, and equally assured of his own manliness and self-control.

But besides this there is the more immediate phenomenon of offcomers in Wanet and the daily threats which they represent. I want to be precise here. I have argued that Doris and Sid's world-views neither add up to a neat, singular or integrated picture of social life in Wanet nor reduce to common denominations and I have argued that despite this 'chaotic relativism' it is these individual orders of diverse landmarks in idiosyncratic landscapes that I was determined to respect. Hence it has not been the commonalities in this conversation that I have emphasised – the sharing of an abstract linguistic code, of a grammar of interaction, and of regular occasions on which it is exchanged – so much as the multiplicities of its participants' motivations and meanings. What is missing from this view, or the wider background which must be added, is the problem of gross difference which the influx of outsiders have caused. Here is a continuous flow of new 'things' and non-habitual happenings which must be codified or ignored. Here are constant challenges to the patterns of order which Doris and Sid would routinely impose and the predictions for the future they would impart. It is not that Doris and Sid are so definite and intent because in offcomers they recognise a common and consistent threat, rather that the threat of difference has been laying siege to many if not all of their world-views alike. In the phenomenon of offcomers in Wanet we see an example of what Devereux has termed 'ego-syntonism' – the coming together of diverse subjective motivations in the same kind of cause or event (1978, pp 127–9). In the offcomer we find the source of potential discomfort to many of Doris and Sid's personae alike, and the alien that must, through definiteness and vigour, be dispelled.

IV

It is the broad question of ego-syntonism in Wanet, of the meeting of individual difference, of community as sameness in diversity, that I take up in the next and concluding part of the book. Let me recap what we have seen. I have described individuals as adopting a number of different personae, and even close neighbours in a small village occupying a miscellany of highly diverse social worlds. I have argued that these cognitively constructed worlds provide the contexts in terms of which individuals' words are to be properly understood: that words spoken should be related to the persona which expresses them and the world-view of which they form part. Moreover, I have argued that individuals' utterances are fulfilments of what their pre-existing world-views lead them to expect of people, objects and events. Their sayings are acts of doing, and what are being achieved are codifications of the universe in such ways as to realise and reaffirm prior definitions in the social landscapes around them.

In interaction, furthermore, it was these personal 'truths' that individuals were found keen to boast. Far from being shared, and a common denomination across the whole of the community, then, meaning in conversation was idiosyncratic and diverse, as individuals continued to understand the universe in terms of very different worlds of verbal association. Hence, I have differentiated between the common linguistic surface of interaction and the diversity of opinion which can be discovered beneath. Beneath the surface of a public and shared system of verbal signs was to be found a multiplicity of private semantic domains, individuals operating with a diversity of modes of interpretation, a diversity of systems of codification. I have argued that exchange can assume an ambiguity, a plasticity, which quite belies the appearance of its singularity and the common structure which it represents, and I have emphasised the distance between what may be signified to different people by the 'same' signifier (verbal or other) in the 'same' interaction. That is, conversational exchange may seem to flow freely enough, if the verbal symbols different speakers use by and large overlap, but there need be no generalised usage. Rather, the exchange may represent the often confused meeting of diverse loops of thought, with the result that individuals can talk past one another unknowingly, misconstruing intended meanings to a possibly farcical extent.

In short, I have argued that a distinction between form and meaning is of overriding import; between the outward structure, the shape, the appearance of items of behaviour perpetrated by members of a cultural group, and the substance, the content, the significance of those actions as imparted by those who are their habitual witnesses, by those who live with the behaviours as parts of their daily lives.

Part III

Meaning versus Form: The Individual and the Community

Si bis faciunt idem, non est idem
(If two people do the same thing, it is not
the same thing).

George Devereux, *Ethnopsychoanalysis*

Meaning versus Form: The Individual and the Community

I

'You'll have to look like a farmer, Nigel, if you're gonna be round here or people will start talking: "who's that on Cedar High?" . . . And you don't see farmers with beards, Nigel, either.' 'Oh, don't you Doris? What about Jonty from Robbgill?' 'Well, he's just young and he's really not from round here . . . And you'll have to say "tup" not "tuhp" when you mean Barney the ram or no-one'll understand you . . . And then when you're wanting to be fed you say "I'm so hungry my belly's touching my backbone". Or else Fred's favourite: "I'm so hungry my stomach thinks my throat's been cut". You'll have to learn our words if you're gonna be local and live here! . . . And don't you ever stroke my sheepdog, Jet, like that again. It spoils them. She's a working dog, not one of your lazy, petted, city dogs. Jet's a farm dog, aren't you Jet? Y–e–s. And she doesn't like these stupid offcomer dogs you see around . . . And Nigel, you know you and me are gonna have a real barney if you drive that tractor by again when I'm milking. I'd just put on the suckers and now you've aggravated the cows and they've kicked them off and shit them all up again. I tell you, we'll have a right set-to, my lad, 'cause then *I'll* be the one who's getting aggravated, and we'll just see who cracks first . . . And what are you carrying two bales of hay at a time for? Do you think you're strong? That's not strong. You're not strong. Fred's strong. He can carry on all day and not stop. That's real manly strength. You haven't got that . . . Now Nigel. When the National Park Inspector comes today, say nowt. Leave all the talking to me and Fred. You just stay outside and drive the tractor up and down the farmyard. Fred and me'll see what he wants and soon sort him out here in the kitchen. Snooping busybodies. But you just say nowt. Look like you had a hard night or something! Okay?'

It was through these sorts of cues that I had learnt to play my part in the routine life of Cedar High Farm, as I outlined earlier in the book. Here are some of what I would call the regularities of behavioural form, from the verbal to the non-verbal, in which Doris instructed me so that we could maintain our regular relations as surrogate parent and child. That is, over the months Doris moulded me into her social universe and I learnt how, as a farm hand, as a kid on her farm, I should fit in with the daily routines. And in case I forgot there was always time for a reminder, as the conversation in Part II exemplified. She had taught me to keep silent, to keep working at a steady pace, to do the simple physical tasks that would ease her and Fred's chores, to speak when spoken to by adults and then not to keep the spotlight any longer than, or in any fashion outside the specific way that they granted it, and to remember that I was on show, as representative of Cedar High, as bearer of Doris and Fred's parental reputations, at all times. And there were similar habits of interaction which I learnt for my relations with Fred (as farmer with farm boy), and then with Sid (as builder with builder's mate). 'Learning to play my part in the everyday life of the farm' meant learning an assemblage of behavioural routines which I played out with each of them; versions of 'good form' which each regarded as normal and normative, to which each felt their behaviour closely approximated, and which each expected to find replicated by others. Of course, my argument has been that what Doris regarded as 'good form' and taught me did not necessarily coincide with Sid's versions. But then this did not threaten the daily life of the farm because there were other behavioural routines for when Doris and Sid interacted with each other, as we have heard above.

The scene in Cedar High kitchen, that is, possessed something habitual: a worried Doris, world-weary, financially burdened and harassed by outsiders, a moody and monosyllabic Fred, a badgered Nigel, anxious and on his mettle, a brazen Sid, worldly-wise, cool-headed and competitive; and quiet and browbeaten children. All of these people were coming together in the kitchen as per usual, the day's work done, Karen doling out the food, the family seated around the supper table, and Sid standing smoking by the Aga, as usual, and exchanging local gossip about the pubs, the behaviour of today's youth, and so on. As a cultural community, the dale of Wanet might be described as composed of an aggregation of routine, regularly enacted behavioural forms of this kind. In this dale, then, people often live in stone cottages and sometimes whitewashed farmhouses. Many earn a living by farming sheep for wool and meat, and cows for milk. Usually they meet their fellow-dalesmen in their farmyards or the fields or on the road or in the pub, and they normally exchange a set of words that are current in dale conversation, catchwords and phrases and whole sets of sentences which are popular at the time. Complaining about adult neighbours or today's youth were widespread refrains when I was living in Wanet, and it is one of Doris's, Sid's and Fred's versions of it which I have focused on above. Doris, Fred and Sid had probably made their arrangement of it chiefly as a trio before my arrival but were nice enough to write me into a minor part of it as we saw. It might have been 'the National Park wardens', or 'the number of coloureds you see about now', or 'the state of the Baineses' allotments', but on this occasion they did part of the 'recreation and today's youth' routine. It locates the three of them as current inhabitants of Wanet, as long-suffering parents, as people aware of the lot of bringing up local children and working the land, and, in the personal touches the three of them give to the Wanet catchwords (Fred's condescending mono-syllables and dampening ripostes, Doris's plotting and ear for others' sarcasm, surreptitiousness and scorn, Sid's idiosyncratic phrasing and wily ploys for preventing his precise position from being 'catched'), it locates them as friends and members of their own private and habitual talking-relationship.

But the behavioural routine is personalised in a far more significant way too. It is animated by a whole host of individual thoughts and intentions which it was the intention of the previous chapters to eluci-date. Talking through the routine was a way Doris, Fred and Sid, as well as Karen and myself, had for expressing and fulfilling a wide variety and diversity of personal meanings. What I mean is that we all personalised the behaviours in this interaction. It looks routine, it was routine. It seems shared, it was shared inasmuch as it was something we all owned between us (had developed, had negotiated between us) and came together to regularly exchange. Of course, some talking-partners were more central, more responsible, more willing than others. Sometimes I felt in these exchanges that it was not just a routine that I was part of but an institution, and that here I was having myself encompassed by the strictures of a disproportionate verbal regimen. But then at the same time the interaction was something multiple and diverse, a form of idiosyncrasy, of creative expression, of escape. The interaction was a form, a visible shared form, but its personal signifi-cance filled up the mould and spilled over the top. The significance gushed and flowed in all directions and this is what I have tried to tap. I have wanted to show how ambiguous the conversational form was, how malleable the words and actions were, in order to slot into very different mental landscapes and so that the overlap of these forms between Doris's and Sid's different landscapes, for example, could seem quite secondary, coincidental, almost accidental.

But of course, the overlaps, the sharing, are not accidental. Far from it. They are constituents of a precisely structured, (possibly) painstak-ingly developed, and carefully maintained exchange between a number of village residents. The beauty of the exchange for me is this awful tension between the surface exchange, the orderly conversational form, the shared knowledge of interactional systematics – how to speak, when, and in what manner – and the unique visions, the limitless avenues of thought, the wild disorders of contradiction that can be motivating the exchange, causing its regular re-occurrence, and dancing delightedly but invisibly around its expression.

Of course, saying this is not saying anything particularly new but it is a matter of emphasis. All too often, it seems, these insights, following Durkheim, are eschewed as social psychology or decried as psychologisms, as if social interaction pertained to a reality external to the individuals responsible for constituting and re-constituting it and could be satisfactorily described in their absence (as if interaction were anything other than the synthesising phenomenon whereby private, individual meanings and public, cultural forms intersect). Following Simmel, I believe this to be a grave error. The distinction I have been using between form and meaning originates with him (e.g. 1971a, 1971b). What he suggested, of course, was that aspects of life exist through conflict and contrast with others diametrically opposed, that opposing entities, processes, tendencies, are ultimately complementary because a constitutive force inheres in the tension between them. In the social realm, we find this fundamental constitutive dualism in the opposition between individual subjects and cultural objects, between meanings and the social forms which they assume. That is, one can envisage the world of cultural objects as a collection of common forms: language, artistic precepts, moral, religious and legal ones; scientific concepts; also educational, historical and economic ones; also 'love', 'painting', 'flirtation', 'prostitution', 'bourgeois households', 'drama', 'sexuality', 'reality', 'knowledge' and 'existence'. (Obviously it is not that great a remove from these Simmelian forms of normal, normative behaviour to Wittgensteinian 'forms of life' and the language-games by which they are expressed in interactional routines.) Individuals then use these objectified forms and make them subjective. They 'consume' cultural objects, incorporate them into their daily lives and, in personalising them, use them to develop a subjective world-view. In this way they also maintain them. Thus, in any social phenomenon form and content constitute one reality. A social form severed from content does not gain existence, and the world only becomes an object of information, of substance and content, if provided with a common form. The content implies goals, motives, purposes, interests. The form implies the shape by which these attain social expression. The form represents a mode of exchange and continuing association between individuals. Forms are the shared vehicles by which individuals and their meanings come together. Moreover, it is because individual contents and cultural forms constitute one social reality that neither can be properly or ideally described in the absence of the other. And, to repeat, it is their meeting in opposition which is socially constitutive.

In the above conversation then, we found Doris, Sid and others speaking together and using common forms of expression while engaged in common behaviours – in this case, eating supper, teaching youngsters, smoking a cigarette, serving food, chatting in a farmhouse kitchen in the early evening, and so on. These were all socially accepted things to do in Wanet, verbal and non-verbal: well-known, often repeated, widely shared, easily instigated; they represent what might be called a finite fund of stable, ubiquitous, malleable, legitimate, apt and appropriate behavioural cliches from which these people gradually concocted their interactional routines. But within these can be seen the play of complex and often diverse individual world-views, common behaviours engaged in for the pursuit and fulfilment of possibly contradictory personal ends. And the one is inevitably rooted in the other. Doris and Sid *et al.* are able to express and realise their idiosyncrasies because they engage in such an habitual social interaction; and an interaction like the above exists in commonality because of continuing individual idiosyncrasies. The social exchange is constituted by this inherent duality.

Such thoughts are not new to social anthropology either. It was a number of years ago that Pocock was advising that society is a dialectical process between principles making for aggregation and principles making for individuation, and urging that their interaction be the object of our study (1961, pp 103, 114). But I feel that the full implications of this view for an understanding of society as symbolic interaction – that the collective structures of social reality can only be fully grasped through an appreciation of the way they are personalised in individual lives, that the objectification of cultural objects is only to be understood in terms of the subjective psychic processes of the individuals who use them in interaction, the intentions which they bring to that usage and the experiences they construe – have yet to be fully spelled out, and that is the intention of this part of the book.

II

A culture, I suggest, might be described as a fund of behavioural forms. This fund, moreover, has a distributional aspect in use. Hence, Doris sees certain behaviours as proper for herself or her family, other behaviours as appropriate for neighbours, for dalesmen, for tourists, for Britons, for foreigners, and some behaviours legitimate for none. Not only should locals of Wanet speak as she instructed me, then, but visitors should not be allowed to bring big cars like Jaguars on to Wanet's narrow and windy roads, while Pakistani immigrants in the cities should not be allowed to rent single rooms in indecent numbers at all. There are two variables in this distribution: like me and mine/ unlike; proper/improper. Doris and Sid barely agreed on either aspect, as we saw, neither on how *they* behaved, and properly should, nor others. But they were alike in thinking in these spectral terms – some behaviours were more local and more proper than others.

The notion of properly local behaviours was widespread in Wanet. Furthermore, they aroused far more concern than commoner proprieties. On my arrival I had thought that I might begin to belong and negotiate relations on the basis of what I regarded as society-wide interests or at least gender-inclusive ones. After all, I was British, middle class, and I knew how to roll up my sleeves and get serious about my darts, over a tankard of beer down the pub, the same as the next bloke. I came to realise, however, that all that these forms initiated, with Doug the landlord, say, or Arthur, one of his regulars, were the polite but distant and superficial reciprocations which Doug and Arthur variously introduced into interactions which they defined as taking place with offcomers. So they would play me at darts, jokingly have bets with me on the outcome of the Triple Crown rugby competition, and voice opinions about machinations at Whitehall, but soon get bored and turn to their more regular talking-partners for more interesting exchanges. The universalistic forms did not lead me to any greater closeness, but, on the contrary, kept me in Doug and Arthur's distanced category of outsider. These were the appropriate ways of dealing with offcomers, and the ways which they probably used when dealing with one another. Being faced by strangers, interaction was certainly safer within this set of limited forms (the code which they seemed to prefer) because you were really never to know what they might do beyond it. Hence, a non-local, non-familiar form helped control the unfamiliar interactant. This was an universal code for hopefully universal protection against all manner of potential randomness in their behaviour. Whenever possible, however, the local forms of behaviour were far more comfortable – they had long been under what felt like personal and community control. So Doug and Arthur soon returned to their more regular, local and private interactions. Indeed, it was a dale-wide talking point when someone eschewed local proprieties and preferred the strange, institutional form (when a neighbour decided, for example, that Arthur's sheep being loose on the road yet again was the last straw, something that had gone beyond the bounds of decent local behaviour and informal arbitration or self-help, and so reported him to Leyton police for driving his tractor with bald tyres). In short, outside forms of behaviour were for outsiders, and their use by locals inside the dale insinuated the same. Talking international rugby or politics was labelling me as an offcomer, rather than a step towards overcoming this divide. To be a local, as Doris advised me, was to interact in local ways. Why talk as just anyone might when in Wanet linguistic forms were a recognisable emblem of a more special belonging, as comfortable as a familiar room or set of clothes, and so clearly and immediately under local supervision and decision. In local forms (from which the outsider was debarred) was a place to feel securely at home.

However, it would be wrong to think of these local behavioural forms in terms of standardised essentials, of standard, agreed-upon relations that held every time a local was polite to an offcomer, or interacted with an offcomer, or indeed with a fellow-local, a farmer or a publican or child. There were frequent mentions of a glorious Wanet past, of the meanness of a particularly seclusive farmer, of the rudeness of a new shopkeeper, of the strangeness of folk in neighbouring dales, but these always took place within the context of a particular habitual talking-relationship, and between them there were less uniform correspondences than 'families of resemblance'. That is, the forms of behaviour in common use in the dale amounted to polythetic categories (ABC, BCD, CDE, DEF etc.; 1234, 2234, 2567, 3234, 3567, 38910 etc.) rather than anything more unitary. In other words, I have said that Doug and Arthur treated me as an offcomer when I arrived in Wanet and we exchanged pleasantries on a number of suitably distant and limited topics. 'Talking to an offcomer' would be something that many people in Wanet would have notions about, even offcomers themselves, notions concerning the proprieties and improprieties of good form. And yet these interactions were still distinctive. Being treated as an offcomer by Doug, the landlord (an ex-offcomer himself) – eager for my custom and yet anxious to run a 'locals'' pub rather than one seen as geared to visitors – was not the same or even especially similar to being treated as an offcomer by Arthur, the farmer – keen to recall army days outside Wanet as a foil to present economic difficulties and disagreements with parochial neighbours.

The particularity and 'polytheticality' of common Wanet forms in use became clearer still as I gained acceptance in local relationships and began to slough off the offcomer taint. For I never became a 'local' per se so much as someone with whom Doris and Fred, and Sid and Joanna, and Arthur and Doug, and Big Bri came to habitually engage in what they regarded as the proprieties of local behavioural forms. I became a local, that is, as Doris's farmhand, as Arthur's domino partner, as Big Bri's cruising partner (out in the souped-up Allegro for a Sunday spin), and as Sid's builder's mate. When they considered our relations, they seemed to them all like legitimate, even typical, ways for locals in Wanet to behave, but there were no more shared or even similar facets to these different relations than this. To be a good local was for me to engage in habitual interaction with others who regarded me and my behaviour as such. True, to be a local and not an offcomer was often linked to one of a set of other apt behavioural forms – throwing a straight 'arrow' at the darts board, bringing up respectful children, working farmers' hours – but these, similarly, would never be expressed in an abstract sense. One would always be talking *about* somebody being a good local *to* somebody, and in a different context (the same interactant perhaps but a different subject, or the same subject but a different interactant, or the same interactant and subject but a different mood or place or time) the same common behavioural form or set of interlinked forms could mean something else. Indeed, assuming that common forms – such as calling pubs by their old names (the 'Haywain'), or finding offcomers who trailed so far from their friends unfathomable – *were* universal and usable by all caused me early woe in the dale, as I have described. It was felt, instead, to be copying and usurpation, even theft. Hence while there were many forms of behaviour which Wanet people agreed in regarding as special to them – being polite to offcomers, being a good local (which in turn included being a good farmer, or helpful to fellow-dalesmen) – I found no standard definitions of what these entailed. Rather, every usage was connected to and expressed within a particular relationship, and a juxtaposition of these usages would reveal not a way of being polite as such, or helpful, or a good farmer, but a wide range of ways of behaving, of interacting, with polythetic not common-denominational connexions. 'Polite' behaviours could be poles apart with nothing in common at all for people in Wanet would personalise the behavioural forms which they heard and saw legitimated by others around them and construct their own versions within the conditions and contexts of their own lives. Hence, the way Sid behaved towards me as an offcomer, an apprentice, a neighbour, was not the same as the way Doris did. Each would see the other behaving, would remember how they had seen offcomers and apprentices and neighbours being treated in Wanet in the past, would take their cues from a variety of sources (Sid, as we have seen, had a liking for the turn of phrase of Radio 2 disc-jockeys), and then place their own signatures on the behavioural forms, coming upon them with different motives, different world-views, and a variety of different meanings to express and fulfil. In short, in use, the forms which many would agree upon as common and proper to Wanet come to be mediated by a diversity of individual ends and are the means for achieving satisfaction of a variety of kinds and amounts.

Nevertheless, the forms can be seen to assist in important synthesising processes by which the threads of different individuals' lives are interwoven, and they meet one another – like Doris, Sid and me – in talking-relationships of greater and lesser familiarity and frequency. This is Devereux's phenomenon of ego-syntonism. A culture offers behavioural forms which members of different motivations can at the same time perceive as suitable for the expression and gratification of subjective meanings and emotions (1978, p. 126). The forms are able to provide for this diversity because of their basic ambiguity and abbreviation. The normative and proverbial as well as the commonplace and routine are expressed and maintained via a great economy of verbal imagery and phrasing so that, as we have seen, differences in workaday worlds do not become apparent. Hence, a language of common forms always mediates between the actions of one individual and the cognitive definitions of another, 'friendly ambiguities', as Sapir put it, conspiring to reinterpret for each the behaviour observed in terms of 'those meanings which are relevant to his own life' (1956, p. 153). At the same time, individuals need to feel that communication is possible and, indeed, successful on a daily basis, and as a result of following simple routine procedures, can be easily met. Doris and Sid can partake of the traditions of their forebears, and engage in organised or spontaneous social processes with their contemporaries with no fear of the loneliness of a monadic universe and the Babel this would represent.

The ambiguity of common forms also affords them a certain inertia. Vague and simplistic outside a social context, they can be handed down between generations, adaptable to a variety of settings. They are ready-made formulae always capable of being substantiated and revived by new motivations and moods (cf. Propp, 1968 [1927], p. 116). Their inertia or conservativeness, their usefulness and prevalence, are an issue of their plasticity, and this point is crucial. The forms of behaviour common to a community such as Wanet are necessary for meaning to be constructed but they do not represent a sufficient precondition. Most of the forms of the English which Doris and Sid use, for example, existed long prior to their usage and will, in all probability, outlive them – and they could not express themselves without them – but they do not tell Doris or Sid what they can or should or must mean. The vocabulary of English and its grammatical construction are limited, the phrasal expressions of behavioural forms common to Wanet even more so ('Village people can't abide being told what to do', 'He's a right twined, narrow-backed bastard', 'Offcomers' plans always get through the Park Committee'), but, as we have see, what Doris and Sid can say through them is not. Indeed, the forms live and carry meaning only in the particular contexts of their use. English lives in Wanet because Doris and Sid and others continually employ it in certain specific ways as their medium of expression. To describe meanings, then, we must look

not to a decontextualised linguistic code, but to individual interpretations in particular situations. Meaning derives from particular meetings
of personal world-views and public behavioural forms. Moreover, the
meetings are not knowable or predictable in the abstract. What Doris
means by 'proper wifely behaviour', for example, depends on her
construction of the talking-relationship, the routine exchange of words
and actions, in which she recognises this form, upon the persona she is
employing and the world in which she is perceiving action to be taking
place. And, of course, this need not be singular. To the one behavioural
form a number of meanings can be imparted simultaneously. Hence,
the relationship between form and meaning is one of interdependence
and multifactoriality. Individuals depend upon these common attributes of their culture for the capacity to make meaning, and yet, the
vitality of the forms depends on individuals with meanings they
endemically want to express through them. Hence, behavioural
commonalities are personalised in usage and come to be animated in
possibly idiosyncratic fashions. They become instruments of diversity
and difference, and yet the conditions of their use remain essentially
public, and it is in coordination with significant others and in certain
routine and limited ways that these meanings come to be made.

III

Interaction in Wanet was constant – people always seeing each other in
the streets, across the fields, at the pubs, on the fells, in one another's
houses. Common behavioural forms (gestures of greeting, words of
enquiry, castigation and advice) were continuously being exchanged.
In their different ways, Doris and Sid also took this as a sign of legitimate local belonging. It was proper for Wanet locals to take an interest
in each others' news and well-being and to pass this information on
when they met. For above all, this was a means which Doris and Sid had
of maintaining their certainty about the ways of the world and assuring
themselves that their expectations were still correct. To know what
fellow-dalesmen were doing and had done, to be able to interpret their
words and actions within the terms of one's established views of the
world, was to secure for oneself the power of understanding and the
ability to react whatever the eventuality. Indeed, to find that despite the
flux of life, of ageing, of moods, of accidents, of political competition,
market fluctuations and factional ups and downs, the old meanings still
seemed to serve was to find in the latter particular security and charm.
In their world-views Doris and Sid possessed funds of data which
served as comfortable rationales for future judgements and explanations, for the discovery of 'new' people and events. In constant interaction, in short, the past was re-told, brought up to date, its relevance

proven again, while the new could be seen as the familiar, and afforded the logic of continuity. Moreover, there was a sense in which Doris and Sid even found the weird a comfort, and would seek it out in inter-action. Hence, when I arrived, a bearded student from the town, Sid would often look for me in the pub to see what this 'mystery man' and 'rum bugger' and 'Professor' and 'Joshua' had got up to now. In the exceptional and strange he found a reminder of the rule-bound and of the prevalence of the normative. In fact, it was often the case that embracing the weird was to discover the normal underneath after all. So Doris found that beneath the beard was an unskilled youngster who needed treating like her others – fed, laundered, protected from night-time thunder, and instructed on the farm. The strange could be dealt with and accommodated in terms of patterns of relations which she knew all too well.

Furthermore, the arrival of large numbers of offcomers who, in recent years, had moved into the dale to live, had greatly increased the value of boasting an understanding of the world, and of finding one's expectations fulfilled in routine interactions. More than a quarter of Wanet's population now consisted of 'outsiders' as we have seen, many of them residing in the more nucleated sections of the dale such as Wanet Town and the hamlets of Robbgill and Thurn, and causing something of a separation between 'town' and valley, at least in terms of the formal commonalities of behavioural style. And yet with this influx the fulfilment of routine worlds became harder to construe. For traditionally, the dale consisted of cognitive 'objects' (people and events) which were all familiar and which one habitually recognised. The physical dale and one's immediate social landscapes more or less coincided, and there were no people or parts of the dale that one did not regularly 'construct' in one or more ways. One had an opinion of them, knew a lot about their activities, and expected the converse – however pejorative and biased one suspected their opinions on one to be. The named 'objects' in Doris's and Sid's socio-cognitive landscapes shared a fair degree of overlap, then, however differently they located and evaluated these landmarks in relation to themselves. Now, however, landscapes had to be reconsidered, and some amendments had to be made to interpretations of behavioural form. Traditionally, for exam-ple, as a Local, Sid expected to give and receive hospitality from his Wanet neighbours – meaning all those who lived inside the dale – and often to defend these borders by being decidedly unwelcoming to outsiders. But with outsiders now living inside, lines of sociality had to be redrawn, otherwise, he would have to be hospitable to outsiders or else inhospitable to neighbours. Similarly, for Doris as a Villager, great store was to be put on living in Wanet and maintaining a traditional way of life. It was easy to see that offcomers living inside the dale did not have the breeding to imitate this latter way and survive – even if they were to try taking up farming. But it increasingly seemed to be the case that one could only maintain oneself in Wanet by catering to outsiders and pandering to offcomer tastes. Doris depended on outsiders staying on her campsite, or in her caravans, or buying her dairy produce, and all the time altering the tenor and destroying the style of local life in order for her to be able to try to preserve it. She had to accept difference, to some extent, in order to stay the same, and so conceptions of localness had to be regauged.

During my time in Wanet, therefore, individuals were active in interaction not merely to reaffirm continuously their knowledge and hence control of the worlds they mapped out around themselves, but also to include in these conceptions an invasion which many chose not to ignore. 'Offcomers', that is, had become a common local linguistic and behavioural form which threw many other, more traditional forms into sharp relief. I do not say that 'offcomers' represented a *Ding-an-Sich* which had forced itself on local attention willy-nilly, nor that, as we have appreciated with Doris and Sid, people in Wanet constructed offcomers in the same, singular, or even compatible ways. But 'offcomers' certainly became a form, a social event, into which much local feeling, thought and emotion could be invested alike. 'Offcomers' became a popular form of legitimate local expression. Doris and Sid appeared to be accommodating 'offcomers' into many of their world-views, then, and much of the tension which I experienced in our interaction – once we had got over the liminal periods of negotiating our own routines – derived, I suspect, from a readjustment of landscapes and a realignment of landmarks so as to clarify their positions. If the dale is not the locality then how is membership to be signalled, and will others know that I still belong? If village life is the best life, which villagers would not want to change, then why can I sometimes imagine the benefits of smart clothes for myself, a fancy car for the family, and a posh education and occupation for the children? The onslaught of strangers, and the sheer volume of irregularity they had introduced into a variety of cognitive landscapes which had formerly housed relatively slowly changing sets of forms and meanings, seemed to make Doris and Sid into anxious people.

I do not believe this to be the reason for the distortion in their communication which I have made the focus of this book, however, at least not directly. Such miscommunication I would see rather in terms of features more basic to the systematics of interaction in the dale, more inherent in the common *style* of exchange of behavioural forms and the *purpose* for which this was done.

IV

Communicational distortion, miscommunication, factors helping and hindering communicability, have been explored from quite a variety of social scientific interests, and a number of variables have been suggested. For example, the capability of 'successful communication' – of the listener understanding the speaker in the way he or she intended – has been linked with the regularity and repetitiveness of exchange: the more frequent the more successful (e.g. Berger and Luckmann, 1966, pp 140–1; Bott, 1964, p. 212), especially if the community is simple and small (Goodenough, 1963, p. 264). Also, communicability has been linked with the exercise of power. The patron, then, is capable of having values of his choosing affirmed by his client – as opposed to mere go-betweens and brokers (Paine, 1971, p. 8), and in great contrast to the poor, whose structural disadvantage makes it almost impossible for them to control the frame of interpretation imposed on their actions by others (Wikan, 1980, p. 42). In similar vein, communicability has been tied to the inequalities of class, the lower class being deprived of speech which uniquely fits their personal intentions and experiences or allows them to elaborate upon these (Bernstein, 1972, p. 476). The ideological dictatorship of the ruling class results in them only having the symbols and predefinitions of a public language, so that all their private meanings are distorted and repressed (Zaslavsky, 1982, pp 83–4). Then again, communicability has been linked with the prevalence of conventionalised forms of stylised speech. The more interactants share a tacit agreement about the official definition of a situation and a working consensus about each others' statuses and role-obligations within it, the more immediate and heart-felt feelings and wants may be suppressed and concealed (Goffman, 1978, pp 20–1). For still others, communicability is a feature of national character or cultural identity. The English, for example, are a dumb people whose spoken platitudes do not describe either their senses or their acts (Carlyle, 1843, pp 135–9), and whose actions must hopefully speak for themselves (Berger, 1967, p. 93). Communicability is seen at least as a feature of cultural vitality and health – the more consciousness and intellectuality is impaired, the more imprecise, incoherent, abstract and stale language becomes, and the more meaning, in the making and the receiving, is lost (Orwell, 1968, pp 360–5; Steiner, 1967, pp 45–6).

While these explanations may offer hints for an understanding of the situation I have described for Doris and Sid *et al.* in Wanet – interaction through an exchange of conventionalised, even cliched, verbal and non-verbal forms limiting, through their very sharedness and publicness, the amount and quality of personal and uncommon information that can be communicated – there is a further important element which has yet to be broached, the question of desire. Successful communication is an aspect of the wish to communicate, and here we find more interesting analogies in the anthropological literature. For these recognise the social truths that, firstly, in the sphere of daily social exchange, the Batesonian distinction between information-seeking behaviour on the one hand (learning about the world) and value-seeking behaviour (judging the world) (Baleson and Ruesch, 1951, p. 179) is collapsed, and no information is constructed value-free. Secondly, communicability is not something objectively measurable in terms of approximations to an ideal linguistic or other standard but is, rather, context-bound and tied to individual purpose and situation. Hence, desirability of communication becomes a variable, for example, where the basic work of interaction is the penetration of one individual's personal space by the words and actions of another, the domination of someone else's persona and the protection of one's own. Here, then, social interaction proceeds through formalised speech and ritualised exchange in order that personal thoughts and events may remain disguised (Weiner, 1983, pp 692–4), or so that at least one's strategy, friendliness and power have to be guessed at, and interlocutors' decisions about ripostes – to fight or truce – are always made more difficult (Favret-Saada, 1980, pp 10–11). Desirability of communication also becomes a variable where interaction is a means of matching behaviour against a clearcut prescriptive and imperative social order, expressed in a clear public code. Here, the institutionalisation of secrecy and lying creates the ambiguities, the flexibilities by which the stasis and clarity of the code and the flux and blurredness of everyday life can co-exist. Through deception and invention one preserves one's honour and dignity, notwithstanding the pessimism, detachment and weakness one feels (Gilsenan, 1976, p. 211). Then again, the desire to communicate may be variable where the social environment is a highly segmented or factionalised one. Here, commitment to certain social truths and opposition to their denial is inextricably tied to partisan membership of certain social groups against others. The 'true state of one's heart' is revealed to co-members but always hidden from rivals (Pitt-Rivers, 1974, pp xvi–xvii), who are met with politeness and avoidance, if not prejudice and violence (Larsen, 1982, pp 159–60). Or again, desirability of communication is a variable where people live in such close proximity that there is the threat they will find out too much about one another, and social relationships will become impossible. That is, relationships between people, as between anything else, depend on those people remaining distinct, being both together and apart. Non-communication and a keeping secret of information become means of maintaining this distinction and hence enabling the relationship. This applies both to dyadic relations, hence characterised by 'beliefs and blindnesses' (Compton-Burnett, 1969, p. 30), or 'kind-ness and lies' (Greene, 1974, p. 58), and also to relations of broader scope. Here too mendacity may be of great service in turning a surplus stock of mutual knowledge into 'ample doubts and few convictions' (Murphy, 1972, pp 227–8). Finally and relatedly, especially where cultural norms recognise the existence and importance of individuals as autonomous social units (such as England [MacFarlane, 1978, p. 5]), desirability of communication may be variable because in the sharing of information there may be a lessening of individual identity. That is, it is not only the relationship which disappears with a total exchange of information but its components too – if individuals communicated everything they would cease to exist as individuals (Pocock, 1961, p. 101). Here, one's value-laden information is not merely an asset, a weapon, not just an indication of one's honour, one's social group and status, one's moral worth, but also a sign of one's social existence and an emblem of uniqueness. Individual differentiation depends on what one does not reveal or seek to share. Others may construe this non-communication as good or ill, but there is always the doubt, and hence the potential for dignity. As G. K. Chesterton pithily phrased it: 'I should think very little of a man who did not keep something in the background of his life that was more serious than all this talking' (1975 [1908], p. 18).

Returning to Wanet then, on this English note, what should be made of the distortion in communication between Doris and Sid (and others too, I suggest, who interact so habitually and so superficially)? That is, to be more precise in my use of the terms 'communication' and 'miscommunication', how is it that Doris and Sid can contextualise the words of their routine exchanges in such diverse cognitive associations as to mean something very different when they refer to them, and yet not recognise these differences when they meet? This is a non-recogni-tion, moreover, which is not merely another politeness, I would argue, but a thorough misconstrual. It cannot be a question of frequency or foreignness, for they are neighbours in a small village community who meet almost every day. Moreover, it is not that they conceal their feelings out of duty to their interrelated roles. Their feelings are often openly admitted and, as they intend, on display. Nor do they suffer from 'structural impoverishment'. They are accomplished and highly skilled, and own their own means of production – in local terms they are not lacking in resources. Certainly they are not intellectually re-tarded or verbally restricted! On the contrary, they are talkative and highly articulate, despite being English.

What I *would* say, firstly, is that Doris and Sid's miscommunication is a question of the proprieties of styles of exchange in Wanet. That is, in habitual interaction with each other, as fellow-adults, Doris and Sid both feel they know what the other has to say, and should or will say. Doris, as English, as a farmer, as a neighbour, as aggrieved, as a friend, as middle class, as a villager, as a mother, as a wife, and Sid, as a craftsman, as a local, as a husband, as a pal, as a father, as a man, as an Englishman, each expect to know what their adult interlocutors mean. In other words, as regards style of exchange, it is legitimate to lecture children at length, to brook no interruption as one elucidates the ways of the world, and it is apposite for children to listen in silence. (Hence, I could learn of Doris or Sid with little verbal prompting or reciproca-tion.) When talking to adults, however, there may be less lecturing and more interrupting, but the interruptions are less searching and the story simpler because adults can be expected to know already, to know of people, to know of events, and to know of the normative ways in which these are to be evaluated. Therefore, talking with fellow-adults is more of an exercise in comparison. One compares one's information to check on one's rectitude, and to confirm the parameters and coordinates and boundaries of one's social landscapes, and this, as we have seen, is generally accomplished.

Secondly, as adults (that is, adult farmers, adult craftsmen etc.), Doris and Sid entered into interaction with each other spurred by contradictory impulses, and in conjunction with the above this amounted to interaction of great complication and duplicity. They wanted to talk in order to realise their expectations and see their world-views fulfilled in each other's actions and reactions. From public exchange they gained proof of their social existence and its nature, and yet they did not want to talk for fear of playing into the hands of the inferior and immoral, and having what they said misconstrued. Doris and Sid talked in order to gain sympathy and support from their moral fellows, to share their fears and to rouse indignation and receive emo-tional compensation for troubles suffered and wrongs incurred. And again, they talked to gain superordination over their worthless fellows, to assure themselves of the latters' continuing immorality, to gain further evidence of their inferiority, tease them perhaps, castigate them a little, without laying themselves open to similar aspersions, or reveal-ing any of their own worries. So they were prepared to talk in order to bolster their fellows and unite with them against common opposition, and yet they did not want to talk in case what they revealed about themselves was misused, taken as a sign of weakness or ignorance, or otherwise fitted into their enemies' machinations, increasing the latters' strength. They enjoyed to talk because this was how people in Wanet displayed and experienced their belonging, and yet they were frightened to talk in case outsiders overheard, and what was common to them was appropriated and adulterated, and lost to the outside. In short, Doris and Sid were almost certain that they could continue to maintain order in their worlds (even with a deluge of offcomers), but they were also afraid that they might one day find out they were wrong. By engaging in routine interactions with each other, exchanging words and actions which were indeed so familiar that they could be taken *in brevito*, even interrupted with ease, Doris and Sid assisted one another in keeping this day well distant. And by regularly coming together and helping fulfil one another's expectations, they succeeded in keeping their worlds very much apart.

V

Things, we heard from Bateson, are epiphenomena of the relations between them, information on their characteristics deriving from how one comes to be related (compared and contrasted, connected and juxtaposed) to another. But there is a further complexity here which Simmel supplies. The information to which the relations give rise feeds back into those relations. The relations constitute the condition under which the information takes this or that shape, but then the relations come to be maintained on the basis of the information which its constituent parts have of it. 'Here', Simmel writes (1950, p. 309), 'we have one of the deep-lying circuits of intellectual life, where an element presupposes a second element which yet, in turn, presupposes the first', and 'one of the points where being and conceiving make their mysterious unity empirically felt'. The being of the relationship presupposes its conceiving and vice-versa. Social life, he explains, is replete with similar 'compresent dualisms', from public and private, to rule and practice, antagonism and solidarity, freedom and constraint, creativeness and structure, rebelliousness and compliance and so on. Indeed, from the constitutive compresence of forms and meanings the very fundamentals of sociation may be said to derive, as I have mentioned. In all these cases, insight is to be gained not from focusing on one aspect of the dualism to the exclusion of the other, nor by collapsing the opposition in a synthesis, but by keeping the tension between the elements alive and making continuous excursions between them. As Forster adjured in *Howards End*, 'Only connect . . .': social life is not to be appreciated by fragmenting dualities and occupying one side or the other; nor is it to be appreciated by attempting to place oneself halfway between the two; rather, the truth of social life is that it is 'alive' and always a coming-together: it must be appreciated by contriving intellectually to occupy both sides simultaneously (1950, p. 174).

This should not sound particularly strange or controversial. Social identities as 'contrastively constituted', by 'playing the *vis-à-vis*';

cultures as 'intrinsically comparative', 'fundamentally beside them-selves', 'autodislocated' and 'inclining towards contrastive others' – after Boon (1982, pp 230–1), this should in fact have a significantly modish ring to it. And yet when it comes to an appreciation of sociation as the meeting of individual subjects and cultural objects, cultural forms and individual meanings, the anthropological eye seems blinkered, and the literature to privilege a system of forms to the almost total exclusion of their individual usage. Indeed, thanks to Durkheim and his emphasis on society as the 'prime mover', the dichotomy between the individual and the collective has been obsessively denied as a false one, and the individuals, their motivations, and the micro-social worlds in which they mostly operate, 'buried under a vast weight' of *conscience collectives* and macro-social role specifications (Brittan, 1973, p. 171). In the grand-theoretical traditions of sociology, individuality and the diversity of meanings-in-use have been largely ignored, and anthropology has not been slow to follow suit.

Thus, the distinction between form and meaning has been customar-ily elided, and the reader fed a notion of overriding consensus or at least organisation as a necessary basis of community life and a sufficient description of it. For the basic foundations, it is often argued, are to be found in macro-structural forms and processes. Hence there is no need to stoop to what Giddens has described as the 'triviata' of everyday life and detail (cited in Brown and Levinson, 1978, p. 244). In sociological analysis, everyday looseness and lack of coherence is to be overcome (cf. Varwell, 1981, p. 6). The language in use in a community, for example, may be taken as one such macro-structure and described as an edifice of external collective reality, a crystallisation of values, norms, categories and conventions which form subjective consciousness into intersubjective, typical and communicable experiences (cf. Berger and Luckmann, 1966, p. 37; 1969, p. 66). Language is seen as coercing speakers into its patterns, constraining actions and experiences. Tran-scending differentiation, it integrates everyday life into a meaningful whole; that is, since language typifies experience and anonymises it, what is said to emerge is a single, consensual, cohesive and objective view of the world as language makes a collective reality into a continu-ing social fact. To learn a language, in this picture then, is to learn a social structure, and to speak it is to cause that structure's replication, because to speak it is to use a range of possible expressions, from a collective arsenal of acceptable formulations. Hence grammatical and verbal restraints become social ones, and individual speech may be reduced to the transmitting of the 'genes' of class sociality (Bernstein, 1964, p. 258; 1972, p. 494; and cf. Gumperz, 1970, pp 292–3). For every word spoken is a sign 'powerfully overdetermined' by the system of collective description, the shared code or matrix of which it forms part, an episodic manifestation of a deducible underlying structure (cf. Hawkes, 1977, pp 20–1; Riffaterre, 1981, p. 83; Gumperz and Hymes, 1972, p. 5). In this way, individual differentiation may be 'overcome', rendered invisible, since, in Sacks's words, it is the 'fine power' of a culture to fill members' minds not just in roughly the same way but 'so that they are alike in fine detail' (1974, p. 218).

Even when individual diversity has been admitted into the sociological picture, the individual is deprived of any responsibility, for the diversity is rather that of contradictory mores, of opposed positional interests, of situational roles, of circumstantial norms, of competing status groups, of a complex system of values and beliefs, of a disequilibriated social organisation, of a social structure in change. It is these collective symbolic systems which become the sources and guarantors of meaningful social behaviour, and these social forces to which individuals perforce respond and of which their behaviour is an expression. That is, individual diversity disappears because individuals are decentred from analysis, dissolved into various systems of convention which are said to be operating through them, constituting their selves. As Foucault praised the process, individual subjects are decentred in relation to the rules of their actions, the laws of their desires, the forms of their language and the play of their mythical and creative discourses (1972, p. 22). Thus individuals become collective constructs. Psyches become defined and realised by society, universes of discourse reflecting social positions (Mannheim, 1970, p. 117; Berger, 1970, p. 375). Selfhood becomes allocated from societal repertoires for use in certain collectively structured worlds of experience, pegs on which items of collaborative manufacture can be hung for a time (Goffman, 1978, p. 245). Roles played become allotted and determined by society, representing bundles of obligatory activity (Goffman, 1972, pp 76–7). Even imaginative explorations become emanations of certain pre-given and pre-structured life-worlds of socialisation (Psathas, 1973, pp 8–9). It is not individuals who think through their myths but myths which think through them, unbeknownst and outwith their control (Levi-Strauss, 1970, p. 20). In short, diversity is socialised and thereby sanitised. It is not the individuals who are diverse so much as the working parts of the complex social systems of which they are components. Their diversity is itself governed and part of a replicated pattern. In fact their diversity becomes an absence of diversity, of individual difference, and a triumph of cultural order. For culture is, in essence, a set of 'control mechanisms', as Geertz would have it, symbolic devices (plans, recipes, rules and instructions) like computer programmes, which reduce the breadth and indeterminateness of individuals' potential lives to the specificity and narrowness of their actual ones (1983, pp 44–5). Here it seems sociological common denominators simply 'solve' the question of individual difference, or at least remove it to the realm of the psychological, and only then do cultural belonging, social coordination, community, come to be born. Diversity rarely if ever equates with individual creativeness or idiosyncrasy, even when admitted, therefore, because it is to collective representations, produced in and for public settings, to which meanings are necessarily tied.

These images of community as inculcated consensus or integrated organisation do not tally with my fieldwork experiences in Wanet. In the earlier parts of the book I have tried to remain true to those particular feelings, and I see no reason to give in to a craving for generality in contempt of idiosyncrasy at this stage. Yet this, it appears to me, lies behind much of the above imaging, where Grand Theories of macrostructures and social systems make monothetic taxonomic concepts – 'community', 'culture', 'society', 'status group' – into analytical constructs, which cut out the mundane and the idiosyncratic as 'noise', without questioning the realities of the formal sameness these constructs are said to encompass or entertaining notions of their polytheticality (cf. MacIntyre, 1972, p. 8; Cohen, 1978a, p. 450). In search of Durkheimian collective solidarities and Marxian structures and Chomskian grammars and so on, highly filtered and homogenised ethnographies emerge which, I would agree with Schwartz, seem 'a great loss of information in a dubious leap of abstraction' (1978a, pp 419–20).

What is more, I find that the images conjured up in this way are anaemic – pale pretenders to a depiction of the complexity of social interaction. The abstraction to universals, to general laws, deadens the motion of circumstances and events, so that what emerges is static and inevitable. If Doris and Sid were reduced to 'ideal speaker-actors', then, and their interactions subsumed in some sort of concept of 'Wanet standard idiom', I should feel that detail was not merely being lost but in a very vital sense adulterated. To see their interactions as organised according to some universal type or types, or even as an interplay between such types, would seem to be doing violence to the genuine variety and contingency of meetings which, as individuals, they have negotiated between them (cf. Blumer, 1969, pp 53–4; Steiner, 1978, pp 162–3; Louch, 1966, pp 207–8; Glaser and Strauss, 1964, p. 675). The only thing that such images do achieve is distance. Behaviour is automatically seen as representative of some generic category, and its perpetrators as components of some larger collective entity, while the logic of explanation becomes self-fulfilling. For from a distance, local experience can be easily 'made visible' in terms of a selection of externally-imposed variables, and assimilated into a few metaphysical formulae, which thus justify themselves and remain empirically irrefutable. All that is situationally discrete is lost, subsumed in the sterility of hypothetico-deductive canon (cf. Harris, 1981, p. 110; Cohen, 1978b, p. 7).

Of course, one must be careful here. I am not advocating pure description in the absence of analysis or aiming at a depiction of everything that everyone did or said during fieldwork, and I do not suppose that any explanatory framework does not also construct its own explicanda. However, I do feel one can achieve a social scientific analysis which retains notions of the individual and his or her idiosyncrasies, and I object to the way I see grand-theoretical approaches treating cognitive diversities as ultimately patterned and therefore irrelevant (certainly non-problematical) when the societal domain is broached. Nor is it sufficient, as some apologists are wont, to say that Grand Theory is committed to large-scale explanatory projects and so is bound to seem out of place and 'vulgar' in the context of the particular case (e.g. Culler, 1981, p. 16). Because it is surely from individual behaviour, from watching what individuals say and do, that any data must derive. It is in individual minds that events occur and it is they who provide what Ayer calls 'final testimony' to the existence of a public world (1968, pp 256–7). As Blumer would emphasise (1969, *passim*), then, in exorcising the spirits of Functionalism and *Structuralisme* we must eschew notions of the institutional and the systemic as entities with mechanisms and dynamics operating in their own right, and recognise instead how these are made up of a complex and continuous interlinkage of individual actions, the connexion, simultaneous or sequential, of a possibly great number of separate lines of interest and activity. These lines of action derive in turn from how individuals define and decide to meet the situations in which they find themselves. Thus the large-scale system of cooperation or conflict (the community, kinship group, class-uprising, political confederation, or religious sect) may be broken down into smaller scale interactions between interpreting individuals in any number of settings and situations.

This is not to say that large-scale projects of societal study are inherently flawed but to argue that they should be managed without losing contact with the small scale. Even if the social group *has* become a machine, a superorganism with a separate existence, this state of affairs should be described as the ongoing construction of the people who serve it, a phantasy of groupness, as Laing depicts it, by members whose individual thoughts and actions are ever necessary for its maintenance (1968, p. 81). In short, social scientific analysis should tackle the interface between aggregation and individuation and to this end retain respect for individual cognitive processes. It should be possible to steer between what might be termed the Romantic image of seeing society as a mere vehicle for the expression of the unique soul of the preformed individual, and the Classical image of seeing in individuals mere bawdy colouring of a society's basic design. If one does this, one can take into account both the individual idiosyncrasy which brings a culture to life and also the cultural commonality which enables individuals to coordinate their activities, to interact, to avert societal dissolution (cf. Schwartz, 1978a, p. 423). In this fashion we might reach a notion of society as encompassing and composed of individual difference – indeed, as has been suggested, in a significant way constituted by this difference: a picture of society as a meeting of ambiguous cultural forms and possibly diverse individual meanings.

VI

The attraction of social Grand Theory, besides the clarity, fixity and inexorability of the picture provided by its 'objective' comprehension, and the distance and multiplicity of circumstances at which this can be applied, must include the overall control over its situated subjects which its exterior logic would suggest is possible. Hence, Roy Harris would tie the rising popularity of Saussurean linguistics in the early decades of this century to the crisis of credibility of the European nation-state as a viable social and political unit (1980, pp 157–8). For in the notion of *Langue* could be found a psychological manifestation of collective uniformity. *Langue* was a common property of the whole community and logically subordinated the linguistic role of the individual. In Saussure's grand picture was explicitly mirrored the ideally integrated and stable (Durkheimian) society which assumed absolute sovereignty over its members.

According to Harris, Saussure's successors in modern linguistics have not improved the situation (1981, p. 54), and, earlier, I stated rather baldly that anthropology still tends to privilege the abstraction of a system of forms to the exclusion of their individual usage, and that a full appreciation of their dialectical interdependence had yet to be arrived at. Let me try to justify this presumption by taking a closer look at the work of Anthony Wallace, still perhaps the most committed attempt to come to terms with individual idiosyncrasy and the diversity of meaning to be found in a social setting (e.g. 1961, 1962, 1964), and the work most frequently referred to in this connection (e.g. Goodenough, 1963; Szwed, 1966; Paine, 1974; Schwartz, 1978a, 1978b). Wallace's opening premise is that the cultural does not form a closed system. It is always engaged with the non-cultural – such as the psychological. Moreover, the dialectical relations between the cultural and the psychological eventuate not in a replication of psychological uniform-

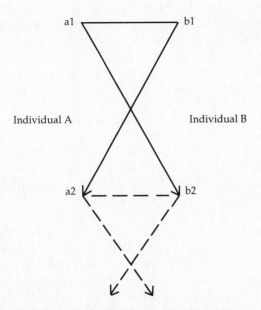

Figure III: A. F. C. Wallace's simple equivalence structure.

ity within a social group, in personalities sharing a homogenous '
cultural' character, but rather in an organisation of diversity. Hence
individuals in any one society need not be found 'threaded like beads
on a string of common motives'. They can still interact in a stable and
mutually rewarding fashion, and organise themselves culturally into
orderly, expanding, changing societies in spite of their having radically
different interests, habits, personalities, customs, and despite there being no one cognitive map that members share. Indeed, the 'mazeway' of
each individual, the mental map of values, plans, techniques, people
and things, the organised totality of meanings which each maintains at
a given time and which is regularly evoked by perceived or remembered stimuli, may be unique. Each individual may possess a complex
cognitive system of interrelated objects which amount to a private
world, and may rarely if ever achieve 'cognitive communality' or
mutual identification with another. To this extent, all human societies
are plural societies.

In fact, Wallace goes on to suggest that cognitive non-uniformity
may be a 'functional desideratum' of social structure, a necessary condition of making social coordination possible, and that if all participants
were to share a common knowledge of the social system, or indeed the
burden of knowing their differences, then the system would not work.
For Wallace's image of the orderly relationships which constitute stable

socio-cultural systems is of what he calls 'equivalence structures' or sets of equivalent behavioural expectancies. Individuals regularly engage in routine interactions with one another because they have developed a capacity for mutual prediction whereby the specific behaviour of one is highly likely to eventuate in the specific response of another, and so on. That is, individual A knows that when she perpetrates action a1 then individual B, in all probability, will perpetrate action b1, which will lead to her doing a2, etc. Meanwhile, individual B knows that when he perpetrates action b1, individual A responds with a1, which he follows with b2. In other words, individuals A and B need not concur on when precisely the interaction begins and whose action is perpetrated first: on who acts and who reacts. Wallace (1962, p. 356) depicts this simple equivalence structure as in Figure III above.

Thus, individuals organise themselves, integrate their behaviours into reliable and joint systems, not by developing uniform cognitive maps or possessing equivalent motives but by learning that under certain circumstances others' behaviour is predictable, and can be confidently interrelated with actions of their own. This system of organising relations, Wallace suggests, fits not only interactions between, for example, the American Indians and the Whites, trading and fighting for years without mutual comprehension, but also between different social classes, who may not share ideologies, and between bus drivers and passengers, whose interests in avoiding traffic jams may be very different and whose cognitive worlds, especially in large and complex societies, may be 'uniquely private'.

Nevertheless, what the bus driver and passenger do share is something very precise. Their interests in keeping to timetables overlap, their motives in riding the bus are complementary, and they possess detailed, mutual behavioural expectancies. Moreover, the relations are standardised between any driver and any passenger within the urban or regional or national system. Wallace calls this a 'contract', something where the equivalent roles are specified and available for implementation to any parties whose motives make their adoption promising. At other times, Wallace also calls it a 'meta-calculus', something which is the sum of at least two parties' particular 'calculi', or recipes of behaviour. And he goes on to say that a culture may be described as a 'family of meta-calculi', a set of standardised models of contractual relationships, a system of interlinking equivalence structures. In fact, culture becomes a consummate equivalence structure over the diverse whole, the sum of all the diverse mazeways of a society's particular sub-groupings and individuals.

In this way, Wallace explains, individuals can together produce a socio-cultural system which is beyond the comprehension of any single one of them. The contracts which they establish for the mutual facilitation of their separate strivings amount to a structured whole, however tacitly and gradually concocted, which is more complex than the cognitive map of any of its members. It is not that the socio-cultural system becomes a superorganic entity in the Durkheimian sense, Wallace insists, of something *sui generis*, even if it does so in a Spencerian sense, individual contracts and group policies adding up to another and higher level of organised diversity.

It is here, however, despite his insistence, that I find Wallace's lead losing its attraction. For with individuals constructing a system which functions as a whole beyond their comprehension we begin to slip towards a more Durkheimian notion of organicism again. Wallace would protest that he sees culture and personality as constructs of different Russellian logical types within a social system, personality signifying cognitive diversity, and culture merely amounting to shared expectations, and that it would be using the wrong metaphors to talk of individuals 'internalising' a culture, or a culture 'moulding' the personalities of its members, almost as if one were to talk of a circle moulding the individual points that constitute its circumference, or the points as internalisations of the equation by which the circle may be described. And yet, Wallace's model *does* take on this shape, and must do so, in order to describe the circle of interactions, the holistic system of interlocking parts, to which individual behaviours come to amount.

For the principle of socio-cultural organisation in his model is the meta-calculus or macro-equivalence structure and its institutionalisation, so that almost any individuals, any assemblage of mazeways, can work as interchangeable components of the system; and one must explain whence this metasystem derives and what the driving force behind it is. Wallace's answer is that culture is the driving force, with cultural forms and standardised contracts becoming autonomous and maintaining themselves by teaching members the mutually predictable behaviours necessary on different occasions. More than this, culture also provides members with their diverse mazeways. It teaches sets of equivalent meanings by which individuals can predictably define stimuli and, just as predictably, act before one another over wide situational parameters. Far from culture deriving from individual invention and continuing decisions about practice, then, culture now acts, and in peremptory fashion, taking advantage of individual cognitive tendencies to make possible a maximal organisation of motivational diversity. Thus, notwithstanding his renunciation of the deterministically superorganic, in the end we find Wallace talking about diverse cognitions being articulated by a society into functional equivalence structures, and a culture as an organisation which is responsible for coordinating its disparate elements and shaping them into relatively consistent patterns. It is very much to a separate societal domain that these elegant meta-calculi belong.

From his premise of individual diversity, then, Wallace reaches a point of gross socio-cultural determinacy, diversity as a cultural task, a social tool. Sometimes this diversity is culturally forbidden, and uniformity is socialised into individual members and rewarded. On other occasions it is 'in the interests of the survival of the culture' to encourage randomness and not to organise individuals at all. But most 'solutions', Wallace concludes, fall between the two and diversity can be organised and used in one or more of four universal mechanisms: 'Inclusive Structures' (a subordinate interactional partner bowing to the calculus, the plan, of a superordinate); 'End-Linkage' (a precise articulation of the calculi of equals in different domains of expertise, a division of labour); 'Ad Hoc Communication' (a warding off of centrifugal calculi and societal dissolution through constant casual intercourse); and 'Administration' (a checking of the large numbers of the above three types of contract in operation by a group of experts who can adjust individual members' calculi as necessary). In sum, with his image of a circle in whose circumference individual points of difference join and submerge, Wallace almost brings us full circle. Individual diversity has become treatable as cultural integration – ideal behaviour which is most often and most closely approximated to – and sociologically it has ceased to have any real relevance. Again we have succeeded to a picture of socio-cultural consensus, a system with a structure of interdependent parts, maintained by standardised behaviours, and ensuring at least some degree of social stability and cultural unity.

Nevertheless, I have wanted to describe Wallace's model at some length because of his recognition of diversity within commonality and his efforts analytically to keep the two in relationship. He recognises that social systems can exist without consisting of replications of uniformity and that cultures need not represent standards, norms, practices, rules, views or beliefs which are shared alike by all members. He shows how individuals might meet in interaction while at the same time executing moves, achieving positions, proclaiming successes and so on, in private and possibly very different game-plans, so that individual constructions of social worlds may have tangential connections, colliding and co-evolving without amounting to a single or even compatible world of meaning. Through equivalent structurings of their behaviours, interaction becomes an ego-syntonic outlet. Parties may use each other as Meadian *alters* in the definitions of their worlds without needing their separate constructions to be in any way meaningfully compatible, yet still they manage to maintain habitual relations with one another. They are not at a loss as to how to interpret each other's words and behaviour, but can regularly and routinely make meanings from them. They expect to meet one another and expect to exchange actions and opinions successfully concerning a number of possible topics, people and events.

Thus, the diversely motivated bus driver and passenger manage to engage in economic exchange while discussing the traffic or the weather or the Prime Minister, in the same way as Doris and Sid share space in Cedar High kitchen and discuss 'Tom Mason' or 'habits at the pub' or 'clay-pigeon shooting' or 'cheeky kids'. Here is a recognition, then, that joint social events need not be singular in order to be maintained, and need not eventuate in singularity either. Individuals need not be in agreement when they begin to interact, and constant interaction need bring them no closer to a joint or standardised consciousness, or a 'correction' of their idiosyncrasies. A great deal of their interaction can go on in a situation of misperception or misinterpretation of one another's motives. In short, in his acceptance of cognitive diversity, Wallace helps eschew the determinacy of interaction and focus our examination on the successful maintenance and replication of the latter not on an ethnomethodology of how meanings come to be interpreted alike but more beneficially on how behaviours come to be regarded as expected and mutually predictable.

What I find less sympathetic in Wallace's portrayal is the way in which individual agency is replaced by that of a cultural force which is seen as accountable for order and responsible for behavioural predictability, the way individual requirements and interests are replaced by those of the organisation, and the way in which the multitude of behavioural contracts are seen as amounting to one neatly integrated social system. For behaviours can be complementary without being integrated together or otherwise subsumed within a structure which is more complex than either. Complementarity need not entail organisational hierarchy (cf. Strathern, 1987, pp 30–4). Hence, the touching of circumferences of two circles does not represent their 'integration' or a point of greater 'complexity'. Doris and Sid are not 'subsumed' by their regular conversational meetings. These represent points of touching, *simple* conjunctions in fact, between otherwise very different verbal worlds. Their meetings exist alongside their private cognitive journeying as two parts of the same reality.

Furthermore, meetings of complementarity, even standardised ones, need not be seen as assuming a life-force of their own. The 'contracts' may be autonomous but the objectification they possess, the order they can instil, is that of the mould or the mask rather than the wind-up model with moving parts. What they can properly be said to exhibit is

inertia, not momentum. It is not that these contracts work, that they
have requirements, so much as they are worked and serve as vehicles
for their users. Moreover, they may be seen to be worked not as a
machine which is switched on and off but as a piece of music which is
jointly interpreted by an orchestra, or as a poem which is written in
metre and engaged by an audience. That is, while it may be incumbent
upon individuals to use standardised forms in order to enter into
exchange, to seem English, reasonable, posh, fashionable, clever, local
and so on, these may serve as avenues of release, of realisation, at least
as much as constraint. The villanelle, in existence as a poetic kind of
contract for centuries, does not force individuals to write one, nor those
who do to write with a specific intent. Indeed, using the form ushers in
the conventions of usage, the subject matter and treatment, the occasions of expression, which normally link writer and audience in a series
of mutual expectancies, but there is still the choice – to use in an
expectable way or to modify. Moreover, thinking with the form may
focus the attention, and release the imagination, so that one comes upon
rhymes, metaphors, correspondences and oppositions not brought to
mind before. Singing rugby songs with gusto in the bath or the pub may
be a requisite expression of manliness expected from team neophytes,
but there will invariably be alternative expressions, a range of versions,
idiosyncratic modifications and eccentricities – ways, in short, of personalising the form as exchanges with team-mates become routine.

To move to linguistic 'contracts' in general, we might say that language provides a fund of precedent cases which individuals adapt to
current communicational requirements, while past linguistic practices
do not determine their present communicational possibilities. Interaction represents a structure of exchange which individuals by and large
make up, without convenor or referee, as they go along. Verbal practice
eventuates in varied and inconsistent usage, with the repetition of
words in a language regardable as only partial replication, language as
a home to polythetic readings without resolved endings. In opposition
to conceptions of structural determinacy, then, a linguistic grammar
should be seen as neither overwhelming nor sacrosanct. Rules of grammar represent only very approximate and unstable summaries of past
regularities, and communities of interactants need not assume any
regimented sameness. For members communicate by internalising neither primers nor dictionaries, and notions of predetermined meanings
make little sense in relation to their construings of acts of communication. Individuals continuously improvise, innovate, and make meaning
as best they can (cf. Harris, 1981, *passim*; also Bruner, 1983, pp 11–13).

In short, individuals do not follow formal behavioural contracts
willy-nilly. Rather, these are available for implementation by those who

choose to adopt them as instruments towards their own ends. For example, Doris and Sid negotiate behavioural equivalences because Doris hopes Sid will lend a sympathetic ear to her financial problems, while Sid hopes Doris will admit his role in Cedar High Farm becoming a financial success and his part in its future. The bus driver and passengers enter into mutually compatible behaviours because the driver and company bosses hope people will get on and pay, while the passengers hope the buses will ferry them to their destinations safely. The jailer and the prisoner adopt the available standardised structure of exchange because the jailer hopes the prisoner will accept the strictures of confinement and serve 'good time', while the prisoner hopes the jailer will go by the book and make his 'porridge' bearable. Admittedly, choice is getting slimmer throughout these examples of contractual behaviours but even in the extreme case of the prisoner, the contract does not run by itself, or for itself. It cannot force compliance and, even when adopted, it does not determine its users' states of mind.

Finally, the multitude of behavioural contracts in use in a cultural setting need not eventuate in one working system, one 'meta-calculus' at all (cf. Moore, 1987, pp 730, 735). The way Doris and Sid have developed relations with each other need in no way constrain them in their negotiations with others. Far from operating together in series, one contract may oppose another – in time, in style, in consequence – or have tangential relations or none at all. Indeed, I would argue that Doris and Sid's different contracts with each other, the different behavioural routines they may engage in – not just the world-weary Doris and the worldly–wise Sid we saw conversing above, but the 'bantering Doris' and the 'pandering Sid', or the 'critical Doris' and the 'conciliatory Sid' – all of these may amount to no single set of equivalencies or overarching compatibility.

In sum, the model I have adopted is still rather different from Wallace's. For I present a society (such as a village community) as neither an holistic entity, with an existence independent of the persons composing it at any one time, whose consciousness and behaviour it immanently moulds, nor a mere aggregation of a multiplicity of individual actions without institutionalised commonalities which serve more than in particular instances of intercourse. Society is a phenomenon of neither objective determination nor mere subjective impulsion but rather, to paraphrase Simmel, where the vitality of individual meanings attain the reality of common forms (1971a, p. 24). The forms do not constitute society, do not determine social order, and severed from content (from individual purposes, motives, interests and desires) they do not gain meaningful existence. But they do facilitate the imposition of individual views of order. Hence society can be conceived of as an aggregation of orders, possibly highly diverse, expressed and maintained in certain limited and common forms. In complex societies, of course, containing a plurality of cultures, these forms will have a particular geographical distribution, and there will be forms special to the Cumbrian Dales, even perhaps Wanet, which are not common in Elmdon, on Shetland, or to Pakistanis in Manchester; and in any society, the forms will have a particular social distribution, between different generational, professional and status groups too (cf. Bakhtin, 1981, p. 293). But over and above the taint of such socio-cultural heteroglossia, the way in which these forms are used, I would argue, is the same. People can be said to be members of communities and living in individual worlds at the same time. Indeed, as we saw with Doris and Sid, the two states may be inextricably related. People are able to become idiosyncratic *because* they engage in habitual social interactions, and interactions exist in commonality *because* of continuing individual idiosyncrasies.

In any understanding of the systemics of society it is this highly complex relationship which surely must be grasped. To talk about the behavioural forms alone, abstracted from individual usage and context, is to produce something reified and sterile, to assign the forms a misleading metaphysic and reality. The necessary focus is instead on specific interactions where individuals regularly meet and interpret these forms, however manifold and intricate the overall picture becomes, and however attractive an hypostatisation of its forms seems. Equally, to integrate these forms into a tight and objectified cultural pattern is to decontextualise the realities of separate situations so as possibly to misrepresent them all. The more vital image is of the complicated and fragmentary, of individuals not as singular persons but as 'communities of selves', in whom private paradoxes may stand forever (cf. Mair, 1977, pp 130–1); and of the cultural forms by which they live as amounting to a shifting collage of behaviours whose pattern no two members may configure quite alike (cf. Sapir, 1956, pp 200–3). Instead of describing culture as a mechanism of encompassment and control, as the abstract ordering of a multiplicity of actions and ideas, then, it may be more properly seen as the means by which a host of individual orders come to be expressed and realised. For through the exchange of common cultural forms we can say that members of a society are able to build one another into characters in a multiplicity of different worlds, and influence one another in all manner of indirect, incidental, contingent, contradictory and changeable ways. A culture comes to be represented not as an entity with a positable, objective significance but as the forms in which subjective worlds develop, interact and are fulfilled and maintained, forms which derive their quickness from individual creativity. It is with individuals' purposes and their reasons for coming together in interaction that the key to our understanding of the social lies.

This model of the social system is not neat. Rather, it is a muddling through, based on possibly discordant variety. It is not final, but dependent on the continual meeting of individuals through common forms. It is not direct, but eventuates from individuals' behaviours influencing one another in all manner of possibly unintentional ways. And finally, it is not singular, but the aggregation of a multiplicity of private orders which collide, abut, overlap, and need not consistently coordinate or coincide. It is a picture of formal regularity, of sameness in ways of behaving, which facilitate and are maintained by difference in ways of interpreting.

VII

McLuhan's image of a global village has proved to be a very powerful one, frequently serving as the metaphorical framework in which to conceive of a world of global media of communication, meeting and consensus, a world where global syncretism and translation have become the rule. And yet, as Strathern has declared, our use of the image is essentially self-deceiving for who ever heard of a village that was not 'riven apart' by conflicting thoughts and interests (1986, p. 48; also cf. Leavis, 1972, p. 184)? In the global village, similarly, it is a dangerous fiction to equate a mutual influencing, an interfering, an 'inter-referencing' of cultural communities with a lessening of significant difference, or a prevalence of cliched communication with an homogenisation of meaning.

Boon describes anthropology as a tricksterish pursuit, straddling boundaries, living in margins, presenting a collage of disjunctions and thus keeping images of differences alive (1982, p. 237). This book has been an attempt to describe such disjunctions in a contemporary English village, to portray the inconsistency, the incomparability, the multiplicity and contradiction that may exist in a social setting beneath the physical contiguity, daily exchanges and uniform contours of behaviour. I have wanted to show that the universal structures of life in a Dales village, as in the global village, may be brought to meaningful life in a variety of ways. On the surface, then, we find a village which, since the opening up of the area to large numbers of visitors by roads and railways in the later years of the last century, and even more the popularisation of the private car in the second half of this, has become increasingly divided between inhabitants who think of themselves as country folk, whose lives are tied more or less closely to agriculture and the local family farm, and those who see themselves as having more or less recently arrived, after leaving the cities to find a different life. Indeed, population figures over the century suggest such an extent of de-population of 'farmers' and counter-population by 'townies' that Wanet would appear to be metamorphosing from a place of work – or, at least, work in a traditional vein – to one of recreation and retirement. In my concentration on two individuals who occupy the local or 'farmer' side of this gross divide, I have endeavoured to get below the surface and demonstrate the diversity this hides. Far from mouthpieces of universal social structures and members of a singular community then, Doris and Sid have been depicted as aggregations of idiosyncrasies whose most vibrant and significant communities were ultimately, perhaps, private to themselves. It was within the boundaries of self that their most significant truths resided. It was not that they did not attempt to communicate, rather that they both wanted to be understood (to share and compare, to boast and reaffirm experiences) and not to be understood (to protect and preserve, to maintain and celebrate individuality) at the same time. This, the exchange of common Wanet behavioural forms enabled them to do. In Simmel's terms (1964, p. 351), Doris and Sid could be described as becoming complete social entities *and* complete personal entities through the same mutual interactive process. Moreover, Simmel claims (1971a, p. 35), this individual duality reflects a societal one – through these psychic realities and psychological processes, sociological fundamentals are also to be understood. Hence, in this concluding part of the book, I have extrapolated from Doris and Sid to broader reaches of sociation. Here too I have suggested that we find a 'compresent dualism' which is constitutive – society existing through a continuous process of the exchange of homogeneous cultural objects and the construction of individual worlds of meaning in the same interactions at the same time.

Afterword: Style Reconsidered

Before the self of the observer was taken seriously as a component in the anthropological enterprise, it was a common (if heretical, if cathartical) flippancy to say that in the field anthropologists learn more about themselves than about anything else. Now, of course, awareness has shifted (as have common flippancies). As canonised by Leach (1982, pp 52–3; 1984, p. 22), every anthropological observer can be expected to recognise in the field something which no other observer will see, a projection of his or her personality; and since this personality 'distorts' the interpretation and analysis of that experience, what is to be discovered in published anthropological accounts is a record of their authors' reactions to the situations in which they were acting, texts full of possible implications and layers of particular meaning, intended and otherwise, but not items which give onto a pristine or objective, external world.

If this is so, then, as I mentioned in the Foreword, I have been mulling over the above projection of my consciousness in an English village in the early 1980s for a decade or more, receiving comment and critique on various spoken and written versions – criticism which no doubt reflects the alternative constructions of other personalities. In this Afterword it is a number of these different and competing conceptions that I want briefly to refer to, an admittance of other social–scientific logics that it has been suggested to me ought to be brought into play, alternative visions of socio-cultural order encompassing the details of Doris's and Sid's lives in Wanet. I do this because I want to end this book with something of the paradigmatic environment in which I have drawn up and selected my own account and, in so far as I can reflect upon my own personality and reactions, to describe what I now feel about the kind of account I have provided here and why.

Criticism has fallen within three broad ranges. These offer alternative answers to the questions of diversity of opinion *within* Doris and Sid (a), and *between* Doris and Sid (b) on the one hand, and on the other offer interpretations which replace notions of diversity all together (c). I might precis them as follows.

(a) *Diversity within Doris and Sid is not a matter of a multiplicity of personae and world-views, but rather:*

• An example of the tension between individuals' conflicting roles in face-to-face society. Doris and Sid each have several different roles to play (as parent, neighbour, villager, spouse) and, as is normal in a small rural community, all before the same audience. But, as is also normal, we find a built-in conflict of expectations concerning the behaviour appropriate to each role. Hence, as Doris and Sid are obliged to do dances of identification between their different, allotted roles, they can seem to be contradicting themselves. But the contradictions are not 'theirs'. Instead they belong to the role-sets, the collectively-managed behaviours which make 'Doris' and 'Sid' what they are. In rural society, moreover, these contradictions are more 'transparent' and tension always more likely to break out into open dispute, and so we have the image of Doris and Sid seemingly at odds with themselves.

• An example of the plurality and competitiveness of normative concepts in complex society. Concepts which components of a social system such as Doris and Sid use to think and express themselves with ('National Park wardens', 'Cedar High boundaries', 'Wanet village') are not necessarily consistent, nor must they form internally coherent and logical sets. To the contrary, societal concepts may be ambiguous and absurd. They might give the impression of possessing consistency but instead be taking on different meanings per context or else lacking in meaning completely. Moreover, these qualities may be socially functional, indeed essential for the functioning of the social system and for endowing the vagaries of societal need with the appearance of external, given and authoritative reality. Hence, what we see in Doris's and Sid's diverse behaviour is the play of concepts: multiple, malleable and manipulated per social context according to social function.

• A case of me not understanding my informants well enough. I have described Doris and Sid as fragmented characters and cognitively dissonant because it was only in odd moments that the logic guiding their behaviour became known to me, probably in those moments when their logic and my own conceptions of feasible behaviour most overlapped. Had I got to know them better, however, and seen them more in their own terms, I would have been able to make out the interconnections between their behaviours, and describe their characters as integrated wholes.

• A case of me not appreciating what kind of social beings my informants were. Because of ethnocentric concerns with my own folk concepts, I had expected discrete 'individuals' with personal 'selves'. Had I immersed myself more fully in the field I might have come to realise the need to replace such mystifying cultural notions with an appreciation of the total, systemic logic of encompassing social situations. I might have realised that it was in the collective discourse (the situation, the relationship, the institution, the organisation, the structure), and not in particular, transient interlocutors that social meaning, order, and consistency lie. What I call 'Doris' and 'Sid', then, are really conventional, shorthand ways of describing the juncture of series of macro-social systems of signs which operate and 'speak' through them.

(b) *Diversity between Doris and Sid is not a matter of incompatible perceptions and ambiguous interactions, but rather:*

• A case of me first forming an understanding of Doris and Sid in relation to myself (how each was like me and how different, how I could identify with and relate to each, how I could imagine myself acting in their places) and then bringing these two refractions of myself together and mistakenly calling this shadow-play 'an understanding of relations between Doris and Sid'. The differences I point up are not between Doris and Sid at all but between Doris and me on the one hand and Sid and me on the other. I only succeed in bringing them together with myself as mediator, whereas I am properly irrelevant and extraneous to their dyadic exchange. The residues and overlaps of perception and the negotiation of routine behaviours between me and them need have little relation to their negotiations with each other.

• An example of a situation of social change from *Gemeinschaft* to *Gesellschaft*. The dale of Wanet is in the throes of modernisation and here is somebody (Doris) in the process of sloughing off the multiplex and total social identity of membership in a traditional community and contracting the simplex relations and outlook of more modern forms of societal association. Of course, relations with neighbours change during this time. Not everybody welcomes modernisation or adapts so rapidly or so well. Some (Sid) resent the change and cling to the statuses of the past. Hence, disagreement increases between them. Not being sociologically aware, however, they phrase their differences in various more immediate and parochial ways.

• An example of the permeability of conventional social boundaries. For here is someone (Doris) in the process of moving across the borders of class, owning and improving their means of production and becoming middle class (or mid middle class) and leaving their erstwhile peers (Sid) and their lower class (or lower middle class) origins behind. Of course, classes in English culture remain even as individuals move between them, so there will be increasing differences between Doris and Sid, and more especially a need on Doris's part to limit or redefine their relations. Sid is more likely to resent Doris's 'departure' and Doris to feel ambivalence and some guilt as she takes on board the accoutrements of capital investor and entrepreneur, and necessarily distances herself from the people and norms of the group she is leaving. From here it is a simple act of transference for Doris to impart her 'fickleness' to them. Hence the tension in Doris and Sid's relations and the frequent *contretemps* between them.

• A case of disagreement over how certain common Wanet norms are to be applied. Doris and Sid share abstract notions about how the world works and how, in theory, people should behave within it. They roughly concur as regards what it means to be a good parent, a good villager, a good local, a good Englishman and so on, and agree on how behaviour has changed in Wanet since the arrival of the offcomers. Where they diverge is over the evaluation of particular people and specific instances of their behaviour. Moreover, they know they have these disagreements, but restrain themselves from referring to them too frequently or blatantly in conversation, and openly quarrelling, because of an overriding agreement as community members and as country folk to stand firm and united against the urban intruder.

(c) *Diversity between Doris and Sid is secondary compared to what they have in common. Their minor disagreements are rather:*

• Epiphenomena of their sharing, without which they would not know how to disagree. They disagree as regards 'second-storey' matters because they build on the same 'first-storey' foundations. Not only is their verbal idiosyncrasy made possible by their grammatical and other deep-structural uniformity, but their individual opinions and interpretations make sense because of the shared social–structural and commonsensical background to which, however implicitly, they always refer. We can think of Doris and Sid as having certain basic cultural scripts or melodies in common, and embellishing these in different ways to produce their own particular variations. If it were not for the scripts they would not be able to meet (to harmonise) in public space and perform and further extend their embellishments. (Nor would I be able to write and publish an account of their diversity and expect someone else to understand it.) It is the shared scripts and melodies which are socially significant.

• The eruptions of widespread rural anomy in the face of unattainable goals. Doris and Sid find themselves in very similar situations. Their world is changing rapidly, their community no longer isolated and separate. The dale of Wanet has become a thoroughfare for urban visitors and is increasingly prey to cosmopolitan influences and fashions, arriving at its door ever more rapidly and overwhelmingly through (computerised) mass media of communication. Inexorably, Doris and Sid succumb to new values and goals which are no longer primarily matters of local decision and debate but set by distant urban centres. Yet Doris and Sid find these goals almost impossibly hard to achieve. Moreover, local people seem disadvantaged when compared to the newcomers in their midst, who seem to succeed primarily because of favouritism and the application of double standards. In short, there is a growing dissociation in Wanet between culturally prescribed aspirations and the social–structural avenues for realising these. Doris and Sid suffer the same anomic reaction, and this expresses itself as the uncertainty, the distaste, the insecurity and so forth which they display before each other.

• The signs of their common alienation from the strange new world of counter-urbanisation and post-industrialism. Suddenly, transience has become a societal norm with people socially, and more especially physically, mobile as never before as the parameters of community change beyond recognition. Outsiders, uprooted by urban change, or uprooting themselves, are moving in and calling Wanet 'home', or at least 'retirement home' or 'holiday home'. Others seem to carry home on their backs and stay for a while, without a past and without roots, before wandering on again. Still others physically separate home and work to such an extent that they regularly commute from Wanet to Leeds, Manchester, even London and Edinburgh. In this situation, Doris and Sid find themselves potentially adrift in a place where old notions of common village space, if not already anachronistic, are becoming so at an alarming rate. So they retreat and we find them both acting withdrawn. Their disagreements are the reflections of social uncertainties foisted upon them by an invading alien world.

• Expressions of their common ageing, and the generation gap between them and their children starting to become politically significant. Doris and Sid are both in their mid thirties. Both have elderly or deceased parents and children who are reaching independence and adulthood. They are both at that age where they become increasingly conscious of their own mortality. Soon their children will be beginning families of their own, soon they will face competition as the sole mature generation which is *compos mentis* and has its hands on the reins of power. Already their oldest children are sowing the seeds of their rebellion. In no time their parents will be grand-parents, relegated to the eldest generational age-group, with only decline and death ahead of them. In this situation, it is normal for Doris and Sid to become nostalgic. They remember dreams of how they thought adulthood and parenthood would be and of what they hoped to have achieved by their mid-thirties. They consider how their present might have been otherwise if other paths had been chosen, or else they determinedly reaffirm the present, justifying it by tracing it straight back to the certainties and the proprieties of the past. Thus, for both Doris and Sid, their past in rural Wanet becomes highly significant and sentimental, if not idyllic.

Adults were friendly before, children were obedient, livelihoods were assured, differences between right and wrong were clear. In their back-ward-gazing and their nostalgia, as generational peers, Doris and Sid are as one. Their conversations demonstrate two close friends sharing the same discontent with the present and comparing the same dreams of resolution and stability in the future, and minor disagreements merely arise out of slightly different personal futures which they plan for themselves . . . .

These, then, are some of the more common ways in which aspects of my account of Doris's and Sid's behaviour have been taken up and fitted into other explanatory paradigms. Of course, these alternative con-structions, pertaining to alienation from modern rootlessness, the disil-lusionment of early middle age, the divisiveness of swapping social groups, or the manners of social exchange, the anomy of relative depri-vation, the heterogeneity of obligations, and the multiplicity of custom-ary rules and conventions in complex society, are not necessarily mutu-ally exclusive or incompatible with mine, and an argument could be made for wider epistemological pluralism in dealing with the Wanet material. Following Devereux, complementarity between them could be advocated, on the grounds that if a phenomenon admits of one explanation then it will admit of any number of others, all just as capable of its elucidation, so long as the phenomenon is 'real', and each explanation logically valid in terms of its own frame of reference (1978, pp 1–2).

However, I have not chosen to travel this route. Nor have I wanted to include these other explanations within the body of my text because I am not happy with them. I will not attempt here their refutation (that I did not naively set out to find holistic individuals, or mistakenly miss them; that I did not allow my feelings for Doris and Sid to over-determine an appreciation of their feelings for each other; that I was not culturally too close to home to recognise the depth of sharing by all) other than to say that they do not ring true to my sense of lives led in Wanet. Partly this is a matter of sentiment, of wanting to remain faithful to interpretations which I can trace back to Wanet and ground in my time there, in specific, situated perceptions of myself and others; and of wanting to retain the vividness, the richness, the complexity of social reality, of particular individuals and events (cf. Fernandez, 1974, p. 132). Partly it is a matter of taste and of style.

Rorty differentiates two distinct styles of philosophical argument, the systematic and the edifying. The systematic style is to construct scientific generalisations, to seek institutionalisation of a particular paradigm and to 'build for eternity'. The edifying style, by contrast, is reactive and peripheral to the mainstream debate, critical and self-conscious. It seeks to 'keep space open for the sense of wonder which poets can sometimes cause – wonder that there is something new under the sun, something which is *not* an accurate representation of what was there already, something which, at least for the moment, cannot be explained and can barely be described' (1979, pp 369–70). Paramount in the edifying style is a consciousness that to define is to limit, that to apply an explanatory code is to threaten an impoverishment, a depletion, of the world, to replace the nuances of living tissue by systematically dissected but dead matter, and that open-ended discussion which entertains *in*comparability is very often more fruitful than any positing of closure (cf. Nietzsche, 1979, p. 25; Wittgenstein, 1980, p. 74; Wilde, 1954, p. 217; Sontag, 1967, p. 7; Ions, 1977, p. 140). It should be clear which style my experiences in Wanet have led me to prefer. It is estrangement from the cold, mechanical models of Functionalism, the distance and certainty of *Structuralisme*, the tautological patness of Neo-Marxism, in fact, the unequivocal, totalising and dominative in any explanation of social life, that fieldwork caused me to feel. Hence the wish to present my account in a style which began from the micro-social and maintained heterogeneity, which focused on the ordinary and the everyday, which emphasised the duplicitous, the contingent, the marginal, the indeterminate, which privileged the imaginative use of cultural forms over political competition to specify their appropriateness for exchange.

Of course, it might be objected that far from deriving from my field experiences, this taste, this style was something which I brought to Wanet with me, and it so clouded and blinkered my vision that what has issued forth is not Doris Harvey, Sid Askrig *et al.* at home in Wanet at all, but rather Nigel Rapport away from home. Here is not Doris and Sid but the disillusioned emigre in search of an England of myth. Here is the person accustomed to defining himself in opposition, afraid of losing sight of his 'uniqueness' if too snug in one social identity or situation, and living in fear of the macro-social and the mean, the tyranny of the majority. Here, as Terry Eagleton scathingly derides them (1981, pp 137–8), are the archetypal idioms of the middle–class Anglo-Saxon academic: a modest disownment of system, a distaste for the definitive, a revulsion from the denotative, a dogmatic privileging of what escapes over what does not, a constant centralising of an irreducible bourgeois subject, and a Forsterian affirmation of a personal preserve. In short, it might be claimed that the feelings of displacement, marginality, uncertainty, and so on, which I have described for Doris and Sid, their multiplicity, contradictoriness, and the chaotic relativism in which I have enshrouded their social lives, are all my own, the result of how I choose to remember their behaviour and construe its significance.

Undoubtedly this is true, in part. It is true that I did not enter Wanet as a *tabula rasa*, however much I tried to become plasticine- or sponge-like, once *in situ*, and I as much believed that all species of Behaviourism were a travesty of individual artistry before my fieldwork as after. But still, the overwhelming immediacy and fullness of the field experience, the effect it had on my social scientific interests and vision, even my awareness of myself, lead me to believe that my account is not wholly 'analogic' or solipsistic but that there is something 'dialogic' in it which arises out of my encounter with strangers. I could not have invented Doris and Sid in this way without meeting them and being strongly affected by routine relations in which we engaged.

This repeated return to my fieldwork experience – its 'vividness', its 'fullness', its 'richness' – as both ultimate explanation and validation of my views may strike some as mere circularity ('my field data mean this because this is what my fieldwork meant') and as theoretically lame. I do not think so. I think that beginning and re-beginning from the intimacies and intricacies of fieldwork and having faith in its disclosures is my chief resource as an anthropologist. This is certainly the sentiment which has imbued this book – that the insights which being an impressible stranger (at once attached and detached, involved and indifferent, near and remote), and only this, affords are the true coin of analytic capital. Nor do I think that this argument is finally circular. Rather it points to the centrality of the 'self' of the observer in the anthropological enterprise, as the interpreter of his or her experience as well as the chief instrument upon which that experience plays. And upon the self of the stranger the resulting notes can be truly other-worldly.

Bibliography

Adams-Webber, J. (1981), 'Personal Construct Theory: Research into basic concepts', in *Personality: Theory, Measurement, Research*, ed. F. Fransella (London: Methuen).

Akeroyd, A. (1984) 'Ethics in relation to informants, the profession and governments', in *Ethnographic Research*, ed. R. Ellen (London: Academic).

Arensberg, C. (1959) *The Irish Countryman* (Massachusetts: Smith).

Ayer, A. J. (1968) 'Can there be a private language?', in *Wittgenstein. The Philosophical Investigations*, ed. G. Pitcher (London: Macmillan).

Baines, E. (1969 [1822]) *History, Directory and Gazetteer of the County of York. Volume I, West Riding* (Newton Abbott: David & Charles).

Bakhtin, M. (1981) *The Dialogic Imagination* (Austin: University of Texas Press).

Bateson, G. (1973) *Steps to an Ecology of Mind* (London: Intertext).

Bateson G. and Ruesch J. (1951) *Communication: The Social Matrix of Psychiatry* (New York: Norton).

Becker, H. (1964) 'Problems in the publications of community studies', in *Reflections on Community Studies*, eds A. Vidich, J. Bensman, and M. Stein (New York: Wiley).

Becker H. (1977) *Sociological Work: Method and Substance* (New Jersey: Transaction).

Bell, C. and Newby, H. (1975) *Community Studies* (London: Allen & Unwin).

Bell, C. and Newby, H. (1977) 'Editorial Introduction: The rise of methodological pluralism', in *Doing Sociological Research* (London: Allen & Unwin).

Berger, J. (1967) *A Fortunate Man. The Story of a Country Doctor* (London: Penguin).

Berger, P. (1970) 'Identity as a problem in the sociology of knowledge', in *The Sociology of Knowledge*, eds J. Curtis and J. Petras (London: Duckworth).

Berger P. and Luckmann, T. (1966) *The Social Construction of Reality* (New York: Doubleday).

Berger P. and Luckmann, T. (1969) 'Sociology of religion and sociology of knowledge', in *Sociology of Religion*, ed. R. Robertson (Harmondsworth: Penguin).

Bernstein, B. (1964) 'Aspects of language and learning in the genesis of the social process', in *Language in Culture and Society*, ed. D. Hymes (New York: Harper & Row).

Bernstein, B. (1972) 'A sociolinguistic approach to socialisation: with some reference to educability', in *Directions in Sociolinguistics*, eds. J. J. Gumperz and D. Hymes (New York: Holt, Rinehart & Winston).

Blumer, H. (1969) *Symbolic Interactionism* (Englewood Cliffs: Prentice-Hall).

Blythe, R. (1969) *Akenfield* (London: Penguin).

Boon, J. (1982) *Other Tribes, Other Scribes* (Cambridge: CUP).

Bott, E. (1964) *Family and Social Network* (London: Tavistock).

Brittan, A. (1973) *Meanings and Situations* (London: Routledge & Kegan Paul).

Brown, P. and Levinson, S. (1978) 'Universals in language usage', in *Questions and Politeness*, ed. E. Goody (Cambridge: CUP).

Bruner, E. M. (1983) 'Editorial Introduction: The opening up of anthropology', in *Text, Play and Story: The Construction and Reconstruction of Self and Society* (Washington: AES).

Bulmer, T. (1905) *Directory of Westmorland* (Preston: Bulmer).

Byron, R. (1985) *Sea Change. A Shetland Society 1970-1979* (St John's: ISER)

Carlyle, T. (1843) *Past and Present* (London: Chapman & Hall).

Chesterton, G. K. (1975 [1908]) *The Man Who Was Thursday* (Harmondsworth: Penguin).

Clifford, J. (1986) 'Introduction: Partial truths', in *Writing Culture*, eds. J. Clifford and G. Marcus (Berkeley: University of California Press).

Cockcroft, B. (1975) *The Dale That Died* (London: Dent).

Cohen, A.P. (1978a) '"The same – but different!": The allocation of identity in Whalsay, Shetland', in *Sociological Review*, 26(3).

Cohen, A.P. (1978b) 'Ethnographic method in the real community', *Sociologia Ruralis*, XVIII(1).

Cohen, A.P. (ed.) (1982a) *Belonging. Identity and Social Organisation in British Rural Cultures* (Manchester: MUP).

Cohen, A.P.(1982b) 'Introduction. Belonging: The experience of culture', in A. P. Cohen, ed. (1982a).

Cohen, A.P. (1982c) 'A sense of time, a sense of place: The meaning of close association in Whalsay, Shetland', in A. P. Cohen, ed. (1982a).

Cohen, A.P. (ed.) (1986) *Symbolising Boundaries: Identity and Diversity in British Cultures* (Manchester: MUP).

Cohen, A.P. (1987) *Whalsay. Symbol, Segment and Boundary in a Shetland Island Community* (Manchester: MUP).

Cohen, A.P. (1992) 'Self-conscious anthropology', in *Anthropology and Autobiography*, eds J. Okely and H. Callaway (London: Routledge).

Colbeck, M. (1979) *Yorkshire: The Dales* (London: Batsford).

Compton-Burnett, I. (1969) *Mother and Son* (London: Panther).

Condry, E. (1979) 'Scottish Ethnography: A report on present and future', paper presented at the SSRC conference on 'Anthropological Research in Scotland', University of Edinburgh.

Countryside Commission, The (1979) *Leisure and the Countryside* (Cheltenham: CC).

Culler, J. (1981) *The Pursuit of Signs: Semiotics, Literature, Deconstruction* (Ithaca: Cornell University Press).

Devereux, G. (1978) *Ethnopsychoanalysis* (Berkeley: University of California Press).

Dewhirst, I. (1972) *Gleanings from Victorian Yorkshire* (Ridings: Driffield).

Dickens, C. (1967 [1854]) *Hard Times* (Harmondsworth: Penguin).

Dumont, J-P. (1978) *The Headman and I* (Austin: University of Texas Press).

Duncan, H. (1959) 'Simmel's Image of society', in *Georg Simmel*, ed. K. Wolff (Columbus: Ohio State University Press).

Eagleton, T. (1981) *Walter Benjamin* (London: NLB).

Economist, The (1985) *Britain's Economy*, March 9th.

Emmet, I. (1982) 'Fe godwin ni eto: Stasis and change in a Welsh industrial town', in A. P. Cohen, ed. (1982a).

Favret-Saada, J. (1980) *Deadly Words* (Cambridge: CUP).

Fernandez, J. (1974) 'The mission of metaphor in expressive culture', *Current Anthropology*, 15(2).

Forster, E.M. (1950 [1910]) *Howards End* (Harmondsworth: Penguin).

Foucault, M. (1972) *The Archaeology of Knowledge* (London: Tavistock).

Fox, R. (1978) *The Tory Islanders* (Cambridge: CUP).

Frankenberg, R. (1957) *Village on the Border* (London: Cohen & West).

Frankenberg, R. (1965) *Communities in Britain* (Harmondsworth: Penguin).

Garfinkel, H. (1967) *Studies in Ethnomethodology* (Englewood Cliffs: Prentice-Hall).

Geertz, C. (1983) 'The impact of the concept of culture on the concept of man', in *The Interpretation of Cultures* (New York: Basic Books).

Gilsenan, M. (1976) 'Lying, honour and contradiction', in *Transaction and Meaning*, ed. B.Kapferer (Philadelphia: ISHI).

Glaser, B. and Strauss, A. (1964) 'Awareness contexts and social interaction', *American Sociological Review*, XXIX.

Goffman, E. (1972) *Encounters* (London: Penguin).

Goffman, E. (1978) *The Presentation of Self in Everyday Life* (Harmondsworth: Penguin).

Goldstein, K. and Blackman, S. (1981) 'Theoretical approaches to cognitive style', in *Personality: Theory, Measurement and Research*, ed. F. Fransella (London: Methuen).

Gomme, G. L. (1890) *The Village Community* (London: Scott).

Goodenough, W. (1963) *Cooperation in Change* (New York: Sage).

Greene, G. (1974) *The Heart of the Matter* (Harmondsworth: Penguin).

Gumperz, J. J. (1970) 'Linguistic and social interaction in two communities', in *Man Makes Sense*, eds E. A. Hammel and W. Simmons (Boston: Little & Brown).

Gumperz, J.J. and Hymes D. (1972) 'Editorial introduction', in *Directions in Sociolinguistics* (New York: Holt, Rinehart & Winston).

Gumperz, J. J. and Tannen, D. (1979) 'Individual and social differences in language use', in *Individual Differences in Language Ability and Language Behaviour*, eds C. Fillmore, D. Kempler, and W. Wang (New York: Academic).

Hannerz, U. (1988) 'The world in creolisation', *Africa*, 57(4).

Harris, C. (1974) *Hennage* (New York: Holt, Rinehart & Winston).

Harris, R. (1980) *The Language Makers* (London: Duckworth).

Harris, R. (1981) *The Language Myth* (London: Duckworth).

Hartley, M. and Ingilby, J. (1968) *Life and Tradition in the Yorkshire Dales* (London: Dent).

Hartley, M. and Ingilby, J. (1982) *A Dales Heritage* (Clapham: Dalesman).

Hawkes, T. (1977) *Structuralism and Semiotics* (Berkeley: University of California Press).

Howitt, W. (1971 [1838]) *The Rural Life of England* (Shannon: Irish University Press).

Hymes, D. (1972) 'Models of Interaction of Language and Social Life', in *Directions in Sociolinguistics*, eds J. J. Gumperz and D. Hymes (New York: Holt, Rinehart & Winston).

Hymes, D. (1973) 'Towards ethnographies of communication: The analysis of communicative events', in *Language and Social Context*, ed P. Giglioli (Harmondsworth: Penguin).

Ions, E. (1977) *Against Behaviourism* (Oxford: Blackwell).

Krech, D., Crutchfield, R., and Ballachey, E. (1962) *Individuals in Society* (New York: McGraw-Hill).

Laing, R. D. (1968) *The Politics of Experience* (Harmondsworth: Penguin).

Larsen, S. (1982) 'The two sides of the house: Identity and social organisation in Kilbroney, Northern Ireland', in A. P. Cohen, ed. (1982a).

Leach, E. R. (1982) *Social Anthropology* (London: Fontana).

Leach, E. R. (1984) 'Glimpses of the unmentionable in the history of British Social Anthropology', *Annual Review of Anthropology*, 13.

Leavis, F. R. (1972) *Nor Shall My Sword* (London: Chatto & Windus).

Levi-Strauss, C. (1970) *The Raw and the Cooked* (London: Cape).

Littlejohn, J. (1963) *Westrigg: The Sociology of a Cheviot Parish* (London: Routledge & Kegan Paul).

Louch, A. R. (1966) *Explanation and Human Action* (Berkeley: University of California Press).

MacFarlane, A. (1978) *The Origins of English Individualism* (Oxford: Blackwell).

MacFarlane, A.(1981) *The Justice and the Mare's Ale* (Oxford: Blackwell).

MacIntyre, A. (1972) 'Is a Science of Comparative Politics Possible?' in *Philosophy, Politics and Society*, 4th series, eds P. Laslett, W. Runciman, and Q. Skinner (Oxford: Blackwell).

Mair, J. (1977) 'The community of self', in *New Perspectives in Personal Construct Theory*, ed. D. Bannister (London: Academic).

Mannheim, K. (1952) *Ideology and Utopia* (London: Routledge & Kegan Paul).

Mannheim, K. (1970) 'The sociology of knowledge', in *The Sociology of Knowledge*, eds J. Curtis and J. Petras (London: Duckworth).

Marshall, J. and Walton, J. (1981) *The Lake Counties from 1830 to the mid-twentieth century* (Manchester: MUP).

Mercer, D. (1988) *Rural England* (London: Queen Anne).

Mewett, P. (1982) 'Exiles, nicknames, social identities and the production of local consciousness in a Lewis Crofting Community', in A. P. Cohen, ed. (1982a).

Mitchell, W. R. and Joy, D. (1973) *The Settle-Carlisle Railway* (Clapham: Dalesman).

Miyamoto, F. (1970) 'Self, motivation and symbolic interactionist theory', in *Human Nature and Collective Behaviour*, ed. T. Shibutani (Englewood Cliffs: Prentice-Hall).

Moore, S. F. (1987) 'Explaining the present: Theoretical dilemmas in processual ethnography', *American Ethnologist*, 14(4).

Murphy, R. (1972) *The Dialectics of Social Life* (London: Allen & Unwin).

Newby, H. (1972) 'Agricultural workers in the class structure', *Sociological Review*, 20(3).

Newby H. (1975) 'The deferential dialectic', *Comparative Studies in Society and History*, 17(2).

Newby H., Bell, C., Rose, D., and Saunders, P. (1978) *Property, Paternalism and Power* (London: Hutchinson).

Nietzsche, F. (1979 [1889]) *Twilight of the Idols* (Harmondsworth: Penguin).

Okely, J. (1983) *The Traveller-Gypsies* (Cambridge: CUP).

Orwell, G. (1968) 'Politics and the English Language', in *Collected Essays* (London: Secker and Warburg).

Pahl, R. (1968) *Readings in Urban Sociology* (Oxford: Pergamon).

Paine, R. (1971) 'A theory of patronage and brokerage', in *Patrons and Brokers in the East Arctic*, ed. R. Paine (St. John's: ISER).

Paine, R. (1974) 'Second thoughts about Barth's Models', *Royal Anthropological Inst. Occasional Papers*, No. 32.

Paine, R. (1989) 'The non-routine, and what it reveals about culture', paper presented at the Dept of Anthropology and Sociology, University of British Columbia.

Palmer, C., Robinson, M., and Thomas, R. (1977) 'The countryside image – An investigation of structure and meaning', *Environment and Planning*, A9.

Parker, J. (1977) *Cumbria* (Edinburgh: Bartholomew).

Parkin, D. (1987) 'Comparison as the search for continuity', in *Comparative Anthropology*, ed. L. Holy (Oxford: Blackwell).

Patterson, W. (1959) 'The new Pennine dairy farming', *Agriculture*, LXVI(8).

Philips, D. and Williams, A. (1984) *Rural Britain. A Social Geography* (Oxford: Blackwell).

Philips, S. (1986) 'Natives and Incomers: The symbolism of belonging in Muker Parish, North Yorkshire', in A. P. Cohen, ed. (1986).

Pitt-Rivers, J. (1974) *The People of the Sierra* (Chicago: Chicago University Press).

Pocock, D. (1961) *Social Anthropology* (London: Sheed and Ward).

Priestley, J. B. (1934) *English Journey* (London: Heinemann).

Propp, V. (1968 [1927]) *Morphology of the Folk Tale* (Austin: University of Texas Press).

Psathas, G. (1973) 'Editorial introduction', in *Phenomenological Sociology* (New York: Wiley).

Rapport, N. J. (1986) 'Cedar High Farm: Ambiguous Symbolic Boundary. An essay in anthropological intuition', in *Symbolising Boundaries: Identity and Diversity in British Cultures*, ed. A. P.Cohen (Manchester: MUP).

Rapport, N.J. (1987) *Talking Violence. An anthropological interpretation of conversation in the city* (St. John's: ISER).

Rapport, N.J. (1989) 'Conversing in Wanet. An anthropologist "at home"', *Journal of the Anthropological Society of Oxford*, XX(1).

Rapport, N.J. (1990) '"And We Shall Build Jerusalem". Stereotypes, cliches and the individual construction of the future', paper presented at the ASA conference on 'Anthropology and the Future', University of Edinburgh.

Rapport, N.J. (1992) 'From affect to analysis. The biography of an interaction in an English village', in *Anthropology and Autobiography*, eds J. Okely and H. Callaway (London: Routledge).

Redfield, R. (1963) *The Little Community* (Chicago: Chicago University Press).

Rees, A. (1951) *Life in a Welsh Countryside* (Cardiff: University of Wales Press).

Richards, A. and Robin, J. (1975) *Some Elmdon Families* (Saffron Walden: Richards).

Riffaterre, M. (1981) *The Semiotics of Poetry* (Bloomington: Indiana University Press).

Robin, J. (1980) *Elmdon* (Cambridge: CUP).

Rollinson, W. (1974) *Life and Tradition in the Lake District* (London: Dent).

Rorty, R. (1979) *Philosophy and the Mirror of Nature* (Princeton: Princeton University Press).

Sacks, H. (1974) 'On the analysability of stories by children', in *Ethnomethodology*, ed. R. Turner (Harmondsworth: Penguin).

Samuel, R. (1975) 'Editorial introduction: People's history', in *Village Life and Labour* (London: Routledge & Kegan Paul).

Sapir, E. (1956) *Culture, Language and Personality*, ed. D. Mandelbaum (Berkeley: University of California Press).

Schegloff, E.A. (1972) 'Sequencing in conversational openings' in *Directions in Sociolinguistics*, eds J. J. Gumperz and D. Hymes (New York: Holt, Rinehart & Winston).

Schutz, A. (1944) 'The Stranger. An essay in social psychology', *American Journal of Sociology*, 49(6).

Schutz, A. (1953) 'Common sense and scientific interpretation of human action', *Philosophy and Phenomenological Research*, XIV(1).

Schwartz, T. (1978a) 'Where is the culture? Personality as the distributive locus of culture', in *The Making of Psychological Anthropology*, ed. G. Spindler (Berkeley: University of California Press).

Schwartz, T. (1978b) 'The size and shape of a culture', in *Scale and Social Organisation*, ed. F. Barth (Norway: A/S Greig).

Scott, H. (1965) *Portrait of Yorkshire* (London: Hale).

Searle, J. (1971) 'Editorial introduction', in *The Philosophy of Language* (Oxford: OUP).

Sedgewick, A. (1868) *Memorial by the Trustees of Cowgill Chapel* (Cambridge: Sedgewick).

Shibutani, T. (1961) *Society and Personality* (Englewood Cliffs: Prentice-Hall).

Simmel, G. (1964) 'How is society possible?', in *Georg Simmel 1858–1918*, ed. K. Wolff (New York: Free Press).

Simmel, G. (1971a) 'The Problem of sociology', in *On Individuality and Social Forms*, ed. D.Levine (Chicago: Chicago University Press).

Simmel, G. (1971b) 'Social Forms and Inner Needs', in *On Individuality and Social Forms*, ed. D.Levine (Chicago: Chicago University Press).

Simmonds, I. G. (1971) *Yorkshire Dales National Park* (London: HMSO Guides No.9).

Sontag, S. (1967) *Against Interpretation* (New York: Farrar, Straus & Giroux).

Speight, H. (1892) *The Craven and North West Yorkshire Highlands* (London: Stock).

Steiner, G. (1967) *Language and Silence* (London: Faber).

Steiner, G. (1975) *After Babel* (London: OUP).

Steiner, G. (1978) *On Difficulty, and other essays* (Oxford: OUP).

Strathern, M. (1981) *Kinship at the Core* (Cambridge: CUP).

Strathern, M. (1982a) 'The place of kinship: Kin, class and village status in Elmdon, Essex', in A. P. Cohen, ed. (1982a).

Strathern, M. (1982b) 'The village as an idea: Constructs of villageness in Elmdon, Essex', in A. P. Cohen, ed. (1982a).

Strathern, M. (1986) 'Out of context: The persuasive fictions of anthropology', The Frazer Lecture, University of Liverpool (Published with commentary in *Current Anthropology*, 28, 1987).

Strathern, M. (1987) 'Partial connections', The Munro Lecture, University of Edinburgh (Published in extended form as *Partial Connections*, Savage: Rowman & Littlefield, 1990).

Szwed, J. (1966) *Private Cultures and Public Imagery* (St. John's: ISER).

Thirsk, J. (1961) 'Industries in the countryside', in *Essays in Economic and Social History of Tudor and Stuart England*, ed. F. Fisher (Cambridge: CUP).

Turner, V. (1974) *Dramas, Fields and Metaphors* (Ithaca: Cornell University Press).

Tyler, S. (1986) 'Post-Modern Ethnography: From document of the occult to occult document', in *Writing Culture*, eds G. Marcus and J. Clifford (Berkeley: University of California Press).

Varwell, A. (1981) *In Search of Meaning*, North Sea Oil Occasional Paper No. 5 (London: SSRC).

Vidich, A. and Bensman J. (1964) 'The Springdale case: Academic bureaucrats and sensitive townspeople', in *Reflections on Community Studies*, eds A.Vidich, J. Bensman and M. Stein (New York: Wiley).

Wallace, A.F.C. (1961) 'The psychic unity of human groups', in *Studying Personality Cross-Culturally*, ed. B. Kaplan (New York: Harper & Row).

Wallace, A. F. C. (1962) 'Culture and cognition', *Science*, 135.

Wallace, A.F. C (1964) *Culture and Personality* (New York: Random House).

Wallis, R. (1977) 'The moral career of a research project',in *Doing Sociological Research*, eds C. Bell and H. Newby (London: Allen & Unwin).

Wallman, S. (1977) 'The shifting sense of "Us": Boundaries against development in the Western Alps', in *Perceptions of Development*, ed. S. Wallman (Cambridge: CUP).

Weiner, A. (1983) 'From words to objects to magic: Hard words and the boundaries of social interaction', *Man*, 18(4).

Wiener, N. (1949) *Cybernetics* (New York: Wiley).

Wikan, U. (1980) *Life Among the Poor in Cairo* (London: Tavistock).

Wilde, O. (1954) *The Picture of Dorian Gray* (Harmondsworth: Penguin).

Wilde O. (1968) *Critical Writings of Oscar Wilde*, ed. R. Ellman (New York: Random House).

Williams, W. (1956) *The Sociology of an English Village: Gosforth* (London: Routledge & Kegan Paul).

Williams, W. (1963) *A West Country Village: Ashworthy* (London: Routledge & Kegan Paul).

Winch, P. (1970) *The Idea of a Social Science, and its Relation to Philosophy* (London: Routledge & Kegan Paul).

Wittgenstein, L. (1980) *Culture and Value*, ed. G.H. von Wright (Oxford: Blackwell).

Wright, G. (1977) *The Yorkshire Dales* (Newton Abbott: David & Charles).

Young, E. (1986) 'Where the daffodils blow: Elements of communal imagery in a Northern Suburb', in A. P. Cohen, ed. (1986).

Young, M. and Wilmott, P. (1974) *Family and Kinship in East London* (Harmondsworth: Penguin).

Zaslavsky, V. (1982) *The Neo-Stalinist State* (New York: Sharpe).

Zijderveld, A. (1979) *On Cliches* (London: Routledge & Kegan Paul).

Index of Names

Adams-Webber, J., 152
Adler, J., x
Akeroyd, A., 74
Anderson, D., x
Ardener, E., x
Arensberg, C., 39
Ayer, A. J., 181

Baines, E., 14
Bakhtin, M., 190
Ballachey, E., 156
Barnes, J., 74
Bateson, G., 151, 152, 174, 176
Baxter, P., x
Becker, H., 34, 76
Bell, C., 38, 76
Bensman, J., 73
Berger, J., 1, 40, 173
Berger, P., 154, 173, 177, 178
Bernstein, B., 173, 178
Blackman, S., 156
Blumer, H., 179, 180
Blythe, R, 32, 34
Bone, V., x
Boon, J., 76, 178, 191
Bott, E., 173
Briggs, J., x
Brittan, A., 178
Brown, P., 150, 178
Bruner, E. M., 188
Byron, R., 32, 33, 35, 37, 40

Carlyle, T., 173
Chesterton, G . K., 175
Chomsky, N., 180
Clifford, J., 74
Cockcroft, B., 19, 32, 34
Cohen, A. P., vi, ix, x, 39, 40, 180, 181
Colbeck, M., 11
Coleridge, S., 19
Compton-Burnett, I., 175
Condry, E., 70
Countryside Commission, The, 20
Crutchfield, R., 156
Culler, J., 181

Devereux, G., 157, 159, 169, 198
Dewhirst, I., 36
Dickens, C., 18
Dumont, J.-P., 69, 73
Duncan, H., x
Durkheim, E., x, 34, 164, 178, 180, 182, 185

Eagleton, T., 199
Economist, The, 20
Eden, F. M., 36
Emmet, I., 50
Engels, F., 37

Favret-Saada, J., 174
Fernandez, J., 198
Firth, R., 69
Forster, E. M., 70, 177, 199
Fortes, M., 69
Foucault, M., 179
Fox, R., 39
Frankenberg, R., 32, 33, 36

Garfinkel, H., 153
Geertz, C., 179
Giddens, A., 178
Gilsenan, M., 174
Glaser, B., 180
Goffman, E., 173, 179
Goldstein, K., 156
Gomme, G. L., 36
Goodenough, W., 173, 182
Greene, G., 175
Gumperz, J. J., 150, 178–9

Hannerz, U., 74
Harris, C., 33
Harris, R., 181, 182, 188
Hartley, M., 12, 32
Hawkes, T., 179
Hobart, M., x
Homans, G., 37
Howitt, W., 19, 31, 32, 37, 38
Hymes, D., 151, 179

Ingilby, J., 12, 32

Ions, E., 199

Joy, D., 37

Kressel, G., x
Krech, D., 156

Laing, R. D., 181
Larsen, S., 50, 174
Leach, E. R., 69, 193
Leavis, F. R., 191
Levinson, S., 150, 178
Levi-Strauss, C., 179
Littlejohn, J., 34, 37
Louch, A. R., 151, 180
Luckmann, T., 154, 173, 178

Macfarlane, A., x, 37, 175
MacIntyre, A., 180
McLuhan, M., 191
Maine, H., 34
Mair, J., 190
Mannheim, K., 153, 179
Marshall, J., 36
Marx, E., x
Marx, K., 37, 180
Mead, G. H., 186
Mercer, D., 23, 24
Mewett, P., 33, 35, 38, 40
Mitchell, W. R., 37
Miyamoto, F., 152
Moore, S. F., 189
Murphy, R., 175

Newby, H., 33, 34, 36, 38, 76
Nietzsche, F., 199

Okely, J., 71
Orwell, G., 173

Pahl, R., 36
Paine, R., x, 156, 173, 182
Palmer, C., 32
Park, G., x
Parker, J., 37
Patterson, W., 23
Peters, E., x
Phillips, D., 36
Phillips, S., 51
Pitt-Rivers, J., 174
Pocock, D., 163, 175
Priestley, J. B., 19, 20, 31, 32
Prindiville, J., x
Prior, M., x
Propp, V., 169
Psathas, G., 179

Rapport, N. J., 75, 155
Redfield, R., 34
Rees, A., 32, 33, 36, 37, 43
Richards, A., 38
Riffaterre, M., 179
Robin, J., 38
Rollinson, W., 12
Rorty, R., 198
Rose, D., x
Ruesch, J., 151, 174
Russell, B., 185

Sacks, H., 179
Samuel, R., 14
Sapir, E., 155, 169, 190
Saussure, F., 182
Schegloff, E. A., 150
Schutz, A., 123, 152, 156
Schwartz, M, x
Schwartz, T., 180, 182
Scott, H., 32
Searle, J., 150
Sedgewick, A., 38
Shibutani, T., 153
Simmel, G., x, 164, 177, 189, 192
Simmonds, I. G., 24
Smith, P., x
Sontag, S., 199
Southey, R., 19
Speight, H., 37
Spencer, H., 185
Steiner, G., 155, 173, 180
Stewart, F., x
Stoller, P, x
Strathern, M., x, 38, 40, 75, 187, 191
Strauss, A., 180
Szwed, J., 182

Tannen, D., 150
Thirsk, J., 12
Tonnies, F., 34
Turner, V., 38
Turton, D., x
Tyler, S., 74,

Varwell, A., 178
Vidich, A., 73

Wallace, A. F. C., 182, 183, 184, 185, 186,
    187, 189
Wallis, R., 76
Wallman, S., 50
Walton, J., 36
Weber, M., 34
Werbner, R., x
Weiner, A., 174
Wiener, N., 152

Wikan, U., 173
Wilde, 0., 75, 199
Williams, A., 36
Williams, W., 33, 36, 37, 40
Wilmott, P., 154
Winch, P., 151
Wittgenstein, L., 164, 199
Wordsworth, W., 19

Wright, G., 11, 20, 37

Young, E., 32
Young, M., 154

Zaslavsky, V., x, 173
Zijderveld, A., 38

Index of Subjects

aggregation, 41, 51, 80–1, 105, 122, 125, 129, 151, 154–5, 162, 165, 181, 189–92

ambiguity, ix, xii, 41, 75, 80, 129, 155, 158, 163, 169, 174, 182, 194–5

associations, verbal, 78–80, 84, 106, 122, 124–5, 155, 158, 175

behaviour, xi, xii, 33, 39–42, 43, 50–1, 69, 76–7, 80–1, 84, 129–30, 154–5, 158, 161–3, 165–72, 174, 179–81, 184–92, 194–6, 198, 200

belonging, 43, 57, 151, 166–7, 170, 180

Cedar High Farm, 62–5, 67, 80–1, 83, 85–6, 96–7, 100–2, 106, 108, 113–15, 126, 132–4, 137–8, 141, 144, 147, 150, 161–2, 187, 189, 194

chaotic relativism, ix, 79, 122, 157, 199

cliché/catchword, 38, 75, 162–3, 165, 173, 191

cognition, x, 51, 80–1, 123–5, 129–30, 153, 155–7, 169, 171–2, 175, 181–5, 187, 194

communication/miscommunication, xii, 35–6, 75, 79, 85, 97, 125, 155, 158, 169, 172–6, 188, 192, 196

community, xi, 10, 11, 32–42, 51, 53, 55–6, 75, 98, 109, 111, 123, 150–1, 155, 157–8, 162, 166, 169, 173, 175, 178, 180–82, 188–92, 194–7

consciousness, 34, 41, 76, 103, 155, 173, 178, 187, 189, 193, 199

context/contextualisation, 39, 76, 79, 80–1, 124–5, 129, 150, 152, 155–6, 167–70, 174–5, 190, 194

conversation, xi, 56–8, 63, 78–80, 95, 122–6, 131, 142, 150–58, 162–3, 165, 187, 199

counter-ubanisation, 19–20, 41, 197

darts, x, 41, 56, 58–9, 62, 98, 109, 128, 140–1, 166, 168

diversity, ix, xii, 40, 42, 122–5, 155, 157–8, 163, 168–70, 178–82, 185–7, 192, 193, 195–6

    organisation of, 183, 185–6

Eagle Inn, 4, 25, 27–8, 42, 58–9, 67, 92, 111, 113, 129, 148–9

EEC, 7, 21, 109, 120

ego-syntonism, 157, 169, 186

ethics, 73–6

expectation, xi, 66, 69, 71–73, 78, 80, 82, 96, 108, 111–12, 122, 133–4, 136, 141–42, 145–6, 148, 150, 153–5, 171, 176, 184–5, 187–8, 194

experience, ix, x, xi, 27, 36, 40, 60, 64–5, 70, 72, 76, 102–3, 107–8, 152–3, 165, 173, 178–80, 193, 199–200

family resemblances, x, 41, 43, 51, 167

fieldwork/field-notes, ix, xii, 55–6, 63, 69–74, 76–7, 122, 192, 199–200

forms, cultural, xii, 39, 41, 150, 155, 158, 161–73, 177–8, 180, 185, 188–92, 199

government (Whitehall), 6, 21, 93, 95–7, 109, 148, 166

Hilltop Inn, 4, 58, 128, 137–8, 140–1, 157

individual/individuality, vi, x, xii, 34–5, 37, 39–41, 43, 51, 60, 70, 72, 74–5, 80–1, 95–6, 124, 132, 152, 155–8, 163–5, 168–70, 172, 174–5, 178–92, 194–6, 198, 200

interaction/interactants, ix, xi, xii, 40–1, 50, 51, 63, 74–5, 78–82, 105, 122–3, 125, 129, 149, 150, 154–8, 162–8, 170–74, 176–7, 180–1, 184–8, 190–92

interpretation, xi, 40, 51, 150–1, 154, 156–8, 169–71, 173, 181, 187–8, 190–1, 193, 195–6, 198, 200

landmark, x, 3, 24, 43, 122, 156–7, 171–2

landscape, 3, 24, 43, 122, 153, 155–8, 163, 171–2, 176

language, 58, 64, 69, 75, 137, 151, 152, 155, 157–8, 164, 167, 169–70, 172–3, 178–9, 182, 188

'locals', 10, 24, 28, 51, 56–7, 108–10, 166–8, 170–1, 176

markets, 7, 12, 14–15, 23, 26, 29–30, 35, 37,
     95–6, 107, 170
meaning, ix, xii, 39–41, 51, 75–6, 80–1, 125,
     129–30, 150, 152–5, 157–8, 163–4,
     168–70, 172–3, 177–80, 182–3, 185–9,
     191, 193–5
Mitre Inn, 4, 27–8, 58, 83, 92, 148

national park, 6, 13, 19–20, 28–9, 64, 80,
     94–7, 109, 111, 123–5, 134, 161, 163,
     169, 194

'offcomers', 20, 24, 25, 28, 49, 51, 57, 59, 64,
     66, 80, 91–3, 109–11, 124, 132, 147–9,
     157, 161, 166–9, 171–2, 177, 196

perception, ix, xi, 35, 50–1, 169–70, 187,
     195, 198
persona, xi, xii, 72–3, 81–4, 122–4, 150, 152,
     155, 157, 170, 174, 193
personal/personalisation, ix, xii, 3, 39–40,
     76, 155, 163–6, 168, 170, 173–4, 188,

     192, 194, 198–9
polytheticality, x, 41, 167–8, 180, 188

sociation, xii, 177–8, 192
society, vi, x, xii, 18, 33, 35, 38, 55, 60, 70,
     74–5, 146, 165–6, 178–86, 189–92,
     194–8
speech, 84, 150–1, 155, 180
structure, social, ix, 33, 35–6, 37–8, 40–1,
     70, 77, 151, 158, 165, 173, 175, 177–
     80, 183, 185–7, 192, 195–7

talking-relations, ix, 39, 58, 62, 74, 76–8,
     123–4, 154, 161, 163, 166–70, 174–5
tourism/tourists, 5, 7, 16, 19–20, 23–5,
     27–9, 32, 37, 43, 45, 48, 55, 59, 62,
     65–6, 70–1, 80, 96

world-view, xi, xii, 80–2, 83–4, 105, 106,
     122–5, 129, 150, 152–8, 164–5, 168,
     170, 172, 176, 193